PIMLICO

658

ROMANTIC AFFINITIES

Rupert Christiansen was educated at Cambridge and Columbia universities. He is the author of *Prima Donna*, *Paris Babylon*, *Arthur Hugh Clough*, *The Grand Obsession*, *A Pocket Guide to Opera* and, most recently, *The Visitors: Culture Shock in Nineteenth-Century Britain*. He is opera critic and arts columnist for the *Daily Telegraph*, and a member of the editorial board of *Opera*. A Fellow of the Royal Society of Literature, he lives in London.

ROMANTIC AFFINITIES

Portraits from an Age 1780–1830

———

RUPERT CHRISTIANSEN

PIMLICO

For my mother

———————

Published by Pimlico 2004

2 4 6 8 10 9 7 5 3 1

First published in Great Britain by The Bodley Head 1988

Vintage edition 1994

Pimlico edition 2004

Pimlico
Random House, 20 Vauxhall Bridge Road,
London SW1V 2SA

Random House Australia (Pty) Limited
20 Alfred Street, Milsons Point, Sydney,
New South Wales 2061, Australia

Random House New Zealand Limited
18 Poland Road, Glenfield,
Auckland 10, New Zealand

Random House (Pty) Limited
Endulini, 5A Jubilee Road, Parktown 2193, South Africa

The Random House Group Limited Reg. No. 954009
www.randomhouse.co.uk

A CIP catalogue record for this book is available from the British Library

ISBN 1-8441-3421-0

Papers used by Random House UK Limited are natural, recyclable products
made from wood grown in sustainable forests; the manufacturing processes
conform to the environmental regulations of the country of origin

Printed and bound in Great Britain by Mackays of Chatham

Contents

Illustrations

Introduction

For the best weeks of three summers, I sat at my dining-room table, trying to pretend that the sun was not shining, enslaved to a slowly diminishing pile of English literature exam papers treating of the period known in trade parlance as 'Romantics: 1780–1830'. It was drudgery—and atrociously paid drudgery at that—to assess and grade those papers with any sort of justice: each year I had to pass verdicts on the work of three hundred wretched seventeen-year-olds turning out, against their wills and the clock, litanies about the originality of the *Lyrical Ballads*, the sensuous imagery in Keats's Odes, the irony of Jane Austen, Blake's dark satanic mills. Three hundred different handwritings, three hundred human souls, but three hundred pretty similar sets of ideas about 'the right answer'. A tiny few transcended the obvious; a larger minority were entirely flummoxed; the great mass communicated only dutiful boredom as they went through the motions and jumped through the hoops towards the modest goal of a pass mark.

It was not only the monotony which depressed me, but the anonymity—I longed for an exposure of Self, a confession, a joke, anything rather than another voice parroting from behind the mask of classroom decorum. How could poetry and prose written so intensely out of the pressures of individual lives and dilemmas, by men and women whose antennae were flaringly sensitive to the shocks of history and the culture of their society—how could this angry, passionate, beautiful, truthful literature come out of the mangle of teenage minds so flat and dehydrated? How could it so fail to *speak* to them?

I was naïve, I know. My perfunctory seal of approval on each of those papers was what mattered in terms of jobs, university places, futures. Why waste finer emotions on an examiner's jaundiced eye? Or rather why should I question again the bankrupt but inexorable examination system?

This book, however, has grown out of that experience, and the subsequent feeling that the wealth of existing textbooks were—well, just not romantic enough. So I have tried here to portray the temper of an age through the medium of the lives and work of some of its most sensitive consciousnesses; to show the electric interaction of, and affinity between, people, language, ideas, and events; and to suggest some of the excitement and urgency that was felt at the time. I have no aspirations to an original contribution to literary criticism or history, no pretensions to a comprehensive or encyclopaedic covering of all the territory, only the desire to bring together a sense of the creative chaos—kaleidoscopic, fragmented, contradictory, like everything else in history—which somehow adds up to an artistic era.

And once past the identifying title, I have also tried to avoid the term 'Romantic', except in the senses in which contemporaries used it; and in the specific literary contexts of the Germany of the Schlegels and the Paris of the 1820s. Elsewhere it seems to me to be one of the many literary terms and categories which confuses even as it clarifies, obscuring complex human and poetic individualities in the name of neatness.

This is not to deny that there is a 'spirit of the age' or that cultures have underlying patterns and tendencies. As Shelley wrote in 1819, 'It may ... well be said that Lord Byron imitates Wordsworth, or that Wordsworth imitates Lord Byron, both being great poets and deriving from the new springs of thought and feeling, which the great events of our age have exposed to view, a similar tone of sentiment, imagery, and expression. A certain similarity of all the best writers of any particular age inevitably are marked with, from the spirit of the age acting on us all.'

But the concepts of 'Romantic Poets', 'Romanticism', and 'the Romantic Age' are very much *posthumous* ones, decisively applied only late in the nineteenth century as a critic's convenience, a means of imposing order on that primal creative chaos. The 'Romanticism' of the critic is like a prison with many cells, wings, and corridors; but a place nevertheless of thick walls and locked doors, in which the inmates are all forced into the same uniform. I have gone beyond the usual boundaries here—as marked by the ill-matched conglomeration of Blake, Wordsworth and Coleridge, Byron, Shelley, and Keats—and scanned a broader European landscape for other, perhaps less familiar, affinities and figures obscured by the separations and categories which the conventional notions of 'Romantic' attempt to establish.*

* One of the most subtle and persuasive attempts to fix the terms for Romanticism is contained in the Appendix to John Jones's *Keats and the Dream of Truth* (1969). I would like to thank Paul Driver for pointing this remarkable essay out to me.

None of the existing definitions of that word and its variants has been shown to work much more satisfactorily than the definition of people according to race, creed, or colour: scholars have been scrabbling around for the last century trying to dig up some unassailable ground-plan of common denominators—but are they ever quite sure what it is they are looking for? Some see Romanticism starting around 1830 rather than in the latter part of the eighteenth century; others say that it has never really come to an end. Some would call Wordsworth a Romantic, but not Byron; others have argued vice versa. All this in spite of the indisputable fact that at the time none of the constellation of English 'Romantic' poets ever once characterized themselves as such, any more than Virgil or Horace thought of themselves as 'classics'.

The debate is further confused by the related changes of meaning in the words 'romance' and 'Romantic' ('Romanticism' has been more stable) over the past three hundred years. To take English alone, in the mid seventeenth century, a romance was an unlife-like fiction (as in the Arthurian romances); in the mid eighteenth 'romantick' meant either 'purely imaginary' or, when applied to the inventions of 'picturesque' painters such as Salvator Rosa, twilit and mysterious, even faintly grotesque. The idea of a Romantic *literature* grew up at the beginning of the nineteenth century, though it was then associated with what we would call 'medieval and Elizabethan' rather than Wordsworth and Coleridge. Only later in the nineteenth century did anyone think seriously in terms of a Romantic Age or Movement—or even of an individual being 'romantic' in temperament or personality. Nowadays, we use the words in two particular conversational contexts: one to suggest the qualities of a love story, the other to suggest expectations pitched too high, an unrealistic intensity about life (as in 'He's too romantic to hold down a nine-to-five job'—or to mark exam papers). Amidst all these possibilities,* however, it is not untrue to say that there is an image of a Romantic poet which has taken stronger hold than any other. An average reader who has not, let us say, studied literature at university level, might well think of him as someone who loved nature, lived his emotions strongly, and had a powerful imagination. He wears black, finds communicating with other people

---

* And there are many more shades and variants to record: see relevant entries in the *Oxford English Dictionary* and the essay on 'Romantic' in Raymond Williams's *Keywords* (1983 edn.). For a fully annotated and comprehensive survey, covering the major European languages and literatures, see *'Romantic' and its Cognates*, ed. Eichner (1972).

difficult, and dies unhappily. Now this is perhaps as accurate and helpful an outline as any other, but it can be nothing more than the merest skeleton. What the following pages set out to do is not to argue through the major intellectual issues nor to work towards a statement of the essence of Romanticism, but to paint the extraordinary variety of ways in which that skeleton was fleshed out. This will be a book of *stories*: of long walks, failed love, bank loans, slammed doors, seedy hotels; of moments that changed lives, of bitterness choked back, of music heard over the water, and notes scribbled at attic windows. It tells tales of hunger, lies, and carnage; of men and women waiting for each other beyond the appointed hour, of running down empty corridors, of confronting death and grasping at joy. It is above all a book of reading, writing, and thinking; of resolution and alteration; of courage and despair in the face of the immense forces of social revolution; of a world like our own, in which nothing made easy sense.

Of the many hundreds of books on these writers and their times, I am most deeply indebted to the following for inspiration: M. H. Abrams, *The Mirror and the Lamp* (1953) and *Natural Supernaturalism* (1971); Marilyn Butler, *Romantics, Rebels and Reactionaries* (1981) and *Jane Austen and the War of Ideas* (1975); J. P. Eckermann, *Conversations with Goethe*, tr. Oxenford (1970 edn.); Norman Fruman, *Coleridge: The Damaged Archangel* (1972); Élie Halévy, *England in 1815* (1949 edn.); Richard Holmes, *Shelley: The Pursuit* (1976); E. S. Shaffer, *'Kubla Khan' and The Fall of Jerusalem* (1975); Stendhal, *The Life of Rossini*, tr. Coe (1970 edn.); E. P. Thompson, *The Making of the English Working Class* (1963).

Chapter 1

Visions Betrayed

The Present and the Past thou hast beheld:
It was a desolate sight. Now, Spirit, learn
The secrets of the Future.

Shelley, *Queen Mab*, viii

He wrote his last poem on a thin strip of brown paper, used for tying round bundles of dirty linen: it was all he could find. When he had first arrived at the prison of Saint-Lazare a few months earlier, conditions were easier, and family and friends had been permitted to bring in supplies; but now, with the overcrowding and a feeling among the authorities that matters were getting out of hand, he was left with nothing.

The handwriting on this strip of paper is minute, partly as a way of avoiding detection, partly to save space. The manuscript shows no sign of hesitation, and there are few crossings-out or alterations. This was a poem which had to be written now or it might never be finished: he faced the possibility squarely. That afternoon, in the intense summer heat, twenty-five of his fellow prisoners had been piled into two hooded carts and trundled out of the courtyard. A purge was beginning. He himself had been questioned by some Jacobin hireling; his father's misjudged appeal to Robespierre had probably done more harm than good in drawing attention to his dossier. '*Peut-être est-ce bientôt mon tour,*' 'Perhaps it will soon be my turn,' he wrote.

The patient work of knitting words and rhythms together into a lucid whole must have consoled and calmed him. He had written several poems of the same type in the last few years, satires of a peculiarly intense kind, grim, urgent, and bitter, born out of the first-hand experience of terror, the world of arbitrary arrest, denunciation, show-trials, and mass executions which have remained repellently familiar to the twentieth century. The great Russian poet Anna Akhmatova kept her *Requiem* in her head, not daring to set it on paper for fear of her son's fate in one of Stalin's labour camps, but perhaps no one else since that night of the 5th Thermidor of Year I,

otherwise 23 July 1794, made such art from the anguished uncertainties of totalitarianism.

> Peut-être en ces murs effrayés
> Le messager de mort, noir recruteur des ombres,
> Escorté d'infâmes soldats,
> Ébranlant de mon nom ces longs corridors sombres, . . .
>
> Sur mes lèvres soudain va suspendre la rime;
> Et chargeant mes bras de liens,
> Me traîner, amassant en foule à mon passage
> Mes tristes compagnons reclus,
> Qui me connaissaient tous avant l'affreux message,
> Mais qui ne me connaissent plus.

(Perhaps within these terror-stricken walls, the messenger of death,
black enlister to the Shades, escorted by vile soldiers, making these
long dark corridors reverberate with my name, . . . will suddenly
force me to leave my verse hanging on my lips; and, loading my
arms with fetters, will drag me out, gathering along the way a crowd
of my sad confined companions, who all knew me before the
terrible summons, but who now no longer acknowledge me.)

The poet's name is André Chénier. He is little read now, even in his
native France, but in the nineteenth century he was a popular as well
as intellectual hero, and his life was subject to what we might call
secondary romanticism or 'romanticizing'. Plays, dramatic monologues, novels, biographies, and, as late as 1896, an over-heated
Italian opera commemorated him, the facts steadily lost to 'romantic'
fantasy. In the opera, for instance, Chénier is accompanied to the
guillotine by his lover, the beautiful Madame de Coigny: they go to
their fate hand in hand, warbling of 'love divine' and 'beauteous death'
uniting them in 'life eternal'. It is doubtful, however, whether they
actually knew each other at all—certainly the real Madame de Coigny
died of natural causes in 1820, having escaped the guillotine by means
of a deftly placed bribe.

Outside his circle of family and friends, the real Chénier was not
mourned for a generation; and what little repute he had as a journalist
was swallowed up in the vicissitudes of the wars which ravaged Europe
for the best part of twenty years. In his lifetime only two of his poems
had been published, and it was not until 1819 that a full edition of his
work appeared in print. A generation of young men born since the
Revolution and in search of heroes and models on which to build a

radically new literature, took him as an ally in their fight against the complacency and inertia of the old poetic order, with its deadening rules of procedure, its rigid forms, and decorous vocabulary. To the critic Sainte-Beuve, Chénier revealed 'a poetry of the future', while Émile Deschamps spoke of him in terms of a return to the purity and freshness of the 'first age of poetry'. Victor Hugo addressed him as '*mon André*' in several short poems and celebrated him as 'a romantic among the Classics'. Alfred de Vigny, in his gripping and now sadly unread novel *Stello* (1832), imaginatively reconstructed Chénier's days in the prison of Saint-Lazare, and thought of him as an example of the way that poets were victimized by state and society; so, in Russia, did Alexander Pushkin, whose long ode to Chénier (1825), promulgating true liberty and an end to despotism, was censored by the tsar's bureaucracy and earned the poet harassment from the police.

Chénier was a dreamer forced to martyrdom. Everything about him, from his mysterious love-life to his early death, brought him near in spirit to the men of the 1820s; and yet he was separated from them by one of the sharpest and deepest of historical chasms.

The problem with this image-making was that it presented Chénier only as a proto-Romantic, a man whose purpose was to anticipate the future. The real André Chénier was no John the Baptist, however, but a man powerfully engaged with the culture and politics of his own time. He was born in 1762 in Constantinople. His French father, a mild and bookish man, traded in textiles; but his mother was of Greek descent and it was from her that he inherited a swarthy Levantine complexion which, combined with his huge head and strong features, always marked him out among the powdered and delicate French.

In 1773, the Chénier family moved back to Paris and set up house, despite their modest income, in the fashionable area of the Marais. Here Chénier's mother determined to make her mark on high society. As she spoke only halting French, she cleverly capitalized on her exotic origin by the establishment of a *salon* centring on all things Greek. At a time when there was a growing interest among intellectuals in primitive and folk culture, it proved a great success. Madame Chénier had her drawing-room panels decorated with scenes from Homer and legend; she displayed her collection of Greek coins and fine weaving; and in costume she performed authentic Greek song and dance, notably the *candiote*, which told in pantomime the tale of Theseus, Ariadne, and the Minotaur. Such original entertainment not only attracted the town; it also gave André a deep feeling for the true spirit of Greece. He was always proud of the Greek blood in his veins, and when he began to write poetry in imitation of the Ancients, his image of Greece—unlike that of his contemporaries—was not of symmetry and order, a sort of Versailles inhabited by men in togas. He knew that Greece had gaiety, colour, eroticism, excitement, and these are the qualities that bubble through even his early verse, such as these palpitating lines from an elegy written in praise of one 'Lycoris':

> *Allons, jeune homme, allons, marche; prends ce flambeau;*
> *Marche, allons. Mène-moi chez ma belle maîtresse.*
> *J'ai pour elle aujourd'hui mille fois plus d'ivresse.*
> *Je veux que des baisers plus doux, plus dévorants,*
> *N'aient jamais vers le ciel tourné ses yeux mourants.*

(Come young man, come; take this torch; come. Lead me to my beautiful mistress. Today I feel a thousand times more ecstasy for her. I wish that no sweeter, no greedier kisses had ever turned their dying eyes towards heaven.)

Another formative influence on Chénier's adolescence came from his school, the small and selective Collège de Navarre, probably the best of such institutions in Paris. Its educational scope was broad, embracing modern history and natural and physical science, as well as the usual run through the classics. Here Chénier wrote his first poetry and won some academic distinction: more important, he was introduced, at least indirectly, to the best thinking of his age, which we now remember as 'the Enlightenment', that broad movement of the European mind which sought to establish humane values, universal education, and religious toleration against the rule of superstition and tyranny.

It is common to say that Romanticism was a reaction against the Enlightenment, with its blithe optimism that all would be well if only men would see reason, but it is equally arguable that the two labels obscure a deeper continuity. Our tendency to think in terms of eras, epochs, and centuries is a weakness of our sense of history, inasmuch as it encourages us to suppose that historical change is tidy and complete: that the moment the 'eighteenth century' became 1 January 1800, everything suddenly became different; or that one year Europe was Enlightened, the next it was Romantic.

But Chénier was certainly well placed to swim in particular intellectual currents. He read Montesquieu, for instance, who praised the political structures of Britain, where power was separated and balanced between hereditary monarch and aristocracy, elected parliament, and the judiciary, proposing this as a model for other European countries where the monarch still monopolized control. Given the inefficiency and blatant corruption of the French court and government, most free-thinking Frenchmen subscribed to this point of view, rather as Keynesian economics was generally accepted in the middle of our own century. Chénier would also have been well aware of Voltaire's attack on the iniquities of the Catholic church. He would have used *L'Encyclopédie*, the great collaborative dictionary compiled under the leadership of Diderot to which virtually every major French thinker of the time contributed and which set out to make available the sum of human knowledge, in the belief that lack of education was at the bottom of persecution and misery. *L'Encyclopédie* popularized the belief that mankind could be happy if only societies were organized along rational principles of utility—a dream that has continued to haunt socialist thought ever since. Then there was the more controversial and emotionally charged work of Rousseau, who proclaimed the underlying natural goodness of mankind, as evinced by the uncluttered societies of antiquity and travellers' tales of distant parts. Through all this ran the implications of what we now describe as liberalism—freedom of trade, freedom of speech, a secular state, and government by broadly elected representatives: none of which France then had.

The culture of the intelligentsia in Chénier's youth valued simplicity of style and manners—much time was spent discussing the writings of the Edinburgh-based historians and sociologists on the subject of primitive societies. There was also something of our own attitude to 'over-consumption': the rich were considered distastefully over-sophisticated, plump with '*luxe*' or ostentatious wealth while others starved. The ornament and wit of the rococo were rejected for the earnest austerity of classical remains. The grandeur of Ossian, a third-century Scottish bard whose stories were 'translated' (in fact, faked) by another Scot, James Macpherson, was much admired, as was the sturdy independence of the Swiss mountain peasantry.

Two of these lines of thought and taste colour Chénier's early poetry. One is a longing for the simple, reflective life, untroubled by material or professional ambition. '*Je ne suis rien, n'ai rien, n'attends rien, ne veux rien,*' 'I am nothing, have nothing, expect nothing, want nothing,' he once wrote, and he often celebrates the idyllic blue-skied world of classical pastoral poetry:

...les plaisirs, la beauté,
Des moeurs simples, des lois, la paix, la liberté,
Un langage sonore aux douceurs souveraines

(... the pleasures, the beauty, of simple customs, laws, peace, liberty, a sonorous language of supreme sweetnesses)

The second runs against this nostalgia for the purity of the past. Chénier shared with the *philosophes* of *L'Encyclopédie* a belief in the real possibility of improvement in mankind's lot and had a consequent fascination for the development of science and social institutions. He not only wrote a poem on the brothers Montgolfier's balloon ascent of 1783, but also planned an epic poem, *L'Amérique*, which would deal with the discovery of the New World and thence the geography of the whole planet, followed by a review of the various sorts of society that man had created over the centuries. This enormously ambitious project, however, was scarcely begun, and another similarly enclyclo-pedic work, *Hermès*, never got much further either. That simple, reflective life which would have allowed him to work quietly at reading and writing was denied him, and his vision of mankind, society, and future happiness was to alter violently.

Meanwhile, in the early 1780s, Chénier had to find a career—but without a title, a patron, or a private income there were many closed avenues in a France rotten with privilege and exclusiveness. Without the cachet of noble birth even a place as an army cadet was only obtained by string-pulling on the part of Chénier's father. In the event, his brief spell in the military proved unhappy and he returned to Paris, opting for the literary life and its eternal melancholy twin, poverty. Already, in his early twenties, he suffered from the agonies of inflamed kidneys ('my burning sands', he called them).

The other agonies in his life were the more familiar amorous ones. Chénier was clearly very attractive to women, and seems to have fitted well enough into the elegant libertinism of which his contemporaries James Boswell and the Marquis de Sade were extreme representa-tives. His love poetry runs through a standard range of emotions—suspicion, jealousy, frustration, and disenchantment dominate—but has the charm of both sincerity and wit. Chénier is never chilly or formal, never the mincing beau one encounters so often in love poetry of this period: he deplored such 'cold and gallant nonsense, which contains no poison barb, and which young lovers can read without a blush'. His own verse is '*pleine de chaleur*', 'full of heat', with a characteristic breathlessness which, as we saw in the lines from the poem to 'Lycoris', breaks up the smooth polish of the rhyming couplet. It gives the impression of artful spontaneity; it has something of the cheeky ardour of Mozart's Cherubino in *Le Nozze di Figaro* (1786).

Chénier moved in the best circles of literary Paris. At the Collège he had made firm friends with some enlightened young aristocrats, and he had no difficulty in gaining admission to the most interesting *salons*. Among his friends and acquaintance were the painter David, the philosopher Condorcet, the Italian poet Alfieri, the playwright Beaumarchais, and an American visitor, Thomas Jefferson. Not everyone was of such high calibre however, and Chénier had the young man's contempt for the successful hacks and time-servers who kept literature of a sort ticking over: another of his unfinished projects was *La République de Lettres*, a mock-heroic satire of the situation, along the lines of Pope's *Dunciad*. He also worked on a long essay, again never completed, which charted the history of the relations between literature and society, and proposed that great writing was not possible in an atmosphere of despotism and corruption. His own personal solution was the fond dream of living, 'without pondering whether circumstances allow it, forever far from worldly concerns, with my friends, in retreat and in a state of complete freedom': only thus could he feel that 'my verse and prose, whether appreciated or not, will be put among the small number of works unstained by base conduct'.

Yet there was a good deal more for an intelligent Frenchman to worry about than the cringing mediocrities of the literary world. Since the death of Louis XIV in 1715, the French monarchy, in theory holding absolute power, had in practice failed to wield it with any force. The void left at the centre of the machinery of state had been filled by aristocrats and princes of the church anxious to consolidate their advantages and advance their own interests. The valiant efforts of reforming ministers such as Turgot were strangled, and France remained a nation without institutions capable of governing it fairly. At the nominal top, the king Louis XVI was full of ineffectual good intentions, while his wife the Austrian Marie Antoinette was high-handed and unpopular: in 1785 she had been implicated in a sordid scandal over a diamond necklace which reflected very badly on the general tone of proceedings in the interminably extravagant court of Versailles. At the bottom were something over twenty million peasants (France was, despite its stagnation, the most populous nation of eithteenth-century Europe) working in a backward and unbalanced

agricultural economy, without much hope of anything but survival—
and in times of famine not even that. For the bourgeois, industry and
trade were inhibited by a shortage of capital and a morass of internal
dues, customs, and taxes which usually benefited the local landowner
and nobody and nothing else. The professional classes were similarly
denied the chance of advancement, but were to prove confident
enough to fight for it. Such a complex of interests, wants, ideas, and
injustices was highly combustible.

Chénier witnessed it all for himself. In 1786 he had travelled
through France en route for Italy and Greece (which illness prevented
him from reaching). What he saw—beggary, military occupation,
ruinous taxation—left him with feelings of anger and hopelessness.
His *Hymne à la Justice*, written in 1787, ends with his determination,
once again, to leave the sinking ship:

> *J'irai, j'irai bien loin me chercher un asile . . .*
> *Où mon coeur, respirant un ciel étranger*
> *Ne verra plus des maux qu'il ne peut soulager,*
> *Où mes yeux éloignés des publiques misères*
> *Ne verront plus partout les larmes de mes frères.*

(I will go far away in search of a haven . . . where my heart beating
under an alien sky, will no longer see evils it cannot assuage: where
my eyes, far from the miseries of the people, will no longer see
everywhere the tears of my brothers.)

Perhaps he was dreaming of the warm south when he wrote these
lines, but at the end of the year his destination was the rather more
prosaic one of London. It was not quite the literary paradise he had
hoped for. At the insistence of his father, he had taken to diplomacy,
one of the few decent professions in France accessible to people of
talent, and landed himself a job with status but no satisfaction as one
of the private secretaries to the French ambassador. His duties were
dismally ordinary—copying documents, keeping an engagement
book, attending to the details of protocol—and made worse by the fact
that he did not like London or the English. He was lonely and bored,
despite the attractions of a city more moneyed than Paris and more
beautiful girls than he had seen anywhere. He read Shakespeare,
about whom he had reservations, Pope, and, above all, Milton; he did
some research for various historical projects, and he continued to
write. But he was isolated from his circle, and probably preferred
cruising through the pleasure-gardens of Vauxhall to standing in the

corners of diplomatic drawing-rooms. He fell into a depression, 'counting the minutes, wishing for death, without the voice of a single friend to cheer me'.*

In the middle of 1789, Chénier was given extended leave and returned to Paris. It was a strange time for a holiday: much of it must have been spent waiting for the next piece of news, as one of the most crucial chains of events in European history was forged. The King, cornered by huge debts, an economic depression, and the breakdown of his system of tax-collection, had been forced to summon to Versailles the parliamentary assembly known as the States-General, which had not met since 1614, to debate grievances and approve new levies. It was in effect an abdication from absolutism, an acknowledgment that he could not manage on his own—and it opened a floodgate releasing centuries of detritus. The States-General was divided into three parts, consisting of the nobility, the higher clergy, and elected representatives of the professional classes: lawyers, administrators, surgeons, engineers, and the like. When the convocation opened in May 1789, the King handled matters very badly, at first trying to subordinate the Third Estate (the professional class) so as to curry favour with the First and Second; then reversing his position. Eventually, the representatives of the Third Estate met on the tennis court at Versailles where they swore to keep solidarity and establish a constitution for France. They were soon joined by members of the other Estates, and by the end of June there was a sufficiently strong power-base to dissolve the tripartite States-General and replace it with a single National Assembly.

Away from Versailles, the small shopkeepers and labourers in Paris became ever more excitable, especially as large numbers of troops were gathering around the city, as if in readiness for civil war. Customs posts were burnt, railings pulled down. In the provinces too, there was continuous unrest, fuelled by that great incentive to revolution, hunger—there had been a bad harvest in 1788, and food prices were very high. On 14 July, Paris felt a short, sharp, and violent explosion of tension. The fortress of the Bastille, believed to be holding troops, stores of ammunition and other dark secrets, was

---

* In 1803, Henri Beyle, alias Stendhal, copied out in a letter some verse by Chénier which he called 'the most moving lines I have yet read in any language'. They reflect the sentiments of Hamlet's 'To be or not to be' speech—'... *Et la mort, de nos maux le remède si doux, / Lui semble un nouveau mal, le plus cruel de tous*' ('And Death, so sweet a remedy of our ills / Seems to him but a new ill, the cruellest of all').

invaded and demolished by a marauding crowd. They found the place virtually empty, but before the night was out the governor's severed head was being paraded around the streets on the end of a pike.

The apparent victory of the Third Estate had the effect of a match thrown into a box of fireworks. Most important perhaps was the uncertainty as to what would happen next, an uncertainty which led to panic and violence on the streets. When Chénier returned to England in November, the questions were multiplying: what would be the fate of the King, forced out of Versailles by a crowd of 20,000 barracking for food, and now resident in the palace of the Tuileries in Paris? Would the National Assembly hold long and strong enough to build a constitution? Were the nobles who had already emigrated plotting to reinvade as counter-revolutionaries? Could the nameless and numberless crowds of armed and easily angered townspeople be restrained? At the same time, there was also widespread optimism, a feeling that once the problems had been ironed out, France would be free and happy. If there was violence on the streets, there was also dancing. Privileges had been eradicated, the legal system reformed, torture abolished, Protestants and Jews granted toleration. The universal cry was for liberty: but how was it to be interpreted?

In London, Chénier would have found the news of the Revolution greeted with some enthusiasm. Conservatives were pleased to be rid of a traditional enemy, the French monarchy; while the intellectuals compared (misleadingly) the events of 1789 with the English 'Glorious Revolution' of 1688 and welcomed the French to the brotherhood of the free. 'What English heart,' wrote the woman of letters Hannah More, 'did not exult at the demolition of the Bastille?' 'I see! I see! glad liberty succeed / With every patriot virtue in her train,' piped a precocious schoolboy, Samuel Taylor Coleridge. In the underworld of radical London, William Blake, poet, engraver, visionary, wrote an epic incantation, 'The French Revolution', in the style of the Hebrew prophets, turning its actions into portents and its actors into symbols of the promised Apocalypse: 'the ancient dawn calls us / To awake from slumbers of five thousand years. I awake but my soul is in dreams; / From my window I see the old mountains of France, like aged men, fading away.'

But Chénier worried at his inability to get accurate news: the émigrés put about all sorts of horror stories and once he read that Paris had been burnt to the ground. His family, he learnt from letters, were now at loggerheads: his father a moderate, his mother subscribing to the fashionable left; while of his brothers Louis-Sauveur and

Marie-Joseph, the former—a lieutenant in the army—was advocating a slaughter of the aristocrats and the latter—a popular revolutionary playwright of no literary merit—was consorting with the extreme democratic club of Jacobins.

Chénier left the embassy in June 1790 and returned to Paris, having decided to involve himself and his talents in the coming struggle of ideas. And so the young man with visions of Greece and dreams of poetic seclusion became a journalist; passionately, intelligently, and consistently dedicated to reform by rule of law and constitution, peace, toleration, a jury-system, and equitable taxation. In thus sacrificing his personal ambitions to the welfare of mankind, he was the fine flower of his century, the honest individual speaking his idea of Truth and Justice without fear or favour. Perhaps with hindsight we could argue that he did not see the roots of the problem, but through all the reversals and cross-currents he kept his integrity at a time when, as he wrote to the German poet Wieland, 'men upright and unvarying in their principles, who want to neither lead nor follow parties, and who abhor all intrigue', found things difficult. In all his often very fierce political writing for the *Journal de Paris*, France's first daily newspaper, he never took up a position on the grounds of expediency or compromise, taking human life as the dispensable means to some abstract political end. He maintained his humanity while around him men and women seemed to become monsters.

Chénier firmly believed that the first stage of the Revolution had been '*une insurrection juste et légitime*', but he was already unnerved by the street violence that was erupting sporadically over Paris—indeed, all over France—without apparent provocation. Caution was his gospel: the tide of foreign opinion was ominously beginning to turn against the French, and Chénier knew from his experience in London how ready the English government was to make some sort of capital out of France's disorder. The Revolution's most significant opponent was undoubtedly the great Irish orator Edmund Burke who had been listening to the tales of the émigré nobles resident in London. Although he had supported the rebellion of the American colonies in 1775, his pamphlet *Reflections on the Revolution in France* came down firmly for continuity and inheritance against change, arguing that societies had a permanent and natural structure that should not be tampered with on pain of anarchy. At one level, he was, in Alfred Cobban's words 'prejudiced, violently unfair, grossly unhistorical', misrepresenting the intentions of the Revolutionaries and taking the émigré version of events at face-value. At another level, he was making a centrally important conservative statement, which the radicals of the next generation would have to answer.

Chénier was furious at Burke's attitude, but his own ode celebrating the Tennis Court Oath of the Third Estate emphasized the need for law and self-restraint, its last stanzas full of Burke's fear of what destructive energies might be unleased by new freedoms and soap-box tyrants. In an essay 'The Altars of Fear', Chénier also mourned that ordinary men and women, himself included, were too cowed to speak out against infamy—'the wicked have the courage that comes from envy and hatred, while the good only have their innocence and lack of courage that comes from virtue'. Such fear was the effect of a centre that did not hold. The constitutional government was fractured and fractious, vulnerable to intrigue from the left and right, as well as the extraordinary volatility of the people of Paris. Power was with those who grabbed at it hardest. Politics had once been conducted in an atmosphere of deference and ritual; now their theatricality had become violently melodramatic (and some of the greatest orators actually borrowed techniques from famous stage-actors of the day).

In 1792, France declared war on Austria. The reasons for this were complex. The King hoped that defeat would reinstate him, while others may have believed that fighting against a common external enemy would re-channel popular violence and bring back revolutionary unity. The result was nothing of the kind. The army was in no state to fight anything, and all that ensued was defeat, slaughter, the fall of another series of ministers, and general intensification of panic. On 10 August a huge crush of Parisians, probably incited by cells of extreme democrats, stormed the Tuileries Palace. Over a thousand were killed in the ensuing fighting. Then, through six terrible days in September, amid false reports of Prussian soldiers at the gates of the city and rumours of a conspiracy, the Parisians once again literally took the law into their own hands and massacred about 1,200 prisoners, most of them simple criminals serving time for a bit of thieving. Towards the end of the month, the monarchy was abolished, Year I of the Republic declared, and Louis XVI became plain *citoyen* Louis Capet, to be duly tried for treason on the grounds of his collusion with the Austrian enemy. The ebullience of 1789 had vanished and Paris became a city of closed doors. Europe was now prepared to be horrified, especially since France had declared its readiness to help all peoples wishing to rise against the oppressors of their liberty.

The hopes of Chénier and the moderates were dying fast. The offices of the *Journal de Paris* were ransacked, and Chénier's name appeared on a list of proscriptions. He briefly fled to Normandy, where he may have been involved in a scheme to help the royal family to escape to America; a couple of months later he contributed to the brief for the King's defence, more out of an awareness of the consequences of disposing of him than from any personal involvement. But the King was found guilty and condemned to death by a majority of one: Marie-Joseph Chénier was among the delegates who voted for the guillotine.

The way was now open for absolute democracy, with the government and constitution whose legitimacy was guaranteed by the great abstraction of revolutionary politics 'the people', themselves led and manipulated by a minority of fanatic intellectuals. The momentum of crisis continued. By the middle of 1793, the new French republic was at war with all Europe, except Switzerland and Scandinavia, without any firm centre to make decisions and implement them. In western France there was a serious outbreak of counter-revolution. Censorship, food riots, and a new law sanctioning summary execution of rebels heralded the worst. 'Anyone who breathes the air of terror is doomed,' wrote the victim of Stalinism Nadezhda Mandelstam, 'even if nominally he manages to save his life.' André Chénier was doomed too, even though he was too sane to martyr himself. After the appalling summer of 1792, he moved to Versailles, now a backwater, where he took a small house surrounded by an orchard. Here he found an extraordinary peace and the solitude he so craved. Three miles away, down a pretty avenue lined with elms, lived an old friend, Madame Fanny Lecoulteulx, for whom he conceived a quiet and platonic affection. He took her baskets of fruit from his orchard, walked with her in the woods, and accompanied her on charitable errands. He loved her, but she was married and virtuous, and he learnt to make do with the spiritual comfort she gave him. In an 'Ode to Versailles' he celebrates in an ironic and melancholy fashion his new life—his house, the countryside, Fanny—which had allowed him '*un peu de calme et d'oubli*', 'a little calm and oblivion': perhaps even a little happiness.

Chénier knew that the idyll could not last. His Ode ends with the greenery of Versailles overcast by the 'bloody shadow of an innocent people'. Through the trees lay Paris, and Chénier was well aware of what was going on behind the thin rustic curtain. An emergency junta, known as the Committee of Public Safety, was establishing a savage sort of order, cutting through the red-tapes of votes, party divisions, debates, and procedures that made the parliamentary Convention so inconvenient. It was a tough, united panel, increasingly dominated by Jacobin democrats and made effective by its huge intelligence budget—secret agents, paid informers, and local surveillance organizations all pulled the net tighter. The Revolution was at war, both civil and foreign: there was no room for the democracy that allows dissent. It was through the Committee of Public Safety that Maximilien de Robespierre, a tight-lipped and fastidious lawyer from the provinces, rose to power. A superb orator, implacably high- and single-minded, Robespierre had been deeply influenced by a then relatively obscure book of Rousseau's, *Du contrat social*, which made the startling claim that power in a society came directly from the will of the people, rather than from a monarch, a constitution, or an elected representative assembly. For Robespierre, the will of the people meant the will of the street revolutionaries of Paris, the shopkeepers, apprentices, craftsmen, and labourers who made up the *sans-culottes*. Because they were poor they were virtuous, 'pure, simple, thirsty for justice and friendly to freedom': the others were 'a pack of malcontents and schemers'. Robespierre's politics hinged, therefore, on virtue and terror: the virtue which he saw shining from 'the people', and the terror which would eliminate all opposition to that virtue. 'If the driving force of popular government in peacetime is virtue,' he asserted, 'that of popular government during a revolution is both virtue and terror: virtue, without which terror is destructive; terror, without which virtue is impotent.'

Terror was the means to the end of universal virtue, and Robespierre had few qualms about intensifying the oppression in the name of that end. 'The Republic owes its enemies nothing but death,' he proclaimed. In July 1793, Charlotte Corday, a girl from Normandy of noble ancestry and liberal views, had with extraordinary but misguided courage taken a kitchen knife and stabbed to death Marat, the terrifying journalist-politician whose demagoguery had done much to provoke the September massacres. Chénier was shocked into writing an impassioned poem celebrating Corday's refusal to sacrifice on the altars of fear. The Committee of Public Safety was shocked into making sure that such a thing would never happen again; charged with the virtue of the people, it considered itself to have a monopoly over the life of tyrants, as it had a monopoly over the press and all organs of government.

In September, new laws suspending ordinary judicial rights were passed: it became, in effect, a crime to be suspected of a crime. Insufficient enthusiasm for the Revolution was a cause for arrest. It has been estimated that over the next nine months some 300,000 were imprisoned and 45,000 officially executed. Among the 'unofficial' atrocities was a purge of the Loire area, masterminded by a Jacobin, in which at least 2,000 people were bound, thrust on to rafts, and then drowned in the river.

Chénier was again shocked into verse—probably his last writing, in fact, before his inevitable arrest in March 1794. He was visiting friends outside the centre of Paris, perhaps to warn them of the possibility of a police raid. There was no proper charge: the register gives only the standard excuse of 'detention for reasons of general security'. A couple of days later he arrived at the prison of Saint-Lazare, a newly requisitioned convent housing at that time about six hundred men and women of all classes, occupations, and ages. At first he may just have cursed his bad luck and hoped that something or someone would turn up to rescue him. The chances were that his dossier would get lost, that his brother Marie-Joseph would have a word with the right person, that a friend would bribe some petty official—such things happened often enough. It was worrying, infuriating, uncomfortable, but the odds were still fairly good.

Chénier continued to write in prison. For some months before he had concentrated on the *ïambe* or iambic—that is, verse written in alternating lines of twelve and eight syllables, with a crisp, sharp metre which the poets of Ancient Rome had thought peculiarly suited to satire. The composition of poetry in classical form may seem a strange way to respond to such an overwhelming pressure of events, yet Chénier's *ïambes* are not poetic or refined, but harsh, disciplined, and direct. Francis Scarfe called them 'anti-poetry'; one also thinks of Brecht's abrasive wit, thrown at an age which needed anger and action more than art. The *ïambes* puncture the official fustian of the revolution, the hymns of praise to the people, the odes to liberty and fraternity, the processions and triumphal arches (one of them designed by David to incorporate guillotined heads). Chénier's *ïambes* are the poetry of the Terror.

The days dragged on in Saint-Lazare. At first, the regime was more like that of an internment camp than a modern prison. Visitors brought in food and took out washing. Ladies received guests in their cells; once somebody even launched a balloon. If the guards were slipped money, further concessions might be made. Sometimes it all seemed like a grotesque parody of ordinary life. Chénier described it witheringly:

> *On vit; on vit infâme. Eh bien? il fallut l'être;*
> *L'infâme après tout mange et dort.*
> *Ici même, en ces parcs où la mort nous fait paître,*
> *Où la hache nous tire au sort,*
> *Beaux poulets sont écrits; maris, amants sont dupes;*
> *Caquetage, intrigues de sots.*
> *On y chante; on y joue; on y lève des jupes ...*

(We live; we live wretchedly. So what? that's the way things are. The wretch, after all, eats and sleeps. Even here, in these parks where Death makes us graze, where the axe tosses the coins of fate, pretty love-letters are written; husbands, lovers are tricked; we sing; we play; skirts are lifted ...)

The fun stops when a messenger appears:

> *Quelle sera la proie*
> *Que la hache appelle aujourd'hui?*
> *Chacun frisonne, écoute; et chacun avec joie*
> *Voit que ce n'est pas encore lui:*
> *Ce sera toi demain, insensible imbécile.*

(Who will be the prey that the axe summons today? Everyone shudders, listens; and everyone realizes with joy that it is not yet him or her. It will be you tomorrow, senseless idiot.)

Chénier too looked for consolation; he may have conducted some prison flirtations. In *Stello*, Alfred de Vigny claims that he was involved with one Madame de Saint-Aignan. More popular is the idea that he was entranced by Aimée de Coigny, an intelligent young *duchesse*, famous for her sexual freedom and considered by Horace Walpole to be 'much the prettiest Frenchwoman I ever beheld'. The tale goes that Chénier's most famous lyric, the ode 'La Jeune Captive', 'The Young Prisoner', was written for and about her. In it, the poet listens to a young girl's plaint that she loves life, for all its hardships: why should she be cut off before her season? When in the nineteenth century Chénier, much like Shelley, was romanticized as a gilded youth who wrote sentimental lyrics, 'La Jeune Captive' was turned into a popular drawing-room song. Considered as a poem written in prison, its beauties of phrase and diction come to seem starker, and its refrain '*Je ne veux point mourir encore*' bleaker. But whether she was *jeune captive* or not, there is no solid evidence that Aimée de Coigny ever exchanged so much as a word with Chénier.

And it is hard to imagine that he had much heart for dalliance, when so much of his emotional energy was being expended on the secretly composed *ïambes*, filled with anger and disgust at the way in which every vestige of humanity had been betrayed by men and deeds that at times he could hardly find words for:

> *Hou, les vils scélérats! les monstres! les infâmes!*
> *De vol, de massacres nourris,*
> *Noirs ivrognes de sang, lâches bourreaux des femmes...*

(Hou, vile scoundrels, monsters, wretches! Fed on theft and massacres, drunkards black with blood, craven executioners of women ...)

His own hopes for deliverance dwindled. No help, no message came. He was not to know that his brother Marie-Joseph, with his friends in Jacobin places, had fallen from favour, while his father had made the mistake of petitioning for his son's release, an action that only aroused suspicion. Meanwhile, Robespierre and the Committee of Public Safety were looking for ways of emptying the prisons and further consolidating the totality of their power. By the Law of 22 Prairial, the courts of the Revolutionary Tribunal were instructed to give only two verdicts—acquittal or death: the implication was obvious. It was also decided to make out that there was a massive conspiracy in progress in the prisons, and spies were sent in to mark down any significant personalities who ought to be eliminated. Lists of prime suspects were duly submitted with headings such as 'Names of detainees whom we believe, to the best of our knowledge and understanding, to be enemies of the people and no friends to the true government of the French Republic'. Among the eighty names from Saint-Lazare was that of André Chénier. On 23 July, 5 Thermidor by the new revolutionary calendar, the first convoy of prisoners were taken off for collective trial. The most one could reasonably hope for was that it would all be over quickly.

The poem that Chénier wrote on the last but one night of his life is a courageous attempt to face up to both the likelihood of death and the achievements of his life. It is clear-eyed and clear-minded: it is also proud, without being self-pitying. As he wavers between a feeling of utter weariness and a desperate desire to live, he is confident that he has been '*l'honnête homme*'. Without blood on his hands, he has fought for humankind:

S'il est écrit aux cieux que jamais une épée
N'étincellera dans mes mains;
Dans l'encre et l'amertume une autre arme trempée
Peut encore servir les humains.

(If it is written in the heavens that a sword will never flash in my hands, then another weapon, soaked in ink and bitterness, can yet serve humanity.)

His last line is a self-conscious, defiant farewell—'*Toi, Vertu, pleure si je meurs,*' 'Thou, Virtue, weep if I die.'

The next afternoon his name was called and along with twenty-six others he was taken to the Conciergerie, where a charge sheet was handed him. The charges themselves were largely hot air about counter-revolutionary activities. Apart from the fact that they had confused him with his soldier-brother Louis-Sauveur, there was little that could be done, since the proceedings of the Revolutionary Tribunal, including the sentences, were all written out beforehand.

Next morning the twenty-seven prisoners of Saint-Lazare were taken to the court to play their roles in the standard travesty. The prosecution drummed up some stool-pigeon evidence; a few questions were asked; but there was no real chance to defend oneself, let alone call witnesses. At noon, the sentence of death was read out and, as usual, one of the twenty-seven was acquitted at random. The rest had their hands tied and their hair shorn. They were then dragged on an open cart to the Barrière de Vincennes (now the Place des Nations). The sight had become so familiar over the months that people in the streets scarcely bothered to turn their heads; but there was always a cackling crowd at the scaffold itself. At about 4 p.m. Chénier was guillotined: a quick, tidy, and theoretically painless method of execution. The day's bodies were then taken about a quarter of a mile away, stripped, thrown into a pit, and covered with quicklime, to stop the rats and the stench. In six weeks of the summer of 1794 a total of 1,306 guillotined men and women were buried in this one mass grave.

'*Toi, Vertu, pleure si je meurs*': did Robespierre think that too, as he was hurried to the scaffold less than two days after Chénier, following a failed suicide attempt? His mistake had been to expect from others the idealism he nurtured in himself. An insistence on a faintly absurd revolutionary religious cult, accompanied by a general lessening of tension following success in the war, had turned public opinion against him. The middle classes did not care for his plans for property redistribution. More than that, his haunting combination of virtue and terror—of virtue enforced by terror—had proved beyond human endurance: it was not a principle on which society could function. The day after his demise, seventy-one of his most prominent supporters were executed, and the most radical phase of the revolution was over. France fell back exhausted.

Hundreds of miles away, on the bleak beach of the Leven estuary in the north of England, a troubled young man, William Wordsworth, asked some passing travellers 'if any news were stirring'. That day he had been meditating on the grave of a schoolmaster who had inspired him with a love of poetry, and he walked in solitary reverie across mountains crowned by a cloudy sunset: he was not ready for the stunning answer—'Robespierre is dead!'—which his casual inquiry elicited. Wordsworth literally whooped for joy. 'A passion seized him, a trance of almost epileptic fervour, prompting him, as he stood alone upon this perilous waste of sands, to shout aloud anthems of thanksgiving for this great vindication of eternal justice,' wrote Thomas De Quincey, to whom Wordsworth later described the incident.

He was not alone in his fervour; but there were some who wept rather than whooped—one Robert Southey declared that he would rather have heard of his own father's death and thought it 'the worst misfortune mankind could have sustained'. Looking back thirty years. later from a perspective that had become deeply conservative, Southey could only explain that 'few persons but those who have lived in it, can comprehend what the memory of the French Revolution was, nor what a visionary world seemed to open upon those who were just entering it.'

Why did the French Revolution come to effect this extraordinary intensity of response? Wars of territory, dynasty, and religion had long produced repression and slaughter on an even larger scale than that of the Terror; Louis Capet was not the first king to lose his head; sans-culottes were not the first band of ordinary civilians to riot in the streets. Nor was the cry for liberty new, for the colonial American war of 1775–83 had issued successfully in a republican constitution. Yet for virtually two hundred years the French Revolution has been regarded as an epochal event, a symbolic point at which, like the Fall of Rome or the atomic explosion at Hiroshima, the range of human possibilities is redefined.

There have been various ways of assessing and interpreting its significance. To some it was a divine revenge on the irreligious

Voltaire and the writers of *L'Encyclopédie*, who had asked fundamental questions, broken long-upheld taboos, and unchained anarchy upon a society previously ordered on principles of social rank and inheritance. To others it demonstrated what happened when the tyranny of a few clashed with the frustrations of the ignorant many: revolutionaries, it was said, must be better educated in future. To others still the crucial mistake was the 1792 declaration of war on Austria. But what everyone, whatever their station in life, realized was that the French Revolution had put politics and political choices at the very centre of society. It was no longer Catholic or Protestant beliefs which determined life or death, but monarchist or republican, reactionary or revolutionary, aristocrat or democrat: the repertory of ideologies gruesomely enacted in the theatre of Paris, with the entire western world its gripped and jostling audience.

And once people were aware that they had to make political choices, came the realization that society was not a permanent and naturally hierarchical structure. The French Revolution had shown how much human force, will, and argument could modify or destroy. Government did not simply exist to remedy abuses and provide security. It could also experiment with completely new ways of organizing humankind into nations and societies. God, a king, nobles, and bishops were no more organic features of the universe than presidents, elections, and committees.

So, for all its horror, the French Revolution (or, more precisely, the phase of it which lasted from the Tennis Court Oath in 1789 to the death of Robespierre in 1794) cannot simply be written off as a bloodbath and a failure, although in the immediate aftermath its effects were largely negative. France was not established as a democratically constituted republic, even if the absolute powers of monarchy, nobility, and the Church had been quashed. The fall of Robespierre did not end the war either—far from it. France continued belligerent, until by the end of the century she was subject to the brilliantly imaginative dictatorship of one of her generals, Napoleon Bonaparte, who had seized power from yet another confused and fragile regime, known as the Directory. All this gave thrust to a fierce reactionary spirit which was to dominate Europe around the turn of the century. Monarchies and aristocracies ceased to negotiate the cautious programmes of reform and social improvement that had been favoured ten years earlier; the nervous enforcement of custom, law, and tradition replaced the Enlightenment confidence in the beneficent influence of reason, education, and science. Networks of spies and informers, sometimes as vicious as anything in the Terror, sniffed out 'French' ideas and stamped on them. The general feeling was 'Give "the people" an inch and they'll take a mile: look at what happened to the French.'

No thinking person found the choices easy. On one side was exhausted and bloodstained idealism; on the other, exhausted and bloodstained reaction. Throughout the nineteenth century those with democratic sympathies were paralysed by the thought that a battle for liberty might bring a Terror round again: it was the price that could not be paid. The German philosopher Hegel, in his history of human consciousness, *The Phenomenology of Spirit* (1807), declared that the Terror represented an ultimate point of crisis for civilized man. 'Better injustice than disorder,' said Goethe in his old age, on a note characteristic of the times. But in 1794, for the poets and intellectuals, the search for a third position, free from blood and tyranny, began.

One thus occupied was Wordsworth. In 1790, down from Cambridge for the summer vacation, he had taken a spartan walking tour through the east of France, en route for the fashionable and much-engraved landscapes of the monastery of the Grande Chartreuse and of Switzerland. In two weeks he walked three hundred miles, carrying his few belongings bundled in a kerchief on his head. Everywhere he went he was greeted as a brother and swept into the fun. 'The whole nation,' he wrote home to his sister Dorothy, 'is mad with joy in consequence of the revolution.' Brought up in the country, sturdily impervious to the glamour of monarchy, and 'a perfect enthusiast in my admiration for nature in all her various forms', he had given little thought to politics or French affairs beyond feeling the common English pleasure in the fall of a tyrant. However, late the following year, partly as a way of shelving awkward decisions about his career, he returned to France for an indefinite stay, ostensibly to perfect his French and find some post as a tutor. His destination was the elegant and Anglophile city of Orléans, but he stopped off in Paris for a week and visited the Jacobin Club, the new Assembly, and the ruins of the Bastille, from which he pocketed some souvenir rubble. Later he recalled how none of it came up to expectations:

> I look'd for something that I could not find
> Affecting more emotion than I felt...

In Orléans, surrounded by bourgeois and royalist acquaintance, he found it hard to understand exactly what was going on; but perhaps, being the sort of person who is content to watch and listen, he did not care that much. After some months of the quiet indolence at which he was so adept, he moved again to Blois where he fell in love with Annette Vallon, a desperately sentimental and clinging young French-woman, whom he made pregnant. It seems to have been a hopeless affair. Marriage would have been difficult: she was a royalist Catholic, he a Protestant with uncertain prospects and a strong distaste for the idea of settling down. To a raw and confused young foreigner the situation must have been, at the very least, anxious—and in the middle of it all came another tremendous encounter.

Michel Beaupuy was a thirty-five-year-old aristocrat, descended from Montaigne, attached to a regiment in Blois and passionately engaged in the revolutionary cause. As a soldier, Beaupuy was no *salon philosophe*, but a man ready to fight and die for his beliefs. For the four months of their friendship, Wordsworth drank in his ardour, his heroism, and his fierce compassion for the poor, all illuminated by 'a kind of radiant joy ... when he was bent / On works of love and freedom'. To Wordsworth, such intensity came as a revelation. Together he and Beaupuy talked out moral and political philosophy, fired by the vision of

> ... a people risen up
> Fresh as the morning star. Elate we looked
> Upon their virtues, saw in rudest men
> Self-sacrifice the firmest, generous love
> And continence of mind ...

When Beaupuy set off for the war (he was to die some four years later on the Rhine Front) he left behind him not only a fervent republican, but also someone brought to an unhealthy pitch of emotion with only one means to channel it: poetry. The closing pages of *Descriptive Sketches*, written between Beaupuy's departure and the birth of Annette's child, may make plain bad verse—thunderous, overwrought, and conventional, all Liberty rising up against Pride's perverted ire—but they reflect all too well their author's hectic frame of mind.

Back in Paris after the September Massacres and the imprisonment of the royal family, Wordsworth was confronted with some of the less attractive qualities of a people in revolution, and his agitation increased. Things were not going the way of the Beaupuys. Although he detested what he saw of the street tactics and power-base of Marat and Robespierre, he also had to deplore the squabbling indecision which undermined the high-minded positions of liberals such as Brissot and Roland.

Now he was forced to leave France, since his guardians had cut off his allowance and he had no other means of support. For some months, he settled in London, keeping himself close to news and activity. Early in 1793, he had two slim and not unsuccessful volumes of sentimental pastoral verse published, but he was still unsure of what to do with his life, and France still dominated his consciousness, especially as in February 1793 England, not without provocation, had entered the Revolutionary wars, a development which caused him terrible shock. The questions hanging over his responsibilities to Annette and his daughter became more insoluble; and his political feelings tugged both ways, for when his own countrymen were fighting heroes of liberty such as Beaupuy, what victory could there be? After one defeat, he found himself bitterly rejoicing in a 'conflict of sensations without name' that the English had been massacred. His dilemma was further complicated by an awareness of the tyrannical activities of the Committee of Public Safety, with its desperate belief that only terror could stop the enemy within. The men dancing in the fields in 1790 were now either hunters or hunted, as the temples of liberty became summary courts of execution. Yet Wordsworth wanted—needed—the vision of mankind that Beaupuy had inspired in him: how could he go on justifying it? Later he wrote of his struggle to keep faith:

> I had approached like other youth, the shield
> Of human nature from the golden side
> And would have fought, even to the death, to attest
> The quality of the metal which I saw.

In London, he wandered round the labyrinth of radical and free-thinking societies and groups which had expanded so densely through the latter half of the century. These organizations had their roots in the great traditions of Dissent from the Established Church of England: their tendencies were rationalist, sceptical, anti-monarchical and anti-clerical, sometimes militantly libertarian and occasionally gingerly approaching the uncharted shore of outright atheism; their democratic procedures and principles of independence and solidarity proved rich soil for sympathy with political revolution, but the gruff and taciturn Wordsworth, full of the exaltation and pain of his French experiences, found no comfortable place among them.

At first, he stood on the ground that a temporary despotism was the inevitable midwife to liberty. In an open letter to the Bishop of Llandaff, a cleric of otherwise progressive views who had inveighed against the execution of Louis XVI, Wordsworth not only put forward a staunch defence of republicanism and an attack on the complacence with which the British constitution was regarded, but also pleaded that 'a time of revolution is not the season of true liberty' and that 'in order to reign in peace' liberty 'must establish herself by violence'. In various forms, this has remained, catastrophically, the argument of authoritarians ever since, even though the simplest questions expose its insidiousness: what, for example, is the limit of this violence, and who decides when to end it? Wordsworth was flailing, and he knew it. In the latter months of 1793 he left London and wandered over England: some think he may have secretly visited France as well. It was a way of putting his fingers in his ears.

A degree of help came from his reading of William Godwin's *Enquiry Concerning Political Justice*, a remarkable book published in 1793 and at once widely discussed. Godwin, a nonconformist minister who had embraced atheism and made his living as a radical journalist, was a philosopher for the post-Revolutionary disenchanted. He jumped the question of political action, firmly denouncing violence, revolution, a large-scale state organization of any kind, arguing that wherever possible we should rely on our own moral judgement rather than submitting to the authority of others. He envisaged a society which we would describe as 'libertarian', in which property would be equitably distributed, small voluntary confederations and co-operative schemes would be the norm, and central government would confine itself to providing security and other such functions.

Godwin also believed, to put it simply, that if humankind's external circumstances were improved, the race would necessarily become more 'benevolent'—but that such improvement would come from reason and education rather than direct political change. 'The road to the improvement of mankind,' he wrote, is 'to speak and act the truth.' Finally, Godwin hoped that men and women would come to the realization that only virtuous behaviour (primarily, working for the welfare of others) gave the doer any lasting pleasure or happiness.

It was a kindly and hopeful philosophy, for a time when people felt little hope, and its impact was summed up by another young man of letters, Henry Crabb Robinson, when he wrote that 'no book ever made me feel more generously'. Wordsworth also clutched hard at the consolations it proffered. He visited Godwin in London and even adopted a friend's little boy with a view to rearing him on Godwinian principles. His letters of the time are full of Godwinian sentiments: 'I recoil from the bare idea of a Revolution ... Freedom of Inquiry is all I wish for: let nothing be deemed too sacred for investigation ... I know that the multitude walk in darkness. I would put into each man's hand a lantern to guide him.' He even proposed to start a Godwinian magazine, to be called *The Philanthropist.* But somehow it did not satisfy. There was a narrowness and glibness about it that could not minister to Wordsworth's profounder emotions, and in some ways it just made his intellectual problems even more complex and baffling. What philosophy of life *did* work, he asked himself, at this deeper level? And what was this level of feeling that Godwin could not touch? He went on questioning, worrying, 'dragging all passions, notions, shapes of faith, / Like culprits to the bar ... demanding proof', up to the brink of mental collapse. One may surmise, although he never mentioned it, that guilt about what amounted to a desertion of Annette and their daughter played some part in all this too. Sick at heart, he turned his mind to mathematics, and reassured himself with the inexorable laws of geometry.

Then miraculously the strength and self-containment for which he would be so revered asserted itself, as he began to build afresh, not on hopes for the future, but on memories of the past. He would eliminate sex, politics, worldly ambition from his life: instead, he would retreat to the simple life of which Chénier had dreamed—with the difference that he was pursuing not the idyllic world the classical poets had celebrated, but his own original self. With the help of a small legacy, he and his sister Dorothy, a wild-eyed, dark-skinned, volatile and sensitive girl totally devoted to her brother, would set up house, peaceably attending to nature and their natural affections. Together they would rediscover the unconscious joy and enraptured sense of the wholeness of life which they had experienced in their rural childhood. Out of this would come vision, inspiration, great poetry, and the wounds of the betrayed revolutionary would be healed.

And so, in the autumn of 1795, Dorothy and William rented Racedown, an isolated house in Dorset, and began their great experiment. It was not particularly comfortable. The area was very poor— Racedown had its fencing stolen for firewood—and its inhabitants mistrustful: Wordsworth's pocket telescope was rumoured to cast the evil eye on local cattle. Dorothy was a frugal housekeeper, they grew their own vegetables, and their entertainment was drawn from long walks and a few books. Yet here, after a period of barrenness and confusion, nursed by Dorothy's constant encouragement and a beautiful landscape, Wordsworth began, with a powerful sense of mission, to dedicate himself to poetry.

His first major effort was a gloomy and quite unperformable play in the German style, *The Borderers*, through which all the accumulated bile of the revolutionary years was purged. The central character Oswald is a hard-hearted cynic who preys on the weakness of others and who has lost his roots in the benevolence of those inborn feelings of love for the natural world, kin and community, which Wordsworth called 'the natural affections'. This sense of 'benevolence' was more mystical and intuitive than that presented in Godwin's rather mechanistic and rationalized version, and it would flow like life-blood through the lyric and narrative poems, such as 'The Ruined Cottage', to which he now turned his powers:

> ... In all shapes
> He found a secret and mysterious soul
> A fragrance and a spirit of strange meaning...

The Wordsworths were keen for visitors to Racedown, but it was not an easy place to get to, and few of their friends ever braved the journey. One who did was a fat-faced young man living with his wife and child on the Quantock Hills, about forty miles away. He was Samuel Taylor Coleridge, who had just had his first book of poems published and whom Wordsworth had met through mutual friends in Bristol. In the summer of 1797 he appeared at Racedown for a three-week visit. 'We both have a distinct remembrance of his arrival,' wrote Wordsworth. 'He did not keep to the high road, but leaped over a gate and bounded down a pathless field by which he cut off an angle.'

If his sister substituted for Annette, Coleridge replaced Beaupuy in Wordsworth's new scheme of things. In John Cornwell's words, they shared their 'inner space' and fed off each other, deeply compatible yet quite unalike. Wordsworth, growing daily in self-assurance and spiritual calm, had stripped his life of extraneous distraction and his mind of extraneous information; while Coleridge, insatiably curious and breathtakingly well-read, was quite unable to master himself or his circumstances as Wordsworth was silently doing. He was impulsive, overtly emotional, constantly harassed. Bubbling over with plans, good resolutions, and visionary schemes, he was at times so buried in a welter of commitments and creditors as to be unable to fulfil any of them.* The sum of his work is a rich and wonderful chaos of

---

* The two projects which he pondered longest, but never managed to write, were an epic poem 'The Fall of Jerusalem', based on Josephus; and a *magnum opus*, summarizing his theology, metaphysics, and moral philosophy. Among literally

fragments—the synthesizing and organizing power that he recognized in Wordsworth was crucially denied him.

But that summer at Racedown the two men each opened up their imaginative worlds and explored each other's domain. For both of them it was an enthralling and enlarging time. Dorothy, echoing her brother, wrote of Coleridge as 'a wonderful man'. Coleridge in turn declared Wordsworth to be 'the greatest man' he knew and thought *The Borderers* 'absolutely wonderful'. (The awe lasted: on hearing of Coleridge's death in 1834, long after their intimacy had faded, Wordsworth still remembered his friend as 'the most *wonderful* man he had ever known'.) Their minds were in many ways complementary rather than identical. Wordsworth's preoccupation with nature, the natural affections, and the revelations provided by apparently commonplace events and ordinary people interpenetrated with Coleridge's more religious, philosophical and psychological interests, especially his concern with the science of perception and the ways in which simple cognition developed into complex mental processes such as 'reasoning' and 'imagining'. Through Coleridge Wordsworth became more intellectually involved in the growth of his own mind, delving back ever deeper into the formative experiences of his country childhood and youth; while Coleridge came to learn the soothing and healing influence of nature's mysterious workings.

Both men were profoundly united in their belief that the world and everything in it—down to the barest motionless existence of rocks and stones—was alive and interrelated, that there was something 'one and indivisible' beneath all the surface diversity of appearance.

> A virtue which irradiates and exalts
> All objects through all intercourse of sense

Out of the moral wreckage of the French Revolution they sought to salvage some single guiding sense of truth on which to base their lives. Their conclusions were not to be the same: but their dialogue over the coming months was to prove one of the most creative in the history of literature.

Samuel Taylor Coleridge was born in Devon in 1772, youngest of the ten children of a kindly, learned, and ineffectual country parson. He grew up 'fretful, & timorous & a tell-tale—& the School-boys

hundreds of other ideas are a 300-line poem on the Nativity, an 'answer' to Godwin, lectures on female education, a series of odes on the Lord's Prayer, a treatise on the Corn Laws, a history of German literature, and a pamphlet on the population question! 'You spawn plans like a herring,' sneered Southey.

drove me from play, & were always tormenting me—& hence I took no pleasure in boyish sports—but read incessantly'. At the age of nine he won a scholarship to Christ's Hospital school in London, where he was put through the tough drilling in the classics and mathematics that shaped a gentleman's education of the time. He also suffered the gentleman's education in flogging and exiguous diet.

> Every morning a bit of dry bread & some bad small beer—every evening a larger piece of bread, & cheese or butter ... For dinner—on Sunday, boiled beef and broth—Monday, Bread & butter, & milk & water—on Tuesday, roast mutton, Wednesday, bread & butter & rice milk, Thursday boiled beef & broth—Friday, boiled mutton & broth—Saturday, bread & butter, & pease porritch—Our food was portioned—& excepting on Wednesdays I never had a belly full. Our appetites were damped never satisfied—and we had no vegetables.

To escape from the misery of it all, he made his own fantasy world, and nourished himself on books—for which, like all great readers, he was indiscriminately greedy, a 'library-cormorant' who by the age of twenty-four claimed to have 'read almost everything'. As a small child, he had been seized by tales 'of Giants, and Magicians, and Genii', and always ascribed to them the origins of the wonder of the sublime mystery of the universe which he never lost: later it was Pope's translations of Homer, the Arabian Nights, and travel adventures. As a London schoolboy, he experienced one of his life's few strokes of luck while walking down the Strand rolling his arms round an imitation of Leander swimming the Hellespont. A passing stranger interpreted this as a new method of pickpocketing, but was so impressed by the boy's earnest explanation that he gave him a ticket to a circulating library in the City. Coleridge took full advantage of the opportunity by working his way through the catalogue A to Z, mastering en route the medical, scientific, and sociological literature of the Enlightenment, along with other books otherwise kept well away from Christian youth.

The result of all this was that on arrival at Jesus College, Cambridge in October 1791, he was a prodigy of learning, with all the emotional imbalance and vulnerability that the term implies. His career at the university was rather different to Wordsworth's, which swiftly sank into relaxed mediocrity. Coleridge had patches of furious energy, winning a medal for a Greek ode on the slave trade, entering himself for all manner of scholarships, and continuing with his frenetic programme of reading. However, a complete lack of discipline, either external or self-induced, meant that he never established any sort of sensible routine. Soon he was drinking and talking the night away with friends, debauching in brothels, and generally running wild. By the time he had notched up an impossible amount of debt—'To real happiness I bid adieu from the moment I received my first Tutor's Bill,' he moaned to his clergyman brother George— failed to draw a winning ticket in the Irish Lottery, and despaired of his courtship of the talkative milliner Mary Evans, the sister of a school friend, his nerve cracked. He skulked off to enlist under a pseudonym in the dragoons (six and a half guineas paid on signing-up) where he proved so ludicrously incapable of sitting on a horse that he ended up cleaning the stables and offering other soldiers advice on the composition of their love-letters. In somewhat theatrical agonies of remorse, he wrote to his brother George to beg him to arrange a release. 'Pardon me, my more than brother,' he begged. 'It had been better for me, if my Imagination had been less vivid ... How many hours have I stolen from the bitterness of Truth ... in building magnificent Edifices of Happiness on some fleeting Shadow of Reality ... I seized the empty gratifications of the moment, and snatched at the Foam, as the Wave passed by me.' His brother wearily paid up and settled the bulk of his debts. Coleridge returned to Cambridge, promising to attend to 'the *meaning* and *duty* of Economy'. The college punished him with a month's gating and the task of translating a drearily obscure Greek treatise.

Yet however overbearing the shadows of reality became, he never stopped building these visionary edifices, and scarcely ten weeks after his chastened return to Cambridge, he was off for the summer on a walking tour of Wales with his pliable friend Joseph Hucks. Their aim was not so much pleasure as fact-finding: what, they wanted to know, was the true state of the nation in the summer of 1794? For one thing, it was tremendously hot—'the roads white and dazzling seemed to undulate with heat', Coleridge wrote; for another, political tensions were running high. A year into the Revolutionary War, the Tory Prime Minister Pitt had suspended Habeas Corpus and was expanding his internal intelligence resources. Twelve leaders of radical movements had been arrested on charges of high treason. The harvest was going to be bad and, with the war blockades, food would be short. Taxation was rocketing—in 1792 the cost of army supplies was under £2 million; in 1794 it was already over £6½ million. The knife-edge possibility of a French-style revolution was the country's suppressed nightmare. In *Europe*, William Blake struck with ominous exultation on his prophetic drum:

> Shadows of men in fleeting bands upon the winds
> Divide the heavens of Europe
> Till Albion's Angel, smitten with his own plagues, fled with his
> bands.
> The cloud bears hard on Albion's shore,
> Fill'd with immortal dreams of futurity:
> In council gather the smitten Angels of Albion;
> The cloud bears hard upon the Council house, down rushing
> On the heads of Albion's Angels.

The student population at Cambridge provided some nests of potential allies to the cause, and Coleridge himself was apparently one of its more rabid supporters. But he was not in reality the Jacobin that his manner suggested. He was certainly noisy against authority, be it of the university or the government. He was certainly a fervent admirer of William Frend, a liberal Fellow of Jesus College, whose pamphleteering against the Church of England led to his dismissal from the university ('Frend of Jesus, friend of the devil' went the graffiti); and he was certainly also engaged with the radical theological speculations of the Unitarian sect, which based itself in a denial of the Christian Trinity and which was fearlessly exploring the degree of historical fact in the Bible. Yet for all this, Coleridge was always sceptical of revolutions, democracy, and 'reform' politics, finding them expedient and narrow in their conception of Truth. What did make the soil for his thinking about man-in-society were elements dug up from a deeper level of experience: 'What is it that I employ my metaphysics on?' he pondered some years later. 'To support all old and venerable Truths, to support, to kindle, to project, to make the Reason spread light over our Feelings, to make our Feelings diffuse vital warmth thro' our Reason—these are my Objects—& these my Subjects.'

That he never did achieve this in a decisive philosophical work was due as much as anything to his impressionability, in the sense of being both extraordinarily receptive to impressions and of being readily impressed by others. There was always a distraction, another point of view, another qualification to be made, until the vision of the Golden City had been enshrouded. 'My thoughts crowd each other to death,' he once admitted. To an outsider, it looked like a bad case of dithering.

All this emerges in the touching and comic story which begins as he and friend Hucks, on their hot, dusty way to Wales, stopped off at Oxford and met a nineteen-year-old member of Balliol College whose name we have already heard, Robert Southey. This stern youth had already won himself a dubious reputation for his fine flowing hair, smooth complexion, and habit of taking to the streets dressed as a girl. Then he had been expelled from Westminster School, after various escapades including a raid on the monuments of Westminster Abbey and an article in an underground school magazine which implied that certain masters were flogging their pupils with a zeal bordering on perversion. He was a firm supporter of the French Revolution, but, like Wordsworth, had been deeply upset by what he called the 'mobo-cracy' of the *sans-culottes*. Now his thoughts had turned to the tales of the South Seas connected with the notorious *Bounty* mutineers, and he was toying with the idea of emigrating there as a way of escaping the clutches of Miss Tyler, the domineering aunt who had largely brought him up and who was determined that he should have a respectable professional future. Meeting Coleridge was to consolidate his dreams dramatically. In August 1794, he wrote to his best friend, Horace Walpole Bedford:

> ... after long deliberation I pronounce—I am going to America. It is my duty to depart. At present everything smiles upon the under-taking. Should the resolution of others fail, Coleridge and I will go together, and either find repose in an Indian wig-wam—or from an Indian tomahawk, but this is the last resource of disappointment and despair. If earthly virtue and fortitude can be relied on, I shall be happy...
>
> Horace, would that state of society be happy where ... the common ground was cultivated by common toil, and its produce laid in common granaries, where none were rich because none should be poor, where every motive for vice should be annihilated and every motive for virtue strengthened? Such a system we go to establish in America. We go at least twelve men with women and children ... We purchase a thousand acres, hire labourers to assist us in clearing it and building houses. By this day twelvemonths the Pantisocratic society of Aspheterists will be settled on the banks of the Susquehannah.

'The Pantisocratic society of Aspheterists'* had been instituted

---

* From Greek roots: Aspheterist, 'without self-appropriation'; pantisocracy, 'the rule of all'.

during three heady weeks of conversation in Oxford. Both men felt that they had found the perfect answer to the post-Revolutionary malaise from which they both suffered. Such schemes were common at the time but Southey and Coleridge's has a peculiar purity of motive. Each contributed, or insisted on, particular items of the plan. Southey had responded strongly to *Political Justice* and subscribed to Godwin's belief in the 'necessary' moral improvement of those living amidst the beneficent surroundings of a small 'voluntary' community. Coleridge approved of the pure Christian denial of personal property (which to some extent was already being practised by isolated Quaker sects). It was also, if you like, a way of dropping out of the rat-race drudgery of a career in the Law or the Church, which was hard for anyone with a degree to avoid; and perhaps the frightening prospect of a Europe plunged into the spiralling anarchy of war and revolution affected them too.

But unfortunately pantisocracy was not very practical. Quite apart from matters of finance, neither Coleridge nor Southey had any very clear idea of what mountainous administrative hindrances lay between them and even just getting to Paradise. They preferred to dwell on the poetry of it all—Southey on how 'when Coleridge and I are sawing down a tree we shall discuss metaphysics; criticise poetry when hunting a buffalo, and write sonnets whilst following the plough'; Coleridge on how 'o'er the ocean swell / Sublime of hope, I seek the cottag'd dell / Where Virtue calm with careless step may stray'.

Coleridge finally left Oxford in early July, in a state of overwhelming excitement, and resumed his walk to Wales. Poor Hucks, who seems to have kept well clear of all the plans, was now very much a second-best companion for a foot-slog over six hundred miles of roads scorching in the summer sun. Coleridge reported back in letters to Southey everything from scenes of spectacular natural beauty, to the romantic ruins of Denbigh Castle, an unlucky chance glimpse in Wrexham of the loved-and-lost Mary Evans, a flea-ridden Welsh democrat who 'grasped my hand with flesh bruising ardour', and the theft of his walking-stick.

In early August, Coleridge ended his tour in Bristol and rejoined Southey, who was there to pay court to Edith, one of the five wretchedly genteel daughters of a deceased wine-and-spirits merchant, reduced to taking in sewing and all desperate for husbands. Coleridge now made his first crucially bad move. On the rebound from Mary Evans, he engaged himself to the oldest Fricker girl, Sara, for no better reason than that their liaison would suit the pantisocratic scheme so well (another of the sisters also being attached to a member). He did not love her then, and try as he might, he never would, for all Southey's insistence that one could love by will. It proved a disastrous piece of self-sacrifice.

The recruiting campaign continued, and won over even Mrs Fricker, who was soon as impatient as the rest. A date of departure was set for April 1795, and a decision made to hire space on a freight ship, carrying out 'ploughs and other elements of husbandry', on a total investment of £125 per male capita. Southey and Coleridge would raise their share by writing, and as part of their effort managed to dash off in three days an incomprehensible play entitled *The Fall of Robespierre*. Coleridge's book expounding pantisocracy never materialized. But not everyone was ecstatic. When Thomas Poole, the Somerset tanner of democratic views who was perhaps the most sane and attractive person in the young Coleridge's circle, heard about the scheme, he expressed doubts as to its Godwinian optimism. Could the community be established, he wrote, 'they would indeed realize the age of reason; but however perfectible human nature may be, I fear it is not yet perfect enough to exist long under the regulations of such a system'.

Coleridge now rushed off to London, where he spent his evenings drinking in a rough ale-house called the Salutation and Cat near Newgate Prison. There he met an old school-friend who had just come back from America and was working as a land agent. Obviously hoping for a catch, this 'most intelligent young man' painted a rosy picture of life on the Susquehanna. Yes, it was secure from Indians; yes, the forest could easily be cleared at little cost; yes, 'literary characters make money there'; no, he had never seen a bison and the mosquitoes were not a pest. All this confirmed Coleridge's idea of America as a blissful stretch of fertile countryside, gleaned from books like Brissot de Warville's *Travels in the United States* and Thomas Cooper's *Some Information Respecting America*. Such authors emphasized the political and religious freedom of the United States, as well as the rapid development of cities, roads, and bridges out of the most unpromising conditions; the danger, disease, and impassable thickness of the forests were not dwelt on, and the Indians were regarded as little more than distantly picturesque. To Coleridge, it was a cultivated land full of cultivated people. He hoped, for instance, that the famous scientist and radical Joseph Priestley, then in voluntary exile in Pennsylvania, would join the scheme; in fact Priestley was one of many engaged in tough capitalistic speculation on land that was often nothing more than swamp, and perhaps Coleridge should have thought himself lucky not to have been swindled out of money himself. Over the next few years, the press in London gave considerable publicity to the chicanery connected with sales of virgin American terrain, but as any reader of Dickens's *Martin Chuzzlewit* will appreciate, the vision of riches, beauty, and peace tragically persisted among the innocent.

Back in Cambridge for his last term, Coleridge's elation began to wane. Amorous complications became inextricable. Southey, still closeted with his aunt in Bristol, accused Coleridge of neglecting Sara Fricker—and Coleridge was indeed enjoying a flirtation with a local actress of literary pretensions. But even worse, he had received a distraught unsigned letter from his erstwhile love Mary Evans, imploring him for the good of his soul to abandon a plan 'so absurd and extravagant' as pantisocracy, which she had heard about from Coleridge's equally worried brother George. The next shock was the news that Southey wanted to bring along his aunt's servant Shad Weekes and his wife, not as equal partners in the scheme, but as second-class citizens ready to attend to their master's laundry. Coleridge was appalled—how could Southey so miss the point of pantisocratic equality?—but went on to express his own fears that the female recruits were not fully aware of what they were letting themselves in for. Southey had a problem too—how would his formidable aunt receive the news of pantisocracy and her nephew's forthcoming marriage to the daughter of a wine-and-spirits merchant?

In December 1794, Coleridge left Cambridge without taking his degree and drifted down to London. Here he wrote a little poetry and journalism, mooned over his 'standard of female Excellence' Mary Evans, and found reasons to put off a trip to Bristol and the embrace of Sara Fricker about whom he felt even more panicky. 'To marry a woman whom I do *not* love,' he complained to Southey, 'to degrade her, whom I call my wife, by making her the Instrument of low Desire—and on the removal of a desultory Appetite, to be perhaps not displeased with her absence! Enough! ... Mark you, Southey!—*I will do my Duty.*' But Southey now became imperious and insisted that Coleridge *did* do his duty and come to Bristol. After he had walked to Marlborough in Wiltshire to meet the 'flying waggon' on which Coleridge had promised to travel and failed to find him there, he stormed up to London himself to drag Coleridge down bodily. 'It was total want of cash that prevented my expedition,' Coleridge meekly explained in a note.

In due course, Coleridge was back with Sara, who made the unwelcome announcement that in her fiancé's absence she had 'rejected the Addresses of two Men, one of them of large Fortune'— thus leaving Coleridge even less room to extricate himself. Southey meanwhile had secretly lost heart. Being of practical and decisive temperament, he had concluded that it was the *American* location of their plans that made it all so difficult and expensive—why should they not break themselves in gently on a farm in Wales? At first, Coleridge was dismissive: 'As for the Welsh scheme—pardon me—it is nonsense—We must go to America, if we can get money enough.' The last clause unfortunately indicates precisely the nub of the problem.

The next fund-raising effort was a jointly written-up series of politico-religio-historical lectures, to be given in Bristol, a city with a lively radical tradition as well as considerable wealth. Southey ploughed diligently and competently over familiar ground; Coleridge was often brilliant, but erratic—once to the point of failing to turn up altogether. A local newspaper also opined that 'Mr Coleridge ... would do well to appear with cleaner stockings in public, and if his hair were combed out every time he appeared in public it would not depreciate him in the esteem of his friends.' The brunt of his message was that political reform must proceed along Christian lines:

> The Patriots of France either hastened into the dangerous and gigan-
> tic error of making certain Evil the means of contingent Good, or
> were sacrificed by the Mob ... We should teach ourselves and others
> habitually to consider that truth wields no weapon, but that of investi-
> gation. We should be cautious how we indulge even the feelings of
> virtuous indignation. Indignation is the handsome brother of Anger
> and Hatred—Benevolence alone beseems the Philosopher ...

Southey found sharing lodgings with Coleridge a terrible trial. What particularly infuriated him was Coleridge's habit of sauntering around *thinking*, while he, Southey, chained himself to his desk, wrote steadily, and kept all his deadlines, as well as working on his epic poem about Joan of Arc. There were several outright quarrels, and pantisocracy receded apace, the *coup de grâce* being a party, where it emerged that Southey was ready to abandon the basic principle of communal property:

> Remember when we went to Ashton on the Strawberry Party. Your
> conversation with George Burnet [another pantisocrat] on the day
> following he detailed to me. It scorched my throat. Your private

resources were to remain your individual property, and everything to be separate except on five or six acres. In short, we were to commence Partners in a petty Farming Trade. This was the Mouse of which the Mountain Pantisocracy was at last safely delivered!? I received the account with Indignation & Loathings of unutterable Contempt...

Southey had heavy-handedly stopped Coleridge wriggling out of his commitment, but he was ready enough to withdraw himself when something better came along. As anticipated, Miss Tyler had thrown him out on hearing of the Fricker-Susquehanna-Wales proposal, but Southey was not one to starve on earth for pie in the sky, and when an ecclesiastical uncle offered him an annual income if he came to heel, he gave in. It was Coleridge's turn to be exasperated – such opportunism from someone he had revered as 'a man of perpendicular Virtue—a *downright upright* Republican'! Finally, he wrote Southey a long, stinging letter that effectively buried the project. 'O God!' he exclaimed. 'That *such a mind* should fall in love with that low, dirty, gutter-grubbing Trull, Worldly PRUDENCE.' Southey was undeterred. In November 1795, having married Edith Fricker, he set off for Portugal.

Coleridge himself had done his duty and married Sara Fricker a month earlier. He bravely tried to snuggle himself into domestic content, but he was now a restless, disappointed man and, with a pregnant wife to support, the getting of money became gnawingly urgent. His next scheme was a one-man political weekly magazine, *The Watchman*, the editorial policy of which would tread between facile radicalism and support for Pitt's ever more repressive regime. After a gruelling tour of the North Country collecting subscriptions and preaching sermons in Unitarian chapels, he was exhausted. 'I am almost heartless,' he wrote. 'My past life seems to me like a dream, a feverish dream! all one gloomy huddle of strange actions, and dim-discovered motives ... For shame! I ought not to mistrust God! but indeed to hope is far more difficult than to fear.'

The strain soon told on *The Watchman*, which folded after ten numbers, and by the end of 1796 Coleridge was sick of the world of 'politicians and politics—a set of men and a kind of study I deem highly unfavourable to all Christian graces'. The staunch Tom Poole found him a mouse-ridden cottage near his own house in the depths of Somerset where, it was hoped, he could quietly recuperate, dig his own vegetable garden, and organize his life. There was a sort of reconciliation with Southey who had returned from Portugal and sent Coleridge a note on which he had starkly written a poignant line from a play by Schiller: 'Fiesco! Fiesco! thou leavest a void in my bosom, which the human race, thrice told, will never fill.' Coleridge was prepared to shake hands, but the scars remained. In any case, he was steadily losing any interest in the systematic, mechanical psychology which regarded human beings as objects which could be formed and reformed according to rules of cause and effect and which had underpinned the idea of pantisocracy. In Wordsworth he found someone who understood all his hopes, fears, and intuitions, and someone who had struck out beyond them to find spiritual peace. The impressiveness of Southey was nothing to the impressiveness of Racedown.

In March 1798, in the middle of a period in which Coleridge came as near to creative joy as he was ever to be, the period of 'Kubla Khan' and *The Rime of the Ancient Mariner*, he wrote to his brother George a letter which embodies his new Wordsworthian direction of mind.

> I have snapped my squeaking baby-trumpet of Sedition & the fragments lie scattered in the lumber-room of Penitence. I wish to be a good man and a Christian—but I am no Whig, no Reformist, no Republican ... And feeling this, my Brother! I have for some time past withdrawn myself almost totally from the consideration of *immediate* causes, which are infinitely complex & uncertain, to muse on fundamental & general causes ... I devote myself ... in poetry, to elevate the imagination & set the affections in right tune by the beauty of the inanimate impregnated, as with a living soul, by the presence of life ... I love fields & woods & mountains with almost a visionary fondness—and because I have found bene-volence & quietness growing within me as that fondness has increased, therefore I should wish to be the means of implanting it in others...

As for pantisocracy, the vision of a community of friends together working the land, rearing children, and writing poetry, untroubled by money, property, or ambition, lingered on. It was an innocent scheme, he thought in retrospect, and 'Wiser men than I went worse astray'. In 1801, when Coleridge was in physical agony and despair at the bitter impasse in his marriage, he proposed to Dorothy and William Wordsworth that they all emigrate to the West Indies 'as a place of repose, not as a scheme of reform'. So the poet-intellectual turns from public reform to private repose—the change in emphasis shows how sharply and quickly the morale and climate of ideas had changed in less than a decade.

As the liberal clergyman and wit Sydney Smith recalled, 'from the beginning of the century to the death of Lord Liverpool [Tory Prime Minister, died 1827] was an awful period for anyone who ventured to maintain liberal opinions ... "Jacobin", "Leveller", "Atheist", "Incendiary", "Regicide" were the gentlest terms used, and any man who breathed a syllable against ... any abuse which a rich man inflicted, and a poor man suffered, was bitterly and steadily resented.' The government was firmly Tory, enforcing policies at best decisive, at worst brutal. The head of steam which could have pushed up major reforms was dissipated, as manpower, energies, and anxieties were channelled into the war against Napoleon; and part of that militarization consisted of billeting the army up and down the country in a network of new barracks, packed with soldiers as ready to put down local insurrections as to fight the French. In place of Godwin's proclamations of benevolence and the future rule of reason, the writings of Thomas Malthus emerged to satisfy the public mood: population, he pointed out in his famous pamphlet of 1798, rises faster than the means of subsistence. Improve the lot of the poor by welfare, and they become lazy, less productive in the fields but more productive of children. Poverty, wars, and vice served the useful function of keeping numbers down. Progress was an illusion—all societies were caught in the population trap—and on balance he thought that a system which kept aristocracy, wealth, and privilege had a better chance of surviving than one which pursued democratic equalities. To Malthus, this was not cynicism, but scientific fact.

Such an apparently inexorable law depressed even the Whig opposition to the Tories. The Whigs remained the party standing for peace with France, Catholic Emancipation, and an extension of the vote through the middle classes, but they were without force or cohesion, preferring to bide their time, compromise, and let the Tories bear the brunt of blame for the war. One typical Whig of this variety, brought to his seat through the usual petty corruption and buying-up of votes, was Timothy Shelley, member of parliament for New Shoreham in Sussex. His father was the baronet Sir Bysshe Shelley, born in America to a failed merchant and quack doctor. The only ingenuity ever recorded of this Bysshe Shelley was his success in eloping with two teenage heiresses who eventually left him rich, titled, and landed. In old age he had turned miserly and eccentric, leaving his mansion empty, moving to a small cottage, and spending his evenings in the tap-room of the local inn, noisily arguing politics. Timothy Shelley, however, was a moderate man, anxious to consolidate his status and ready to sacrifice principle to expedient. He made little impression in Westminster and was clearly happier as a country squire, surrounded by his wife and six surviving children in their home at Field Place, a pleasant Tudor farmhouse modernized in Georgian style, near Horsham. Timothy was an affectionate father, and he had great hopes that his elder son Percy Bysshe, born in 1792, would follow him into the Whig parliamentary interest and keep up the family fortunes. But the boy was wild, fanciful, and intellectual, with an unhealthy interest in the lower depths of Gothic horror, which he read compulsively in cheap blue paperback editions. Hauntings and pursuits, female good and masculine evil, the potency of the unnatural, the extremes of human emotion, fed his psyche, and in the grounds of Field Place he gave full rein to his fantasy life, dragooning his adoring younger sisters into adventures charged with the *frisson* of terror that children find so pleasurable. An alchemist sat in the attic; a sea serpent lurked in the pond; dressing up as ghosts and setting fire to things; digging a cave in the orchard ... It was a wonderful childhood, in both senses of the adjective, and it is easy to interpret the adult Shelley's life as an effort, at some unconscious level, to regain its freedom and security and excitement. In particular he was to look to *sisters* to provide him with emotional satisfaction. The psychology of sisterhood fascinated him too—'In no other relation could the intimacy be equally perfect,' he told his friend Hogg—but it was a fascination that would prove dangerously misleading.

At his first boarding school the young Shelley developed more scientific interests. 'He astonished his schoolfellows,' wrote a contemporary, 'by blowing up the boundary paling of the playground with gunpowder, also the lid of his desk.' Back at Field Place he put his sisters hand-in-hand round the nursery table and informed them that they were to be electrified and their chilblains cured. His family could indulge such eccentricities; when he was sent to Eton his audiences were more hostile. A delicate and *farouche* boy who ran up and down stairs chanting the spells of the witches in *Macbeth* was what to thirteen-year-olds is the most despicable of beings—an outsider, ripe for the merciless bullying that flourished unhindered in public schools of the era. The ordinarily gentle Shelley responded with fury, and was once goaded into stabbing a tormentor with a pitchfork. Biographers like to claim that he was traumatized by the cruelty and isolation of it all, but perhaps Eton's primary effect on Shelley was a partially useful one: it taught him to hate, passionately and contemptuously. What is more he survived to become a poised and sophisticated senior, eschewing the dull and cultivating the brilliant, and the author of some lurid verse and fiction, most of it in obvious imitation of the Gothic style through which he found a channel for his frustrations and fantasies.

This 'Gothic' literature had been popular since the middle of the eighteenth century: its appeal was based in its exploitation of sadistic psychological violence and other aberrant mental states, inverting the quotidian world of common sense for one in which broken taboos, voyeurism, and obsession were the norm. Such narratives were always 'distanced' either geographically or historically (more strictly, 'Gothic' denotes what we would call 'medieval'), and the supernatural elements of the plots were usually explained away at the denouement as tricks or illusions, but the excitement of Gothic was its sensational immediacy of impact, its playing with the sexual charge of suspense and its ultimate release. For Shelley there was also the fascination of the point at which the scientific and rational met with the inconceivable and irrational—a fascination which would become one of the parents of his future wife's extraordinary contribution to the Gothic genre, *Frankenstein.*

At Eton, Shelley also found a mentor and father-figure who could foster his twinned enthusiasms for ghosts and gunpowder. Dr James Lind had recently retired from an exasperating position as one of George III's physicians at Windsor Castle. Shelley was infatuated by this old wizard, with his tall, spindly frame, wisps of white hair, and a breadth of mind and experience that Timothy Shelley signally lacked. Lind was a keen amateur chemist, astronomer, and student of the occult; he had travelled as far as Iceland and China; in 1789 he had opened Edward IV's coffin and put the contents under chemical analysis; he ran pamphlets off his own printing press. His reading spanned Oriental sages to Voltaire and Godwin, and together he and Shelley pored over Lucretius' philosophy of Nature and Plato's philosophy of Forms, both of which would underlie Shelley's greatest poetry. Lind himself makes an appearance as the mysterious hermit in Canto IV of *The Revolt of Islam*; and in Shelley's later paranoid reconstruction of the way his family had persecuted him, it was Dr Lind who stopped Timothy Shelley sending him to a madhouse.

In 1810 Shelley went up to University College, Oxford, then an institution completely stifled by the values and personnel of the

Church of England. Timothy Shelley may still have hoped that his son, if treated tolerantly, would settle down, but it turned out that by its very mediocrity Oxford set him on a more dangerous course. 'He was all passion—passionate in his resistance to injury, passionate in his love,' wrote his bosom Oxford friend Thomas Jefferson Hogg—and it was a passion fanned by the ashes of apathy around him. At first he turned his rooms into a laboratory. Hogg recalled that

> his hands, his clothes, his books and his furniture were stained and corroded by mineral acids. More than one hole in the carpet could elucidate the ultimate phenomenon of combustion ... It seemed but too probable that in the rash ardour of experiment he would some day set the College on fire or that he would poison himself, for plates and glasses, and every part of his tea equipage, were used indiscriminately as crucibles, retorts and recipients, to contain the most deleterious ingredients ...

But the obsession with chemistry was soon supplanted. Hogg himself posed a new set of questions—he claimed to be an outright atheist and shook Shelley out of the woolly indifference to the matter that his family and the deist tradition of the Whigs had communicated to him. 'Down with bigotry! Down with intolerance!' wrote Shelley, no longer the dilettante silk-pantalooned Etonian, in a letter written at the end of his first term at Oxford. Not only the Church, but the Christian religion itself was repressive and irrational: in March 1811 Shelley and Hogg published a brief anonymous pamphlet with the provocative title *The Necessity of Atheism* to argue their case. It was not as sensational as it sounds: there was little in it that could not have been found in certain of the Enlightenment freethinkers, and it proceeds on soberly logical grounds—'It is easier to suppose that the Universe has existed from all eternity, than to conceive a being capable of creating it ... Every reflecting mind must allow that there is no proof of the existence of a Deity. QED.' Blasphemy, however, was a serious legal offence (it remains on the British statute books to this day) and *The Necessity of Atheism* was actionable. The university authorities traced the culprits and expelled them—though apparently they were more appalled by their intransigent refusal to confess authorship and answer questions before a tribunal than by the mere avowal of atheism.

At first it looked as though the affair might be untangled. A lawyer friend of Hogg's father wrote to him that, 'These two young Men gave up associating with any body else some months since; never dined in college; dressed differently from all others ... as much as to say "We are superior to every body" ... There is no striking impiety in the pamphlet ... It is a foolish performance so far as argument goes.' Timothy Shelley was shocked and upset, but he believed that apology and renunciation could put the matter to rights. He went to see his son, who had moved to London and taken rooms in Soho, but the interview was a disaster—Shelley fell off his chair in a fit of high-pitched hysterical laughter at his father's remonstrations and demands that he dissociate himself from Hogg, return to Field Place, and put himself under the guidance of an approved clergyman. A few days later Timothy restated his position in a sad letter headed 'My dear boy' and signed 'your most affectionate and afflicted father'. The impasse continued, with both sides parrying threats and peace proposals. The bottom line was that the family estates were entailed on Shelley, and if he renounced his inheritance—which for an immediate cash income he was prepared to do—the property would be broken up and the hard-won status of the Shelley name reduced. What Timothy simply could not understand was the full sincerity of his son's burgeoning idealism, nor his increasing scorn for his father's 'worldly prudence'.

But Shelley felt a good deal shakier than he appeared: at eighteen, he was young to be at war with everything and everyone that had given him security. Hogg had negotiated successfully with his own father and gone home, leaving his friend alone and penniless in London. 'Certainly this place is a little solitary but as a person cannot be quite alone when he has even got himself with him, I get on pretty well,' he wrote, putting a brave face on it. 'I have employed myself in writing poetry, & as I go to bed at 8 o Clock time passes quicker that [sic] it otherwise might.' Every day he would take long, sometimes aimless walks: once he was discovered at 5 a.m. curled up asleep on the pavement of Leicester Square.

In May, Shelley returned to Field Place and managed to wring £200 a year out of his father, who at this point seems to have given up the struggle. The atmosphere remained uneasy; he was cordoned off in two small rooms apart from the rest of the household, lest he spread the fumes of atheism. His mother—a woman of whom we know very little—spoke to him only of the weather. Meanwhile he slipped out to Horsham for conversation with a newly discovered fellow-spirit, Miss Elizabeth Hitchener, a tall, earnest, and awkward schoolmistress of twenty-nine anxious to further her intellect. This remarkable woman, a staunch radical and feminist, was in a painful position, stuck out in a respectable country town with few resources or contacts. Her publican father had previously been a smuggler and she had educated herself: what she needed was advice, books, names, ideas—and with these Shelley eagerly obliged. When he left Field Place at the end of June, he began a substantial and revealing correspondence with her. Unfortunately, in his excitement at meeting a woman as ardent as himself, he failed to consider certain more delicate matters of personal feeling. She assumed silently that their union would be more than mental; he never dreamed of her as more than the 'sister of my soul'.

In fact, all his amorous thoughts now turned sharply on a 'little friend' he had made in London, Harriet Westbrook. She was the sixteen-year-old daughter of a Mayfair coffee-house owner, infinitely trusting and ready to be impressed, if not moulded. Shelley, perhaps unconsciously, set to work to indoctrinate Harriet with a set of opinions and attitudes that would suit him very nicely. Harriet was thrilled and horrified by such notions, while Shelley neurotically harped, quite without foundation, on the tyranny that her father was imposing over her.

When he received a desperate letter from her, begging for his 'protection', Shelley insisted that they took decisive action to unite their fates. After a whirlwind of letters and travel, they eloped and were married in Edinburgh at the end of August. Timothy Shelley was not deceived by prevarications and at once cut off the £200 allowance. 'God only knows what can be the End of all this Disobedience,' he lamented. Further communications with Field Place brought no relenting, and culminated in Shelley's most livid screech of rage against his father:

> ... if *you* will not hear my name, *I* will pronounce it. Think not I am an insect whom injuries destroy—had I money enough I would meet you in London, & hollow in your ears Bysshe, Bysshe, Bysshe—aye Bysshe till you're deaf.

Over these months, stimulated by his contact with Elizabeth Hitchener, Shelley moved away from his absorption in atheism towards a broader political perspective. He wrote to her of the 'empire of terror' established by Religion, which had Monarchy as its 'prototype' and Aristocracy as its 'essence'. He admitted that 'Equality in politics like perfection in morality appears now far removed from even the visionary anticipations of what is called the wildest theorist,' but then declared himself—'*I* then am wilder than the wildest theorist.'

It is not hard to write off this and other extreme statements of

Shelley's politics as a neurotic compensation for his family's reject-
ion of him—and if his bitterness towards his father was uninhibitedly vocal, then his virtually complete silence on the subject of
his mother is even more psychologically sinister. Certainly his
anger went deep into his childhood as the spoilt first child, growing
up in a thoroughly privileged and pleasant environment, surrounded by adoring women, before being flung into the horrors of
the public school system. Then it should also be said that much of
what he thought and wrote about the Established Order would
have seemed much less shocking twenty-five years earlier: many of
his religious and political ideas were drawn from the Enlightenment thinkers of the 1780–90s. In that respect, one might even call
him old-fashioned, as he dug up principles and ideals that had
long been buried under the rubble of a revolution he was too
young to recall.

But neither of these necessary qualifications, nor any amount of
finger-pointing at his hobby-horses and inconsistencies, can cancel
the impressive truth that from this period until his death, he held
firmly to a belief which he simply expressed in a letter of 1819: 'The
system of Society as it exists at present must be overthrown from the
foundations.' How that system could be overthrown was less certain.
Political reform could only be a preliminary; an instant transfer of
power to the people would lead to anarchy and violence; hearts and
minds were the deepest source of change. As to what should replace
the present system, Shelley was not ashamed to be utopian, as the
visionary panoramas of the last act of *Prometheus Unbound* and the last
two cantos of *Queen Mab* both reveal; but he was also to become an
increasingly astute and well-informed social critic, grasping hard
economic facts and power structures with a vigour and clarity that his
sweeter lyric poetry never suggests.

In the early months of his marriage, Shelley had the notion—
perhaps in tribute to Dr Lind—that he could better serve mankind by
becoming a physician rather than a man of letters. The idea was soon
superseded, without his ever finding another satisfactory channel for
his philanthropic instincts. His immediate responsibility to Harriet,
with her giggling naïveté and unquestioning dependence, never fully
engaged his interest. He and Elizabeth Hitchener had been firing off
on the evils of marriage, and Shelley had called himself an 'antimatri-
monialist', excusing his own surrender on the grounds of protecting
Harriet from vulgar prejudice. 'Marriage is monopolizing exclusive
jealous,' he wrote, 'an evil of immense and extensive magnitude, but I

think a previous reformation in morals, and that a general & a great one is requisite before it may be remedied.' He proposed to Elizabeth the formation of some sort of commune—'My friend Hogg and myself consider our property in common: that the day will arrive when *we* shall do the same is the wish of my soul.'

Everything depended on establishing a *modus vivendi* with Field Place, and in the middle of October, Shelley left York, where he and Harriet were now living with Hogg, in an effort to raise funds. He returned empty-handed to a caricature of his communal hopes: after a good deal of innocent flirtation, Hogg had attempted to seduce Harriet against her will. Shelley felt profoundly betrayed. Hogg had taken the noble principle of free love as an excuse to indulge mere lust. A complex of feelings were raised by this uncomfortable incident. Harriet and Shelley abruptly left the scene of the crime for Keswick in the Lake District, and Shelley wrote Hogg a series of dizzying letters in an effort to sort out the confusions of his passion:

is it so ... are we parted. you—I. Forgive this wildness I am half mad ... dearest best-beloved of friends will *you* come. Will you share my fortunes, enter into my schemes ... love me as I love you. be inseparable as I once fondly hoped you were ... your letters came directly after dinner. How could anyone read them unmoved ... How cd I forbear wishing that death wd yawn. Adieu. Follow us not ... Dare to be good.

Shelley had one very material purpose in making for the Lake District—to get the ear of the Duke of Norfolk, a leader of the reforming wing of the Whig party who owned estates in the area. In the interests of keeping the Shelley dynasty neatly under the Whig umbrella, the Duke was acting as go-between for Shelley and his father. With his bluff parliamentary approach, he succeeded in imparting a little calm to the hysteria, and after Shelley had at least apologized for the 'uneasiness which I have occasioned', Timothy grudgingly restored his annuity.

But the Lake District also attracted Shelley for other reasons. Although the 'Lakists'—Wordsworth, Coleridge, De Quincey, Southey, and many lesser figures—were now associated with a quietist conservatism far from his anti-monarchic and atheistic ideology, it was still a place of extraordinary glamour to any young intellectual. During his stay in Keswick, Shelley met only Southey, now the successful author of several biographies, histories, and exotic epic poems, but it was a fruitful encounter.* The older man saw the image of his own radical youth as an Oxford undergraduate: 'Shelley acts upon me as my own ghost would do,' he wrote. Southey gave him the run of his library and they discussed political questions of the day, as well as the French Revolution and the problems of religious belief. Perhaps they talked of pantisocracy too. Southey said that he considered a revolution in England 'inevitable', and in late 1811, with the start of the machine-breaking campaigns of the Luddites and a severe economic depression following on trade embargoes and a very poor harvest, it must have seemed that the ghosts of 1794–5 were rising again too. Southey's tactic was to let Shelley talk but, in Kenneth Cameron's words, to get 'his youthful feet on the laurel-strewn path to orthodoxy and Toryism'. Shelley was not so easily fooled. He was stimulated by Southey's knowledge and experience, but ultimately infuriated by his condescension. 'He has a very happy knack when truth goes against him, of saying "Oh! when you are as old as I am, you will think with me," ' he complained. Yet he listened—and it was Southey's influence that led him to write two hundred pages of a now-lost novel, *Hubert Cauvin*, 'in which I design to exhibit the cause of the failure of the French Revolution'. It was also Southey who informed him that Godwin was still alive and resident in London, working in obscurity as a writer, publisher, and bookseller of educational children's books. Shelley was thunderstruck: here, at last, might be the man he was seeking—a father-figure, a radical atheist hero who had undergone 'no soul-chilling alteration' of mind.

He began by bombarding Godwin with self-introductory letters. Although the premise was that he was a copybook convert to Godwinism—'I am ardent in the cause of philanthropy and truth, do not suppose that this is vanity ... I imagine myself dispassionately describing the state of my mind'—the underlying intention was to dramatize himself as a victim of persecution—'passive obedience was inculcated and enforced in my childhood. I was required to love because it was *my duty*.' But Godwin's response was encouraging, although he urged that Shelley refrain from rash political activism. His motives were not altogether pure either: chronically short of money, he saw in his young aristocratic admirer the possibility of

---

* In 1830 Coleridge expressed regret at having missed the chance of meeting Shelley—he had been away in London at the time. 'I could have done him good,' he said, 'I should have laughed at his atheism. I could have sympathized with him ... shown him that I had been in the same state myself, and I could have guided him through it.'

patronage. Nor did he inform Shelley that he now felt a little differently about the positions put forth in *Political Justice*. Not a 'soul-chilling
alteration' perhaps, but, for instance, he had long since been talked
out of atheism by Coleridge himself.

Shelley was once again plunged into a state of excitement, marred
by blinding nervous headaches. He made further efforts to gather his
informal commune, not as a pantisocracy so much as what he called
'an asylum of distressed virtue' or 'the rendez-vous of the friends of
liberty and truth'. He summoned Elizabeth Hitchener who said that
she would come bringing friends, pupils, and her mentor, a Miss
Adams, whom Shelley agreed to regard as 'mother'. Perhaps Godwin
would come as well, to the ghost-ridden castle 'in a romantic spot' that
he envisaged as the location. 'These castles are somewhat aerial at
present,' he admitted, 'but I hope it is not a crime in this mortal life, to
solace ourselves with hopes. Mine are always rather visionary.' More
culpably he wrote to his twelve-year-old sister Hellen at Field Place
(mercifully the letter was intercepted by Timothy Shelley), suggesting
that she ran away to join them: 'They will not let you walk and read
and think (if they knew your thoughts) just as you like tho' you have as
good a right to do it as they.—But if you were with me you would be
with some one who loved you, you might run & skip read write think
just as you liked.' However, he reminded her, '*thinking* & thinking
withou[t] letting anything but *reason* influence your mind is the great
thing'.

After his return from an expedition to Ireland, where he had
valiantly but hopelessly tried to influence the clamour for independence and Catholic emancipation, Shelley failed to persuade Timothy
Shelley to advance him £500 towards a farm in Wales, which could
serve as the commune, yield an income, and allow him to write his
radical broadsides in rural tranquillity. The collapse of this scheme
led them to a cottage overlooking the sea at Lynmouth in Devon,
where Elizabeth Hitchener, nervous of scandal, finally joined them.
Everything began well. Harriet liked the new arrival and thought the
village 'a fairy scene'; Shelley worked on a defence of the free press.
Together they sent out copies of a poster anonymously proclaiming a
Declaration of Rights: thirty-one mostly Godwinian principles, concluding with a call '*Awake—arise—or be forever fallen!*' Lynmouth is
still a small and isolated place, surrounded by wooded cliffs, and as
one of the most popular tales of Shelley has it, the best means of
distribution proved to be stuffing the poster into bottles, which were
then flung out to sea in the hope that they would float up the Bristol

Channel to some useful destination. Some were even launched in tiny silk balloons, fired by a spirit-soaked wick. More prosaically, Shelley sent his Irish servant Dan out on the roads to pin copies to any prominent wall or tree.

Given the tensions of 1812, with the Prime Minister Spencer Perceval just assassinated, the military called in to quell riots all over the country, and angrily renewed campaigns for parliamentary reform, such activities were not going to be overlooked as adolescent pranking. Shelley was no undergraduate freak, but part of a cresting wave of radicalism; and he had been under official surveillance ever since the Home Office had been alerted to a package intercepted between Shelley and Miss Hitchener, found to contain Shelley's Irish propaganda and other 'treasonable' items. When the wretched Dan was arrested with the posters in a nearby town, the links with the stranger who dropped bottles into the sea and sent off 'so many as sixteen letters by the same post' were immediately made. A month later Godwin appeared in Lynmouth, where he hoped at last to meet his young apostle. He was disappointed to discover that he had left three weeks earlier, leaving word that he would soon be in London.

In fact, this was a false trail designed to mislead government spies. The Shelley *ménage* was now back in Wales, having fallen in with William Madocks, a Whig MP of the Duke of Norfolk's faction engaged in a celebrated land reclamation and town-building project in Tremadoc, Caernarvonshire. Madocks was struggling to keep the project alive after part of a dam had collapsed. Shelley undertook the role of fund-raiser and went to London. He first approached the Duke of Norfolk in the hopes of both a contribution and further mediation with Field Place: neither application was successful. He also finally and happily met up with Godwin, who approved his philanthropic interest in Tremadoc; and he again saw Hogg, now a law student who for all his earlier undergraduate iconoclasm was quite unimpressed by Shelley's fierce new political views. But they renewed relations, and on his empty-handed return to Wales, Shelley wrote to his old friend of another casualty of Shelleyan domestic idealism— Elizabeth Hitchener. Harriet claimed that she had tried 'to separate me from my dearly beloved Percy, and had the artfulness to say that Percy was really in love with her', but Shelley's letter to Hogg on the matter is a baffling mixture of repulsion and shamefacedness. The only certainty is that she had returned to Sussex, that Shelley had paid her off with the promise of an annuity he could ill afford, and that she was still slandering him and threatening exposure to the government.

'She says that her Reputation is gone, her health ruined, her peace of mind destroyed by my barbarity ... This is not all fact, but certainly she is embarrassed and poor, & we being in some degree the cause, we ought to obviate it. She is an artful superficial, ugly hermaphroditical beast ... What would Hell be were such a woman in Heaven?'

An even greater mystery ensued. Shelley worked hard for the Tremadoc project, but his customarily uncompromising attitudes made him several enemies among the local gentry; he was also severely in debt. One stormy night he heard a noise and went downstairs to investigate. He claimed that an unknown assailant had fired at him shouting, 'By God I will be revenged.' Glass was broken and spent bullets found. Beyond such facts, no one has ever decisively explained the incident, though every Shelley commentator has had a pet scenario. Some believe that the whole thing was a hallucination of a mind too full of Gothic paperback fiction; others that Shelley engineered the attack as an excuse for leaving Tremadoc and his debts; others suggest that he was wanted out of the area for political reasons; and it was even said locally that a mountain farmer was fed up with Shelley's mercy killing of wounded sheep and had taken revenge in kind!

Back in London after a few weeks lying low in Ireland, Shelley struggled on with the negotiations over his inheritance. Less wearily, he was seeing his first major poem through the press—a poem composed over the last fifteen hectic months that was a passionate summation of all his thinking since Oxford. *Queen Mab* has been called 'the most revolutionary document of the age in England', and in 1813 it was too hot to handle as anything but an underground publication—with the result that the few hundred issued copies quickly vanished. Shelley himself later blushingly called it 'villainous trash', but no other work of his had such massive immediate appeal to those very men and women he was so concerned to liberate. For years after his death it was an important source of inspiration and information to working-class radicals.

The plan of the poem is epic, covering a vast range of time and space in its dealings with major philosophical and political issues. Chénier had the same encyclopedic vision for his unfinished epics *Hermès* and *L'Amérique*, as well as the same ambition to make contemporary scientific knowledge into poetry—but he would have had no truck with the fantastic glittering apparatus which propels Shelley's poem. Mab, the all-knowing, all-seeing queen of the fairies, is drawn in a magic car to the bedside of a sleeping girl. This Ianthe is 'good and sincere', a doughty fighter against 'the icy chains of custom', and her soul's reward is a ride through the heavens during which the secrets of the universe are revealed to her. They pass through the ruins of past civilizations, on which Mab moralizes, and move into a 'gorgeous palace', where the tyranny of a monarch and his aristocrat 'drones' is compared to the destitution and famine suffered by their subjects. Then, with obvious reference to Napoleon's catastrophic retreat from Moscow in 1812, they see the horrors of warfare. Mab links this to the exploitations of commerce:

> The harmony and happiness of man
> Yields to the wealth of nations; that which lifts
> His nature to the heaven of its pride,
> Is bartered for the poison of his soul

which even sinks to the selling of Love. Finally she excoriates the superstitions, priesthoods, and Gods 'of human error'. The last two cantos leave past and present behind for the vision of a pastoral and egalitarian future, glowing with Reason, Science, and Godwinian benevolence. Ianthe is sent back to bed with an injunction to fight the good fight

> With tyranny and falsehood, and uproot
> The germs of misery from the human heart.

Although it has its moments of quaint beauty, much of it, as Shelley admitted, is perfunctory poetry. But the point of the poem is as a vehicle for Shelley's ideas—or rather the ideas he had eclectically been garnering from the French Enlightenment *philosophes* and historians, from Plato and Lucretius, from Godwin and many others. Where the verse gives out, long prose notes and quotations, some of them from Shelley's own pamphlets, take over the argument. In summary it may sound a mish-mash, but in the reading its strange juxtapositions of fairy-tale fantasy with modern science,* of invectives against the power-structures of the present with boundless hopes for the future, have a unity that is unmistakably Shelleyan, born of an indignation that may have been self-centred in origin, but which expanded into a compassion for all humankind.

And that is the quality which unites the four great poets whose lives have been touched on in this chapter. In everyday speech, we may

---

* Mab's magic car, for instance, has an actual correspondence with the new possibilities of aeronautics—only weeks before Shelley's arrival in Oxford, James Sadler had made a sensational balloon ascent over the city.

think of a 'romantic' as being someone detached from ordinary considerations, untouched by the reality of the world outside their own consciousness—but nothing could be less true of the so-called Romantic poets Chénier, Wordsworth, Coleridge, and Shelley, as we have seen them. They were all 'men speaking to men', urgently engaged with what Shelley, in a letter to Byron, called 'the master-theme of the epoch'—the French Revolution and the questions it inspired. They saw poetry as a weapon in a larger war, not as an end in itself; they all intensely admired Milton as the poet of the past who had played his part in shaping the destiny of his nation. Wordsworth said that 'he had given twelve hours' thought to the conditions and prospects of society for one to poetry'; while Shelley considered poetry 'very subordinate to moral and political science'. All four men spent a lot of energy on prose polemics when they thought it necessary.

Yet poetry was centrally important to them as a means whereby the revolution which had failed politically could be carried on in hearts and minds. Robespierre and Pitt, Voltaire and Godwin could only do so much with their legislation, exhortation, and rational argument: poetry had its effect at a deeper level. It was through the stimulus of poetry that the imagination could lead man to the truth that politics and revolutions had failed to deliver. The pleasure of poetry could teach joy, hope, community, and love. It kept alive *vision*, in the sense of seeing through and beyond the petty self-interest and 'worldly prudence' which they all so despised about their world as it was.

The vision was not a single definitive 'Romantic' vision; it modified with time, and varied between individuals. For the Wordsworth of the turn of the century, it was based in the wisdom he felt emanating from the natural world. For the older Coleridge, it was an attempt to save Christianity from the cynicism of an Enlightenment thinker like d'Holbach (who characterized the Bible as 'oriental fiction, distasteful to all rational men') by combining it with the truths of modern philosophy. Chénier and Shelley both cherished a vision of the 'firm yet flowing proportions' of the Ancient Greeks, which they shored against the vileness that Chénier confronted in the *Iambes* or Shelley in his *Lines written during the Castlereagh Administration*:

> Corpses are cold in the tomb;
> Stones on the pavement are dumb;
> Abortions are dead in the womb,
> And their mothers look pale—like the death-white shore
>   Of Albion, free no more.

To bear visions of such contrasting force is a terrible mental burden, and the other theme that runs through these poets' lives is the longing to escape from the noise and division of a world eaten up with politics and ideology, to recover peace and simplicity, surrounded by nature and a few loved ones, forgetful of the encroaching horror. Only Wordsworth succeeded in any degree, and for a sane and orderly life in the country he paid the price of his creative faculty. Chénier walking down the elm-lined avenue with baskets of fruit for Fanny; Coleridge dreaming of pantisocracy on the banks of the Susquehanna; Shelley summoning his friends to an 'asylum of distressed virtue': all came near to it and failed, flung back into the maelstrom of a war-torn Europe. As we shall see in the next chapter, the gap between the vision and an even more aggravating present of bills and headaches was one which might be quite unbridgeable.

Chapter 2

'Despondency and Madness'

> We Poets in our youth begin in gladness;
> But thereof in the end comes despondency and madness.
>
>   Wordsworth, 'Resolution and Independence'

The rhyme rolls off glibly—'gladness / madness' has the banal ring of 'moon / June'—but the fear behind it was real and deeply felt. Poets lost their vision, betrayed by history and a society too cruel or crass to nurture them. Poets finished up mad—it was, if you like, a simple statistical fact. Certainly at the time he wrote these lines, Wordsworth was confronting the painful mental decline of his closest friend Coleridge and groping after some basic unalterable truth of existence which would feed his soul and keep him steady. He remembers coming across an old man calmly wading round a pool on the moor, attempting to scrape a living by gathering blood-sucking leeches, which were then sold medicinally. Wordsworth is flabbergasted—if someone in this position, naked before life, can maintain his spirit and endure poverty without rancour or envy, why cannot he, Wordsworth, master his gloomy fears and fancies?

> I could have laughed myself to scorn, to find
> In that decrepit Man so firm a mind.
> 'God,' said I, 'Be my help and stay secure;
> I'll think of the Leech-gatherer on the lonely moor.'

The connection between poetry and madness is as old as Socrates.* In the *Ion* dialogue, Plato reports his view that the poet is 'a light and winged thing ... never able to compose until he has become inspired, and is beside himself, and reason is no longer in him'. The inspiration of the Old Testament prophets was a sort of poetic madness too, and

---

* And was recently subject to 'scientific confirmation', according to the *Sunday Times*. In 1985, Dr Kay Jamison of the University of California made a survey of the mental history of forty-seven contemporary writers and artists. Ten of the eighteen poets involved 'had been treated for mania with strong anti-depressant drugs such as lithium, and had voluntarily had electro-convulsive therapy or spent time in hospital'.

one that Coleridge, in 'Kubla Khan', had tried to recapture. But what worried Wordsworth was the opposite of a creative exaltation—Freud, in his great essay 'Mourning and Melancholia', called it the 'collapsed ego' and described the symptoms as 'a profoundly painful dejection, cessation of interest in the outside world, loss of the capacity to love, inhibition of all activity, and a lowering of the self-regarding feelings to a degree that finds utterance in self-reproaches and self-revilings'. The early nineteenth century was a time when such feelings were endemic. Europe was at war, and the poet's dreams buckled under the carnage of Napoleonic imperialism. The sense of rebirth, of hope for a kinder and wiser future, that had blossomed in the early 1790s was dissipated. In his satirical novel of contemporary attitudes *Nightmare Abbey*, written in 1818, not three years after Waterloo, Thomas Love Peacock tried to open up a brighter perspective—'The little wisdom and genius we have seem to be entering into a conspiracy against cheerfulness,' he wrote. Maybe the visions have failed, but need all our artists and intellectuals be quite so breast-beatingly miserable?

The cloud of despondency and madness was not confined to the literary sphere, however. Just as we now (erroneously) think of Sweden as having the world's highest suicide rate, so it was then generally thought that England was a peculiarly depressive nation. Dr Johnson, himself a manic depressive, found comfort in a treatise dealing with his condition entitled simply 'The English Malady'; the French pundit Madame de Staël put it all down to the violence of English public opinion and the ease with which reputations could be ruined. What put the matter most sharply into focus was the 'clinical' insanity of King George III, a disorder from which he suffered in bouts of increasing length and violence until his death in 1820. Some doctors tried to leech the 'poison' from his brain; others resorted to the straitjacket and even, it was rumoured, beatings.

Such methods were commonplace in the treatment of mental disease, on the basis of an idea that the body could be physically purged of the infection of madness, and well into the nineteenth century one school of doctors made use of blood-letting, forced vomiting, steam-baths, and rotating chairs in its efforts to evacuate the root of the evil, black bile, or whatever. But there was also a more enlightened trend towards a science of psychology, in which the emphasis was put on stimulating the individual's will-power to fight back against the mania or melancholy by drawing out the residual strength of the patient's saner moral self. In other words, the mad were not just to be written off as plain mad, and the best therapy was to treat them as though they were sane. A symbolic turning-point came in 1792 when at a Paris asylum one Doctor Pinel, attuned to the radically liberating mood of the times, unlocked the chains which for years had restrained his 'patients'. Elsewhere, the Marquis de Sade's establishment at Charenton encouraged amateur theatricals as a means for the inmates both to channel and play out their frustrations; while Tuke's 'Retreat', opened in York in 1796, was specifically designed to provide a harmonious and restorative environment far removed from the squalid straw-covered cells of the public asylums. There was also a humane tendency to keep the mentally ill out of institutions altogether—both Dorothy Wordsworth and the German poet Friedrich Hölderlin were fortunate in this respect, the knots of their dementia loosened by the attentions and acceptance of a domestic community. Even the violently manic depressive Mary Lamb, convicted of her mother's murder, was allowed to return home to the stuttering care of her anxious brother Charles: throughout their troubled life together, Lamb's biographer Barry Cornwall recalled a poignant regular scene: 'Whenever the approach of one of her fits of insanity was announced by some instability or change of manner, he would take her under his arm, to Hoxton Asylum. It was very afflicting to encounter the younger brother and his sister walking together ... They used to carry a straitjacket with them.' Theory and diagnosis developed too, and much research centred on the notion that a person's mental condition could be detected visually from their facial expression and external mannerisms (*see plate 3*). This may seem crude to us, but it represented a considerable advance over superstitions about spirit possession and malign fluids—and by the 1820s, another French doctor, Georget, went so far as to ascribe certain forms of madness to the pressures of an unstable society and the effects of commerce, war, and political factions (rather as the radical psychiatrists of the 1960s blamed schizophrenia on the 'nuclear family').

But the prospect that concerned Wordsworth was not so much the loss of his reason as the numbing of it, in that state of non-feeling which empties life of value and meaning. Suicide was the bottom line—an act which every ingrained piety resisted. The taking of one's own life was firmly illegal, and the Church still enforced its ban on the burial of suicides in consecrated ground: killing oneself was not allowed to imply eternal rest. The incidence of suicide among poets was high, or at least highly publicized. The thresher poet Stephen Duck drowned himself in a trout-stream during a 'fit of despondency' in 1756; William Cowper left a macabre circumstantial account of his early attempted suicide which he survived only to spend the rest of his tremulous life in periodic retreats into insanity. The fate of Thomas Chatterton (1752–70) provided perhaps the most haunting archetypal image of what a poet could expect from the world. As a resourceless lad of fifteen, apprenticed to an attorney in his native Bristol, he had begun to fake a series of medieval ballads, which he claimed to have transcribed from parchments he had discovered in an old chest in his local church of St Mary Redcliffe. The mystery surrounding these brilliant pastiches, known as the 'Rowley' poems after their purported author, won him some notoriety and raised his hopes of fame and fortune. After two suicide attempts, he was released from his indentures and made his way to London, where he tried to set himself up legitimately in the literary world. Proud and ambitious, but exploited and refused help at every crucial point, he became unhinged, staring fixedly at people 'for quarter of an hour or more till it was quite frightful'. Reduced to near-starvation, he wrote home to his mother, 'I am about to quit my ungrateful country. I shall exchange it for the deserts of Africa, where tigers are a thousand times more merciful than man.' But a week later, still only seventeen, he bought some arsenic from a druggist and was discovered dead in his filthy garret, the floor strewn with torn-up fragments of his verse. The last lines he wrote were:

> Have mercy, Heaven, where here I cease to live,
> And this last act of wretchedness forgive.

The myth of Chatterton grew (he features alongside André Chénier in Vigny's novel *Stello*, where he is made the victim of unrequited love for his landlord's wife), even after the 'Rowley' fraud had been exploded. Every aspirant to the ranks of English poets mused on how he had died,

> Stung by the world's neglect and scorn
> While conscious merit fir'd his mind,
> Unfriended, foodless, and forlorn ...

The seventeen-year-old Coleridge wrote a 'monody' on Chatterton, and was married in St Mary Redcliffe. In 'Resolution and Independence', written in the metre of Chatterton's 'Ballad of Charitie' and echoing its subject, Wordsworth pays tribute to his 'sleepless soul' in its unblessed grave. Shelley's elegy for John Keats, 'Adonais', raises the spectre of Chatterton, still in 'solemn agony'; while Keats himself wrote a doggerel sonnet beginning 'Oh Chatterton! how very sad thy fate', later inscribed *Endymion* 'to the memory of Thomas Chatterton', and recorded his opinion that Chatterton's 'medieval' idiom showed him to be 'the purest writer in the English language'.

It was not Chatterton's poetic experiments, however, that made him so sharply remembered, but the fact that the story could be interpreted to show that poetic genius could find no soil in England. Only mediocrity flourished: 'society' destroyed Chatterton. This, of course, has always been a convenient idea for artists of all sorts, inasmuch as it allows a lack of worldly success to be explained away as the fault of 'something out there', but in the late eighteenth century it also reflected a burgeoning belief that 'art' and 'artists' existed on a plane higher and purer than that inhabited by this normal eating, sleeping, and earning run of society. Another poet who captured the imagination on this score was the sixteenth-century Italian Torquato Tasso, a man of strongly independent spirit who was under the patronage of the Duke of Ferrara when he had the termerity to fall in love with the Duke's sister. To keep the two apart the Duke locked Tasso up, leaving him to fester in a cell for seven years, driven insane by anger and despair but still retaining his essential nobility of heart. Such was the tale (as with Chatterton, the facts are considerably more complicated) and among those who responded strongly to its implications—again, that the Poet will be scorned and driven mad by hostile worldly forces—were Goethe, Shelley, and Byron, who actually had himself shut in Tasso's cell in Ferrara, so as to experience something of what the seven years' incarceration must have been like.

No wonder that Peacock could talk of an intellectual 'conspiracy against cheerfulness'. Optimism, wit, and sociable good humour had not been fashionable among the ordinary reading public for three quarters of a century, since Richardson's heroine Clarissa died from the shame of rape, Ossian mourned the doom of brave warriors, and Goldsmith reflected on the Deserted Village.

Most sensationally melancholy of all truly popular pre-Revolutionary works was Goethe's novella *Die Leiden des Jungen Werthers* (1774). Composed as a series of letters, the story is told with concise intensity, and without the rambling prolixity of other epistolary fiction. The hero is a young man typical of the alienated over-educated intelligentsia that the German states found so difficult to employ constructively. At the beginning of the book he comes to the country to recuperate from various pressures and miseries. He is charmed by the sunshine and simplicity around him, reads Homer, and dallies with Charlotte, a delightful local girl who shares his taste in poetry. But she is betrothed to the dull honest Albert, and in an attempt to avoid confrontation, Werther leaves to take up a footling official post. Absurdly snubbed by the petty aristocracy and deeply in love, he resigns and returns in a dazed state to Charlotte, who rejects him. Now he pores over Ossian and reflects despairingly on life and human passions. The idyll has darkened—what seemed a world of sunlight and grace now appears stormy and cruel. After elaborate preparations, Werther shoots himself with a pistol lent by Charlotte and Albert.

The sensibilities of Europe, at every level, were struck by the crisis of feeling that this book articulated so sharply. Even Napoleon himself, as a seventeen-year-old recruit to the French army, wrote how 'always alone among people, I return home to dream by myself, and submit to the liveliness of my own melancholy: what turn will it take today? towards Death ...'; over twenty years later he would tell Goethe that he had read Werther at least seven times. In the Italian Papal States it was considered sufficiently shocking to be banned; in England it quickly went through fourteen editions and was turned into both a poem and a play. In fact, so finely attuned was it to the contemporary raw nerve that it sparked off something like a suicide epidemic:* Goethe himself was particularly perturbed in 1777 when a woman who drowned herself in the river near his home was found to have a copy of the book in her pocket; while in London in 1779 James Hackman was condemned to death for the murder of Martha Reay, the mistress of the Earl of Sandwich: a copy of Werther's last letter to Charlotte was found on the ground next to the discarded pistol.

In other more familiar ways Goethe was plagued for the rest of his life by Werther's fame, particularly by the celebrity-hunters who wanted to uncover 'real-life' sources and identities. In his auto-biography Goethe reveals that he had combined the suicide of a student contemporary of his Leipzig days—a young man who, like Werther, wore a striking blue jacket, read English literature, smarted from the snubs of the aristocracy, and was carried off by a passion for a

---

* Suicide has always shown a strong tendency to occur in localized epidemic waves. In 1772, for instance, fifteen soldiers hanged themselves from a single hook protruding from the ceiling of their barracks; an appalling modern instance is the suicide in 1978 of eight hundred members of the People's Temple in Jamestown, Guyana. Suicide is the second largest cause of death in the fifteen to twenty-four age group in the USA—and an article by W.J. Weatherby in the *Guardian* of 29 October 1984 details a rash of such cases in the 'paradise' suburban areas of Putnam, Westchester, and Rockland counties.

married woman—with memories of his own crisis of feeling over one Lotte Buff and a period when suicide was on his mind to the extent of taking a dagger to bed with him. Writing *Werther* served Goethe as therapy, but even so it was a book he hardly dared read again 'lest I should once more experience the peculiar mental state from which it was produced'.

'Wertherism' is one manifestation of the disease of the age: the excessive surrender to personal feelings criticized by Jane Austen in *Sense and Sensibility*, and the Byronic gloom of *Childe Harold* and *Manfred* are others. Of course, melancholy, depression, and intro-spection are universal, part of the biology of the human psyche, and there is as much despondency and madness in Greek tragedy, Shake-speare, or modernism, as there is in this epoch of literature. When Coleridge cries out in a letter of 1804, 'I am heart-sick and almost stomach-sick of speaking, writing, and thinking about myself,' he is not being peculiarly 'Romantic': Hamlet and D. H. Lawrence could have made the identical complaint. Yet there is something extra-ordinarily intense and pervasive about the mental problems of the intellectual and middle classes in the post-Revolutionary era. One possible explanation is the unprecedented amount of moral, religious, and political choice that the Enlightenment and its consequences had made available—not so much a crisis of belief, as a crisis of *what* to believe. The central unifying figure of an authoritarian God, dispens-ing wrath and justice—Blake's 'Nobodaddy'—omniscient and omni-potent, commonly worshipped by Catholic and Protestant alike, no longer bound Christendom together, as it had for well over a thousand years previously. Scepticism, not faith; change, not permanence: a hundred different sects, a hundred shades of belief and ways to shape your mind—all promising Truth, all possibly illusions turning to dust and ashes in the hand. Nothing causes depression like the inability to make a decision, whether practical or philosophical, and decisions were what the tumultuous alterations of the times constantly demanded. A wrong decision, however intellectual in nature, can hit as hard as the failure of a grand passion: abstractions can become life-blood, ideas so much more than the toys of after-dinner conver-sation. And for some, the voyage through the fogs of uncertainty—what to believe, and why; what to do, and why—was a stifling one. To stand and dither was not self-indulgence, but the result of real, deep pain.

The despondency of Coleridge, for instance, has nothing glorious or proud about it; the heroism he showed in response was a long

grinding struggle against a weakness of will that often took the upper
hand. Although there was no real victory, he turned out to be a dogged
survivor, the weak will countered by a strong conscience and a wry
sense of his own shortcomings. He admitted that there was much of
the Hamlet in his make-up, and saw himself as the victim, not the
agent of his own destiny—a line of self-defence embodied in some of
his greatest poetry. In *The Rime of the Ancient Mariner*, the central
figure is hounded and harrowed for an initial crime, the shooting of a
bird, that scarcely merits such persecution; while a weird game of
demon possession is played out in the unfinished *Christabel*:

> In the touch of my bosom there worketh a spell
> Which is lord of thy utterance, Christabel . . .

The failure to complete this poem was characteristic of Coleridge:
but whereas most of his schemes simply evaporated, the unfinished
Christabel continued to haunt him as marking the drying-up of his
poetic inspiration and the beginning of a tumbling downward spiral.
In October 1800, he starkly recorded the moment of realization in one
of the notebooks in which he recorded so much of his inner life: 'He
knew not what to do—something he felt must be done—he rose, drew
his writing-desk suddenly before him—sate down, took a pen—and
found that he knew not what do do.' This feeling of helplessness
welled up a few months after he had moved to Keswick in the Lake
District, so as to be near William and Dorothy Wordsworth. His third
son had just been born; his energies were consumed by hack journalism and translation work. As the antagonism with his wife Sara
became more violent, he felt himself falling in love with another
woman, of whom we will hear more. And even more gravely, his
health was breaking down. The dampness of the Lakes aggravated a
childhood rheumatic condition, a weak heart, and a tendency to
puffiness and congestion. In everything that follows, we must bear in
mind that Coleridge, not yet thirty, was a physically sick man, poorly
served by the medicine of the time. In May 1801 he told his friend
Thomas Poole the beginning of the story of 'my Health & it's
Downfalls':

> During the whole Fall of the year to Christmas I had been harassed
> with all sorts of crazinesses, blood-shot eyes, swoln Eye lids,
> rheumatic pains in the back of my head & limbs, clusters of Boils in
> my neck &c ... slight changes of weather affected me, & *Wet*
> cloathes, tho' pulled off immediately on my entering the house,

never failed to throw me on my back.—The new year was ushered in with what I believed a Rheumatic Fever tho' no doubt part of the pains were nephritic.—This was followed by the Hydrocele [a swollen testicle, which he was too embarrassed to show to a doctor] ... I relapsed—and a Devil of a Relapse it has been, to be sure!? There is no doubt that it is irregular Gout combined with frequent nephritic attacks— ... in general it was my left Knee & Ancle— here the Disorder has been evidently attempting to fix itself—my left knee was most uncouthly swoln & discolored, & gave me night after night pain enough, heaven knows, but yet it never came to a fair Paroxysm.—All this was mere nothing—but O dear Poole! the attacks on my stomach, & the nephritic pains in my back which almost alternated with the stomach fits—they were terrible!

This is only one of many such catalogues, for Coleridge was deeply fascinated by his own condition— 'I tried a multitude of little experiments on my own sensations, & on my senses,' he told Poole—and in particular by the relation between his mental and physical states. It was Coleridge who coined the term 'psychosomatology', as he noted how any feeling of guilt or anxiety would immediately stimulate a physical symptom: arguing with his wife, for instance, would 'like a flash of lightning, shoot thro' my Bowels, and bring on a temporary diarrhoea'.* He also tried a number of remedies, including a bewildering range of diets, all totally opposed to any modern conception of healthy eating. In 1802 he tells Southey that he is refraining from alcohol, vegetables, tea, and bread, and living 'almost entirely on Eggs, Fish, Flesh & Fowl'; and a few months later the therapy is coffee and lightly boiled eggs. There were periods too, when he recovered an extraordinary degree of strength, such as the holiday in Scotland in 1803, when he walked 263 miles in eight days. But in general the picture was bleak, and he was not helped by constant recourse to the most common pain-killer of the day—opium, usually taken in tincture as laudanum.

Opium was a standard analgesic of the early nineteenth century, cheap, legal, and widely available: for the few literary and middle-class people who were addicts (the essayist Thomas De Quincey and the slave-trade agitator William Wilberforce were two others), there were probably thousands of working-class people who drugged themselves and their children out of their misery. Opium's status was

* He also foresaw the principles of Freudian psychoanalysis, proposing a system of medicine which would force 'the will and *motive faculties* into action'.

perhaps comparable to that of Valium today, inasmuch as the taking of a small occasional dose was scarcely remarked upon, and although the danger of becoming addicted was understood, many doctors of the time considered it less harmful than tea. Quite how Coleridge fell is hard to determine, because he consistently lied, even to himself, about the matter. He seems to have taken it first during a childhood illness, and in 1796 a letter mentions the taking of laudanum 'almost every night' and sometimes every five hours, to relieve an attack of neuralgia. In 1816 he was to claim that 'Kubla Khan' had been composed in 1797 under the spell of an opium-induced trance, but this is quite possibly an opportune fiction. He also claimed that he only took it for strictly medical purposes, never for the pleasures of hallucination and relaxation—but again there is evidence to suggest otherwise. One thing is fairly certain: during the period which he describes in the letter to Poole quoted above, he was taking large quantities of the stuff (swallowed in a swig of brandy) and for the rest of his life he was never able to keep away from it for long. In 1814, in what seems as truthful an account as any, he wrote that he had been 'seduced into the ACCURSED habit ignorantly', after reading that laudanum worked a cure for those 'swellings in the knees' which caused him such pain. After a 'miracle' cure, the complaint returned and more laudanum was taken—'but I cannot go thro' the dreary history', he breaks off. It sounds plausible, but the trouble is that whenever Coleridge protests himself in outraged tones to be a mere INNOCENT victim, he is very likely lying. He might even lie about his lying: thus in 1814 he admits, 'I have in this one dirty business of Laudanum an hundred times, deceived, tricked, nay actually and consciously LIED,' while less than two years later he can announce to another correspondent, 'You will never *hear* anything but truth from me ... prior habits render it out of my power to tell an untruth.'

A further barrier is the veneer of cheerfulness and normality which, like so many addicts, Coleridge was masterly at maintaining and which can give a misleading joviality to his letters. He used this surface manner to keep his secret life under cover—a life of fibs, evasions, broken promises, unopened letters, and forgotten appointments. Parallel to this ran a bizarre career in literary plagiarism. This was not just a matter of drawing on a common pool of images and concepts; it frequently involved the surreptitious literal translation of large chunks of little-known German works which were then silently inserted into his own argument (or, as in 'Chamouny; the Hour before Sunrise', his own verse). In these cases, there is really no justification for accepting

Coleridge's own wide-eyed explanation when challenged, that it was simply a matter of coincidence. Rather, it looks like a neurotic compulsion, a form of kleptomania. There must have been occasions when he resorted to it as a way of meeting a deadline or of filling up space, but just as often it seems totally unnecessary—no one would have thought any the worse of him for making and acknowledging an open quotation. To complete the labyrinth of deceit, Coleridge was often vigorous in his denunciation of other people's plagiarism.

One does not lightly make judgements of Coleridge, however. He was a man in chronic pain, and it could be argued that his survival was a triumph of that very will-power—'voluntary' power, as it was then called—which he is widely supposed to have lacked. His lonely fight to get himself off opium is dreadful to contemplate. The drug soon became a necessity to him, not a short cut to hazy ecstasies. The visions he had were sexual nightmares, grotesque and taunting. All he hoped for was 'repose', mere blank relief from the neurotic guilt and paranoid delusions that crowd into 'The Pains of Sleep', a poem that records the effects of withdrawal. It was what such a state of mind revealed about his own soul that terrified him more than anything:

> ... the fiendish crowd
> of Shapes and Thoughts that tortur'd me!
> Desire with Loathing strangely mixt,
> On wild or hateful Objects fixt;
> Pangs of Revenge, the powerless Will,
> Still baffled, and consuming still,
> Sense of intolerable wrong ...

Locked in all this agony and the secrecy that surrounded it, Coleridge looked desperately for the consolation and companionship of human love. His wife could not provide it, despite the brief bursts of affection in the first years of their marriage, recorded in poems like 'The Eolian Harp'. Sara was an ordinary woman, with ordinary suburban ambitions to see her husband do well. She had married him on the understanding that he was a genius, and that a genius would rise to worldly consequence. She expected to be materially comfortable and secure, with Coleridge showing himself to be as 'steady' a character as her sister Edith's husband, Southey. She was disappointed to find instead someone unstable and pathologically unmethodical, whose hours of reading, scrawling, and messing about issued in no visible return.

Then there were his new friends, the Wordsworths—Sara was shut out of their world of nature, imagination, and meditation: they did not much like her, and she reciprocated the feeling, although hostilities were never overt. Coleridge, however, lavished all his attentions and intensity on them, to the point at which Sara was left completely out of touch with his intellectual and spiritual life. While he was on an extended trip to Germany (during which Sara had to cope with the death of their second son), she wrote in exasperation to Thomas Poole—the one friend of her husband's who seemed to her to have some common sense—'It is very unpleasant to me to be often asked if Coleridge has changed political sentiments—for I know not properly how to reply—pray furnish me.'

When Coleridge insisted on moving up to the Lake District and the Wordsworths, the rift in the marriage sharpened. Sara was cut off from her West Country family and friends, to be thrust into a milieu where long walks and poetry were the staple diversions—neither of which she cared for. But she was not the wilting sort. Deeply involved in her children, a skilled housekeeper against considerable odds, and possessed of a certain toughness of mind, she fought back with some hard, conventional marital tactics. Coleridge listed 'ill-tempered speeches sent after me when I went out of the house, ill-tempered speeches on my return, my friends received with freezing looks, the least opposition or contradiction occasioning screams of passion, and the sentiments which I held most base ostentatiously avowed—all this added to the utter negation of all, which a husband expects from a wife.'

Their quarrels were violent and recriminatory—Coleridge never forgot that he had been pushed into the marriage against his better judgement, and she must have remembered her other rejected suitors. But in an age where divorce was virtually impossible, they tried to conciliate. 'She promised to set about an alteration in her external manners and looks and language,' Coleridge wrote in 1803, 'I, on my part, promised to be more attentive to all her feelings of pride etc., etc., and to try to correct my habits of imperious censure.' That 'etc., etc.' embodies all the gritted-teeth irritation that Coleridge felt; and also his fundamentally patronizing approach to her side of the case. 'Permit me, my dear Sara,' he wrote in 1803, as they sank into frosty courtesies,

without offence to you, as Heaven knows! it is without any feeling of pride in myself to say, that in sex, acquirements, and in the quantity and quality of natural endowments, whether of feeling or of intellect, you are the inferior. Therefore it would be preposterous to expect that I should see with your eyes, and dismiss my friends from *my* heart; but it is not preposterous in me, on the contrary I have a *right* to expect and demand that you should to a certain degree love and act kindly to those whom I deem worthy of my Love ...

And there was another woman in the case, although it is unclear as to how much Sara ever knew about her. Sara Hutchinson, whom Coleridge first met in 1799, was the sister of Mary Hutchinson, whom Wordsworth married in 1802. Sara—or Asra, as Coleridge called her to mask the unfortunate coincidence of name—was an odd object of obsessive desire, for she was a short and plain woman without any erotic mystique or even any particular intellectual bent. Her manner was sunny and warm, however, and she had the simple instinct to listen to people's problems and help them if she could: it was this as much as anything that Coleridge needed. There does not seem to have been any sexual intimacy in the course of their relationship, but in thought and word Asra, or the idea of her, was the vessel for all his thwarted emotions, a centre of value when everything else—his poetry, his marriage, his health, his self-respect—had failed him.

In 1802, he wrote Asra a letter in verse, which tries to grapple with the problems of his despondency. This is a first and infinitely more personal and moving version of the poem that he later bowdlerized as 'Dejection: An Ode'. In this letter Coleridge, like so many depressives, does not put his gloom down rationally to its material causes: bad diet, illness, or drug dependence. He concentrates on a metaphysical symptom—his inability to *feel* the world to be the source of beauty and joy he has known it to be. He recalls a magical evening spent with Asra and her sister:

> Dear Mary! on her Lap my head she lay'd—
> Her hand was on my Brow,
> Even as my own is now;
> And on my cheek I felt thy eye-lash play.
> Such Joy I had, that I may truly say,
> My Spirit was awe-stricken with the Excess
> And trance-like Depth of its brief Happiness.

Now he muses on Asra's absence, the difficulties of marriage, and the 'heartless mood' with which he looks at his children and the glories of nature:

I were sunk low indeed, did they *no* solace give;
But oft I seem to feel, & evermore I fear,
They are not to me now the Things, which once they were.

Eighteen months later, his frame of mind is the same, as he writes in one of his notebooks:

Tomorrow my Birth-Day, 31 years of age!—O me! my very heart dies! ... why have I not an unencumbered Heart! These beloved books still before me, this noble room, the very centre to which a whole world of beauty converges, the deep reservoir into which all these streams and currents of lovely forms flow—my own mind so populous, so active, so full of noble schemes so capable of realizing them ... O wherefore am I not happy!

There was only one possible solution that anyone could suggest: Coleridge should go abroad, away from his wife, Asra, the damp, and his bad habits. The Azores, the West Indies, Portugal were variously mooted, but lack of money or a travelling companion, the hindrances of the Napoleonic Wars, and his own inertia, prevented a decision until 1804, when, with the help of his friends, he made his way by sea to Malta. Here, after some string-pulling, he took up a post as secretary to the High Commissioner. The experiment was not a success. He had taken a large amount of opium and laudanum with him and the silent signs are that he was dosing himself uninhibitedly. The job was steady, but dull and routined. An initial improvement in his health faltered. Apart from a mass of notebook jottings, he did almost no creative work of his own. Worst of all, he was desperately lonely and homesick. The war made communications difficult and few of his letters reached their destinations, but one of them, to his wife (for whom one might expect a cooler tone), shows him still in a maudlin state: 'I do not know what it is to have one *happy* moment or *one* genial feeling! Not one!—so help me God! No visitations of mind or of fancy—but only the same, gnawing pain at the heart, sometimes indeed, tho' seldom, relieved by a flood of tears when I can say aloud to myself—My children! My children!'

In August 1806, after a sojourn in Rome and various delays, Coleridge slipped back into London. In his mid thirties, he felt and looked like an old man. The Wordsworths, devastated by the recent drowning of their sailor-brother John, had worried about him constantly; now they hoped he would return to Keswick, resign himself to 'an agreement to disagree' with his wife, and settle down to produce a solid corpus of major work which would complement William's own labours on a projected vast epic poem, *The Recluse*.

This was not to be: Coleridge's first and perhaps only determination was to negotiate a permanent separation from Sara—an idea to which she put up screaming resistance on the sole grounds that 'everybody will talk'. Eventually she was obliged to give way; but the arrangement hardly left Coleridge better off. He was soon back in London, picking up any freelance literary work that came his way. In 1808 the Royal Institution announced that he would give a series of lectures on 'the Principles of Poetry'. These mark the beginning of his sustained writing as a literary critic, but in early form they proved fairly disastrous. Some were cancelled because he was ill or simply did not appear; some evenings, probably under the relaxing influence of opium, he would 'free-associate', rambling happily along streams of thought which had nothing to do with the advertised subject; on another occasion, he could hardly move his jaw—his lips baked and black, he only kept going by gulping down copious amounts of water. A young journalist Henry Crabb Robinson recorded in his diary that for all their sporadic wisdom and brilliance, the lectures contained 'too much apology, too much reference to what he had before written, too much promise of what was to come'. For Coleridge, the most upsetting episode of the period was the reappearance of his first love Mary Evans, now a Mrs. Todd, who had seen the lectures advertised. She was as unhappy in her marriage as he had been in his: Coleridge stared at her, thought of what might have been—but there was nothing more to say.

The bread and butter of these next years was paid for by newspaper writing, mostly in the form of the anonymous political commentary we now call 'leaders'. Admirers might deplore this humiliation of his genius—'What is become of all this mighty heap of hope, of thought, of learning, of humanity?' asked William Hazlitt. 'It has ended in swallowing doses of oblivion and in writing paragraphs in the *Courier*—such, and so little is the mind of man!'—but Coleridge took the work seriously, and reading his paragraphs now, it is impossible not to admire his grasp of the issues, the height of his moral perspectives, and his ability to see, without smugness, the virtues of both the progressive and conservative positions. He detested Napoleon, and was forced to accept the idea of a 'necessary war' against him—but he never lost either his pity for the victims of a ruthless social order or his anger against the oppressors. Unlike the politicians around him, he managed to refuse expedients, stand firm on Christian principles, and yet remain sharp-eyed and realistic.

In the summer of 1808 Coleridge returned to the Lake District and moved into the Wordsworths' uncomfortable new house in Grasmere, where Asra was also living. The plan now was to write, edit, and publish a weekly magazine to be known as *The Friend* which would deal at length with matters of morality, politics, religion, and letters, as well as providing 'sources of consolation to the afflicted'. Neither the Wordsworth household nor anyone else could be very sanguine about the enterprise. For one thing, 'setting up shop' (as Coleridge contemptuously called it) required financial and administrative work of which he was obviously incapable—and indeed even the delegation of the paper, printing, proofs, and postage was beset by constant blunders and miscalculations. When the magazine finally made its appearance, the general response was embodied in Dorothy Wordsworth's judgement that despite beautiful passages in which 'the power of thought and the originality of a great mind' were displayed, the overall effect was 'very obscure'. Whereas the newspaper writing had perforce been brief and benefited from being produced to deadline and order, *The Friend* had no such perimeters, no editorial blue pencil. At times the argument of the essays became so diffuse that even its author seems to have forgotten what its original drift was. 'I earnestly entreat the reader not to be dissatisfied either with himself or with the author,' he writes at one point, 'if he should not at once understand every part of the preceding number': 'I do not understand it either,' one expects him to add.

That *The Friend* lasted as long as nine months (with a few breaks) amazed everyone—but its survival was due as much as anything to Asra's devoted secretarial and copying work. When she caved in under the strain and left Grasmere to convalesce with her brother in Wales, Coleridge lost heart completely. The reluctance of a large percentage of his readers to part with the money they owed for their subscriptions meant that the final losses amounted to something like £300 or the equivalent of a decent annual income.*

This, at least, is one side of the story. Behind *The Friend*, various personal tensions were reaching breaking-point. For some time, the friendship between Wordsworth and Coleridge had been growing more difficult. Through the years of their relationship Wordsworth had gradually secured his material and spiritual stability, buttressed by

* Even in 1818, when *The Friend* was reissued in revised book form, Coleridge's preface is still pleading for those who owe him money to pay up.

the tireless attendance of his wife and sister. Coleridge's adulation of Wordsworth's genius was unfailing, too: 'I dare affirm that he will hereafter be admitted as the first and greatest philosophical poet,' he proclaimed in 1804, and he made a great point of comparing the worthlessness of his own efforts to those of his friend. 'If I die,' he once wrote, be sure to say that heaven 'by showing to him what true poetry was ... made him know that he himself was no poet.' But a psychologist as perceptive as Coleridge should have recognized that such protestations could mask other layers of feeling. In fact, he was beginning to become openly irritated at the way that Wordsworth's womenfolk coddled him. 'Almost his very Eating and Drinking are done for him by his Sister, or his wife,' he wrote, 'yet have I no dear heart that loves my verses.' There was, of course, the canker of envy in this, for Coleridge would have liked nothing better than to be at the centre of female attention. Yet envy is not a sufficient explanation: Coleridge wanted Wordsworth's moral strength, his very soul—'O that my spirit purged by death of its weaknesses,' he wrote in Malta, 'might flow into thine, and live and act in thee, and be Thou.'

Wordsworth, for his part, became increasingly exasperated by Coleridge's inability to organize himself, and having him to stay only confirmed his worst suspicions. He wrote to Coleridge's friend Poole that 'Neither his talents nor his genius, nor his vast information will avail him anything; they are all frustrated by a derangement in his intellectual and moral constitution. In fact he has no voluntary power of mind whatsoever, nor is he capable of acting under any *constraint* of duty or moral obligation.' The most sensitive factor, however, was not opium or indolence: it was Asra. The Wordsworths had probably hoped that she would have completed the family circle by marrying their drowned brother John, and they had good reason to be unhappy about the possible pitfalls in her relationship with Coleridge. His notebooks evince how overmastering his passion for this dumpy and cheerful woman remained: 'I fear to speak, I fear to hear you speak—so deeply do I now enjoy your presence, so totally possess you in myself, myself in you. The very sound would break the union, and separate *you-me*, into you and me. We both, and this sweet room ... are all our thought, harmonious imagery of forms distinct on the still substance of one deep feeling, Love and Joy.' But the notebooks also hint at Asra's rather less intense response to his attentions, as when he accuses her that 'you never sate with or near me ten minutes in your life, without shewing a restlessness and a thought of going *etc.*, for at least five minutes out of ten.'

Coleridge hatched paranoid feelings both that the Wordsworths were scheming to antagonize Asra against him, and that Asra was transferring her attentions to Wordsworth himself—he who already enjoyed more than his portion of woman's love. 'It is not the voice, not the duty of his nature, to love any *being* as I love you No! he is to be beloved,' Coleridge wails, 'I alone love you so devotedly & therefore Sara! love me! love me.' After Asra's departure for Wales, which must have been preceded by a sharp recital of brute facts and which in effect marks the end of this hopeless romance, Dorothy Wordsworth voiced her relief in a letter to a friend. Coleridge 'harassed and agitated [Asra's] mind continually and we saw that he was doing her health perpetual injury ... his love for her is no more than a fanciful dream.' Of her remaining house guest she despaired: 'We have no hope of him ... If he were not under our roof he would be just as much the slave of stimulants as ever; and his whole time and thoughts (except when he is reading and he reads a great deal) are employed in deceiving himself and seeking to deceive others.' He was listless and surly, rarely rising before midday and prone to pretending that he was on the verge of finishing a new number of *The Friend*, when it was obvious that he had not written a single line. 'We have no hope of him.'

In the autumn of 1810, Wordsworth's friend Basil Montagu offered to take Coleridge to London in his carriage and gave him lodging. Wordsworth discouraged the idea, warning Montagu what to expect. But Montagu persevered, and when Coleridge proved every bit as bad as Wordsworth had indicated, Montagu tactlessly blurted out what had been said, to the effect that Coleridge was 'a rotten drunkard' and an 'absolute nuisance in the family'. Coleridge was profoundly shaken. That his soul-mate of the great days of 1797–8, with whom he had so rapturously shared his vision, should turn against him was more than he could bear, especially as Montagu had implied that Wordsworth intended his verdict to reach his ears. 'W. authorised M. to tell me, he had no Hope of me! O God! what good reason for saying this? ... No Hope of me! absol. nuisance! God's mercy is it a dream!' He felt 'whirled about without a center—as in a nightmair—no gravity—a vortex without a center', and on 3 November in a shabby hotel in Covent Garden he made a massive effort to review the bases of his life: perhaps he felt himself on the verge of suicide. The notebook entry begins with an almost melodramatic summary of his Christian faith, his belief in a supreme being of infinite power, inscrutable to human reason but sensed by human conscience: in the incarnation of the Son and the descending grace of the Holy Spirit. Nothing, however, can console him for the terrible knowledge that 'No one on earth has ever LOVED me.' He can blame himself for 'a want of reliability in little things, the infliction of little pains', but as 'the events of the last year, and emphatically of the last month, have now forced me to perceive', he sees that the love he gave to Asra (which 'to an Angel alone would be intelligible') and to Wordsworth ('a man whose welfare never ceased to be far dearer than my own') has not been reciprocated. The sad irony is that it was now if ever that Coleridge needed and deserved the patience of his friends, for he was in the middle of a last-ditch effort to wean himself off opium. He consulted at least eight different specialists, none of whom can have given him hope of anything but a lifetime of controlled doses and unremitting self-control: all the heavy drinking and lying late in bed were symptoms of a despairing preference for oblivion over the daily struggle against temptation. Back in London, demoralized and deserted, he plodded the treadmills of political and literary journalism. There was a brief glittering interlude when his play *Remorse* had some success at Drury Lane; there was an unenthusiastic mending of the quarrel with Wordsworth; and there were still the perfunctory smiles and surface jovialities—if you could ignore the way his hands shook.

In December 1813, when he seems to have been taking an enormous four ounces of opium every day, a climax to the crises was reached. In the Greyhound Inn near Bath, Coleridge went through a week of delirium tremens so terrible that he begged to be consigned to a madhouse. 'An indefinite, indescribable, TERROR, as with a scourge of ever restless, ever coiling and uncoiling SERPENTS drove me on from behind ... From the sole of my foot to the crown of my head there was not an inch in which I was not continually in torture,' he described it. Few understood or even sympathized: 'Did you ever hear of Jesus Christ?' wrote one evangelical friend unhelpfully, 'Come and be healed.' But the healing that Coleridge needed would be constant and enlightened medical supervision, and from 1816 until the end of his life he was fortunate in being 'referred' by one of the physicians he consulted to somebody who could combine that sort of skill with the sympathy and affection of which he felt so starved.

James Gilman was a young surgeon who lived with his wife Maria in Highgate, then a pretty wooded village a few miles north of London. They took Coleridge in as a paying guest—although they never pestered him for money—watched him like hawks, doled out minimal doses of opium, and, most important of all, gave his life a degree of stability. The great defining philosophical project remained, perhaps inevitably, in fragments; and much of the rest of his work was a matter of restitching old patches (sometimes not his own patches either), but he was now able to write in a more sustained and regular way.

There was only a little more poetry, none of it generated by the excitement of his earlier work, and he did not follow up his initial success as a playwright, despite the encouragement of no less than Lord Byron—but he did not regard this as calamitous, for there was much else he wanted to say. In 1817, for instance, he published *Biographia Literaria*, a miscellaneous study of his intellectual development embracing reminiscence, philosophical speculation, and literary criticism: Wordsworth was not amused by the strictures passed on his *Lyrical Ballads* and theory of poetry. One of Coleridge's preoccupations in this work is the definition of the poetic imagination, or the poet's mental processes, as distinguished from other forms of perception: what, in other words, makes a poet? It was part of an attempt (with some covert help from the Germans) to break new ground and introduce new terms and categories into the language of philosophy. As with structuralism or psychoanalysis in our own century, it provoked a great deal of complaint about 'obscurity' and 'jargon'—in Peacock's *Nightmare Abbey* (1818), for instance, the Coleridgean Mr Flosky announces 'This distinction between fancy and imagination is one of the most abstruse and important points of metaphysics. I have written seven hundred pages of promise to elucidate it'. The Prime Minister Lord Liverpool was baffled by a long letter Coleridge sent him, noting that its subject seemed to be the desirability of running his government on Christian lines, or 'at least, I believe this is Mr Coleridge's meaning, but I cannot well understand him.' Coleridge himself could make a joke of it, as when he described, not inaccurately, his principles as those of a 'Spinozo-Kantian, Kanto-Fichtean, Fichto-Schellingian revival of Plato-Plotino-Proclian idealism', but it would be wrong to think of him as ending his life doddering about in a private fantasy world. He remained as concerned with the moral health of society as he had been in the years following the French Revolution, and in a last series of works—*Lay Sermons, Aids to Reflection*, and *On the Constitution of Church and State*—he turned over the great questions of the nature of human spiritual growth and the promotion of 'culture'; of the separation of superstition from faith, and the restoration of this latter to a central place in the Christian religion; of the balance necessary between 'permanent' and 'progressive' social forces. All the long-winded obscurity and logical dead ends in such books did not prevent them from becoming enormously influential on the next half-century of theologians and moralists, especially those in the Christian Socialist and Broad Church Movements.

In the 1820s his reputation spread as much through his talk as his writing, and his small Thursday soirées in Highgate became a sort of religious service for the London literary world. The grand old man of letters would sit in his parlour, reported a newspaper gossip column in 1824, 'looking all sweet and simple and divine things, the very personification of meekness and humility'. There was little conversation—*one*-versation would be the more appropriate word, as Coleridge admitted in a typical little pleasantry—for the function of the small gatherings was to allow him to deliver free-ranging sermons to an audience all too ready to acknowledge the impenetrable aura of genius. It was a strong man who could be sceptical in such an atmosphere: one such was a fierce young tiro of a Scot, Thomas Carlyle, who could harshly judge the fashionable Sage to be a 'mass of richest spices putrefied into a dung-hill'. 'To the rising spirits of the young generation,' he wrote, Coleridge 'had this dusky sublime character; and sat there as a kind of *Magus*, girt in mystery and enigma ... I have heard [him] talk, with eager musical energy, two stricken hours, his face radiant and moist, and communicate no meaning whatsoever to any individual of his hearers.' Posterity is fortunate to have some record of Coleridge's talk, sharply edited by one of his nephews; but that coruscating book of brilliant nuggets *Table Talk* gives no impression of the hypnotising flow of indirections, digressions, and spirals which structured his monologues and which to some extent must have been the result of opium.

The façade of wisdom and benevolence was misleading. Coleridge was not a mellowed and contented old man, but a prematurely aged drug addict, well aware of what he had failed to achieve. Life had flogged him into submission. Some sensitive observers, like Carlyle's friend John Sterling, detected the unease beneath: 'It is painful to observe in Coleridge that, with all the kindness and glorious far-seeing intelligence of his eye, there is a glare in it, a light half unearthly, half morbid. It is the glittering eye of the Ancient Mariner.' The scandals of opium and a broken marriage were by now generally known. The chicanery of publishers left him as impoverished and as enslaved to hack commissions as ever before. There was another tragedy too, in the fate of his adored firstborn, Hartley, a wonderful child, 'the darling of the sun and the breeze', who inherited too much of his father's temperament and grew into a dwarfish, twitchy young man with a shock of black hair which gave him an uncannily Oriental appearance. Coleridge had experimented on his infant psychology with ruthless fascination—'Don't ask me so many questions, Papa! I can't bear it!' he once screamed out—and the result was a neurotic lopsided prodigy with a drinking problem. His irregular behaviour lost him a prestigious Oxford fellowship and he ended up as an eccentric recluse in the Lake District, writing occasional sonnets and doing odd jobs of school-mastering.

Other relationships steadied. He saw Asra once or twice without anguish, and in 1828 accompanied Wordsworth and his daughter on a tour of Germany and the Low Countries. He could meet his wife with equanimity when necessary, and was pleased by his clever and beautiful daughter Sara who, having been born in 1802 and brought up by her mother, he scarcely knew. A lot of the time he fell prey to illnesses symptomatic of his ever-worsening heart, digestive and rheumatic conditions, but there were times when he could be quite ebullient, as at the 'bachelor party' of 1829 which ended with some triumphant glass-smashing; and there were times when he managed to smuggle in a little extra opium. It was not a glorious end, but neither was it the catastrophe that the years 1801–4 had threatened. As he lay dying in 1834, after a last long physical decline, there were consolations to be found in the devotion of the Gilmans and a faith in the Christian ethics and mysteries which had never failed him.

Coleridge had religion to hold on to; Wordsworth found a base-level truth in the Leech-Gatherer: what of those who found nothing to clutch at? For the young writers and intellectuals of Germany, the world seemed altogether unfathomable, cock-eyed, even absurd— appearances were untrustworthy, perhaps only the unreal was real, and life could be turned into a game of illusions and tricks. Germany was certainly no very reassuring place. As a nation it only existed in the form of a chaotic jumble of small states and principalities, weak, quarrelsome, and restrictive. At best such places were backward and inert. Even in Prussia, the most powerful of these units, with its streamlined government and bureaucracy inherited from the Enlightened monarch Frederick the Great, the economy had slumped, leaving an extensive Enlightened educational system producing highly qualified graduates for whom there was no work. All the most respected professions were still riddled with prejudices of rank and class—the poison pinprick way in which Werther is snubbed during his brief period of diplomatic employment was typical of its time. Thousands of would-be writers had no one to write for, since the German reading public thought their own language barbarously coarse and preferred the more urbane tones of English and French. It was a situation which left a whole class of young Germans thumb-twiddling and broody, staring out of windows, waiting.

In the 1780s these frustrated energies found a channel of expression in the plays of *Sturm und Drang* (Storm and Stress). These violent historical tragedies—of which Goethe's *Goetz von Berlichingen* is a prime example—are full of dynastic feuds, rampaging villains, and slaughtered innocents, all shot through with wildly rhetorical verse in supposed imitation of Shakespeare. In the early 1790s these passions were re-focused on real history, real violence, in the hope that the French Revolution would sweep through the musty ducal halls of Germany and provide the dynamism for change. But the course of the reaction to the first five tumultuous years up to the death of Robespierre was similar to that in England, and towards the end of the century there was a distinct loss of faith in external political change. A writer like Schiller, with his proclamations of liberty, justice, and the family of humanity, came to seem naïve and limited. So, having discovered that social-political change foundered between noble sentiments and the guillotine, a new school of writers and thinkers—the first to play consciously with the idea of being 'Romantic'—turned to the idea of a revolution within the individual—the individual with the soul of a poet, the imaginative capacity to transcend and transform the world of appearances, seeing deeper into the significance of things and the mysterious connections between them.

In the first volume of the short-lived journal *Athenäum* (1798–1800) around which much of this first named Romanticism was communally explored, Friedrich Schlegel published the following rhapsodic vision of what a Romantic literature might be. Uniting, animating, embracing, it becomes a mirror of the world, and yet 'can raise this reflection to higher and higher powers and multiply it, as it were, in an endless series of mirrors ... its essential nature is that it is eternally becoming and can never be perfected. No theory can exhaust it ... It alone is infinite, as it alone is free; its supreme law is that the caprice of the author shall be subject to no law.' This means everything and nothing; it means, as Schlegel intended, what you want it to mean, because in a Romantic world everyone is free to make up their own meanings. The Romantic poet simply conjures up, 'in an endless series of mirrors', magical visions without the forms or limits of convention. Writers like Tieck, Jean Paul, and Novalis (otherwise Friedrich von Hardenberg, a mining engineer) produced works in which all the barriers between history and fantasy, reality and dream, subject and object are broken down. Space and time contract and dissolve; characters assume supernatural powers; plots are inconsequential and liable to change direction drastically, obeying only Schlegel's supreme law, the caprice of the author. Whether fantastically witty (Jean Paul) or motivated by a Dantean spiritual quest (Novalis), these writers all escaped the stolidity of German life by constructing an imaginative world based on infinitudes of possibility. This led to an art with little sense of responsibility towards nature, moral experience, or social and political dilemmas. It had its own sort of narrowness, its own blind spots. When it was out of fashion in the 1830s, the acerbic Heinrich Heine could look back and see that it had 'judged the past and prophesied the future', but ignored the present. Even in its brief prime around the turn of the century, it was regarded with considerable scepticism.

One young writer who stood at a quizzical angle to the Romantic liberties was Heinrich von Kleist. The world, he felt, was not miraculous so much as radically uncertain. There are no revelations, only impenetrable puzzles. Humankind lays plans and fixes on good intentions; but there is no telling how the world might parry. His own surviving prose fiction is in the form of the novella or long short story, the subject-matter being some strikingly odd chain of events, taking place in recognizable historical circumstances and related in the impersonal tones of a newspaper report. He does not analyse or explain; he offers no answers or reassurances, finds no havens of peaceful resolution. The chilly atmosphere in Kleist comes from his uncanny presentation of some of the more unpleasant depths of human psychology, particularly the capacity for murderous violence. The horse dealer Michael Kohlhaas starts off as 'a paragon of civil virtues' until the high-handed behaviour of a local nobleman propels him to ruthless *Sturm und Drang* outlawry. The Marquise of O—— finds herself pregnant without recalling any instance of sexual intercourse; an impeccable Russian officer finally reveals that he raped her while unconscious, having rescued her from a gang of his own soldiers with similar intentions. An earthquake in Chile saves two innocent young lovers from the death penalty exacted for adultery and allows them a brief rural idyll before they are slaughtered in a riot outside a church.

Kleist the narrator shows no compassion or outrage on behalf of these people: that is not his point. His imagination was unmoved by the ecstasies of the *Athenäum* group. He wanted only to give the lie to the idea that law, love, or reason might put life in order. He does not lament the loss of a sense of wholeness and joy. In his despondency, he turned to self-discipline and service to the state rather than messy emotional dependencies and opium. His final solution was the clean snap of a pistol shot.

He was born in 1777, his family numbering eighteen generals in their dynasty, as well as some notable literary connections. At the age of fifteen he was commissioned as a corporal in the King's Guard and took brief part in the revolutionary wars against France. In 1799, he petitioned for and won his discharge, on the grounds that he wished to continue his studies. The military style had not suited him: too much standing on ceremony and 'so many officers, so many drill masters, so many soldiers, so many slaves'. He came back into civilian life with what he called a *Lebensplan*, a life-plan, confidently based on Enlightened ideals of progress, education, and happiness as the inevitable reward of virtue. 'A free and thinking person does not remain where chance happens to have pushed him,' he proclaimed, as he set about an earnest course of study in mathematics, philosophy, and physics.

But almost immediately his certainties were rattled: virtue was not evidently being rewarded. He hectored his fiancée Wilhelmine with lists of knotty moral questions: 'Is it better to do good, or to be good?' 'Which member of a married couple loses more by the death of the other?' Behind his irascible and distracted manner, he worried about his career—for, like the rest of his contemporaries, he faced an unattractive little set of options.

He had to travel, he announced suddenly, and made a secret trip on a false passport to Würzburg, where he seems to have undergone some mysterious medical treatment on what he would only refer to as 'the most important day of my life'. Back in Berlin, he admitted: 'The inside of my head looks like a lottery bag, one big winner and a thousand blanks.' Then he read the philosophy of Immanuel Kant, which had recently set out the profoundly challenging view that human perception is structured in such a way as to prevent us ever apprehending more than a conditioned version of reality. In his vulnerable state of mind, Kleist felt the foundations of his *Lebensplan* give way. 'The very pillar totters that I have clung to in this whirling tide of life,' he explained to Wilhelmine, for after Kant, 'We can never be certain that what we call Truth is really Truth, or whether it does not merely appear so to us.'

A period of extreme changes of geographic and mental direction followed. He went to Paris—which he hated—with his cold and 'mannish' sister Ulrike, whose temperament he found distasteful (she may have been hermaphroditic: certainly she had no difficulty in passing herself off as male when she wanted to attend some university lectures on physiology); then he tried a solitary Rousseauan life as a peasant farmer in Switzerland. He abandoned his engagement, and threw enormous emotional energies into relationships with a strongly homosexual character. Out of all this repression and confusion Kleist slowly found his vocation as a writer. His creativity was agonizingly brought to birth, however, and his first major work, a grandly conceived tragedy which would combine the Greek and Shakespearean styles, was abandoned in despair. But if writing gave him a vital sense of purpose, thoughts of death—his *Todplan*, as it were—never left him. 'I have no other wish,' he wrote to Ulrike in 1802, 'but to die if I might achieve three things: a child, a beautiful piece of writing, and a great deed. For life holds nothing nobler than this: to be able to throw it away with a noble gesture.'

All he had thrown away so far was his tragedy, a gesture which was followed by another panicky trip to Paris, where he pleaded hysterically with one of his closest friends to join him in suicide. The friend had a rather more commonplace set of problems and refused: Kleist ran off and was discovered a few days later in Normandy trying to join up with an expeditionary force that Napoleon was assembling for the invasion of England. His brain splitting with violent headache, he wrote to Ulrike that he was hoping to 'die a beautiful death in battle'. Fortunately he was waylaid by an army doctor and forcibly returned to Germany in a state of catatonic depression.

His family pushed him on to a training course for government service which they hoped would lead to a respectability commensurate with the noble name of Kleist, but he was soon ill again with a series of psychosomatic disorders (one of his letters discourses on 'the amazing linkage of the mind with a bundle of bowels and entrails') and he discharged himself. Writing was pulling him back inexorably. Rarely in the history of literature have works as fine as the short stories 'The Marquise of O—' and 'The Earthquake in Chile' or the fantastic comedy *Amphitryon* worked themselves into artistic order out of a mind as unstable as Kleist's was at this period.

There was another focus now emerging in his troubled life, although this again was hardly a conventional stimulus to great writing. After Prussia's defeat at the Battle of Jena in 1806, Kleist conceived a neurotically intense hatred of France and a Prussian government which only passively resisted—and later cringingly compromised with—Napoleon and his imperial aspirations. For five months in 1807 Kleist was imprisoned in Châlons-sur-Marne, on mistaken suspicion of espionage, but even so, his feelings went far beyond a natural sense of anger and patriotism into the realms of obsession. He wrote some stern and lucid essays on the importance of conscription, of sacrificing individual scruple to the national cause, of the necessity for total war. Even more chilling, however, is the brutal play he wrote in 1808, *Die Hermannsschlacht*, based on a battle in AD 9 where the chieftain Hermann rallied German tribesmen to defeat the Roman invaders. The play beats an insistent drum for war: it has none of the doubleness of attitudes and values, the 'Falstaff' elements, of other war plays like Shakespeare's *Henry V*. *Die Hermannsschlacht* is propaganda which blatantly rejoices in the slaughter of the enemy and proclaims the honour of death in battle. It is as stark and powerful as Eisenstein's *Battleship Potemkin* or *Alexander Nevsky*.

A play written some months earlier, *Penthesilea*, based on the Greek myth of the Amazon warrior queen who fought at the siege of Troy and fell in love with Achilles (and perhaps on his mannish and breastless sister Ulrike as well), is much subtler, though no less discomforting, in its exploration of the behaviour of human beings at war, here explosively combining aggression with sexual attraction. The love of Achilles and Penthesilea is like the stalking of two hungry animals on heat—crouching, snarling, clawing at the air in tense readiness for the next move—and it culminates in Penthesilea tearing the body of Achilles to pieces in orgasmic frenzy, before dropping dead herself, drained of life by the anger of her love. Written in a strange distorted syntax and moving abruptly through changes of mood and action, *Penthesilea* is a powerful example of the many attempts in this period to recharge the bland marble image of the Classical world with a new relevance and directness.

Kleist made a major tactical error in sending the play to the revered Goethe, probably in the secret hope that he would want it for the court theatre at Weimar of which he was director. But Goethe's notions of the moral order in the Greek spirit were very different from Kleist's, and he was clearly affronted by the younger man's savage conception of human nature: the letter he wrote in response to *Penthesilea* witheringly implies that it was designed for a theatre and an audience that did not yet exist. To add injury to insult, the performance of *Der zerbrochene Krug* (or 'The Broken Jug'), Kleist's rumbustious comedy of cuckoldry mounted the next month at Weimar, turned out a fiasco. Incompetently produced and acted, the play was virtually hissed from the stage. Kleist was inclined, not altogether unfairly, to blame Goethe personally and at one point was on the verge of challenging him to a duel. 'I'll tear the wreath from his brow,' he bellowed. Later he resorted to printing snide limericks about Goethe's peccadilloes in his literary journal *Phöbus*—to which Goethe, calling it *Phebus*, or bombast, had refused to contribute.

None of this helped Kleist to settle down, and on top of a further cataclysmic defeat for the anti-Napoleonic cause at Wagram, he suffered another prolonged mental collapse. But the play which followed his re-surfacing is an altogether calmer, even at times lyrical work, in which measured acceptance plays a larger part than destructive passion. *Prinz Friedrich von Homburg* tells of a prince who longs for love and honour. In battle, however, his dreaminess leads him to disobey orders impulsively, and although his action leads to victory, military law decrees that he must die. At first he assumes that the magnanimous Elector will pardon him; when he discovers that this will not be so, he screams with terror like a child. The Elector announces that he will leave it to the Prince to decide the justice of his sentence. The Prince is jolted by the gesture into discovering that he cannot take the craven and ignoble way out. He knows he must accept death as just retribution for putting himself above the Law, a phenomenon which the individual will cannot flout. He goes to his death calmly, but is given a last-minute (and less than convincing) reprieve. The Prince's dilemma and decision recalls Kleist's letter of 1802—'For life holds nothing nobler than this: to be able to throw it away with a noble gesture'—and it was to haunt his own last months. Could he find it in himself to make that ultimately noble sacrifice of self, to throw away life with a noble gesture?

Perhaps he felt that there was not much to sacrifice—certainly he had won little recognition outside coteries, and he never saw his two major tragedies, *Penthesilea* and *Prinz Friedrich von Homburg*, performed. His one moment of public success came in 1810, when he set up and edited one of Germany's very first daily newspapers, the *Berliner Abendblätter*. This published some of his shorter work, including gnomic anecdotes, epigrams, and essays, but its main purpose was to disseminate news with as little as possible censorship and as much possible speed. Kleist also wrote up a lot of the reportage—scandalous crime stories, reports of balloon ascents, unverified rumours. So much sensational content pushed circulation up to such proportions that the authorities, recognizing the dangers in Kleist's ambiguous tone, sly juxtapositions, and sometimes barefaced cheek, forced it to print official announcements 'bearing on the public welfare'. The new government line, against which Kleist put up a brave but hopeless stand, made the newspaper so dull that the sales dropped as sharply as they had risen and it soon closed, leaving Kleist with another painful weight on his soul as well as an impossible burden of debt.

His emotional life was no happier. He was on bad terms with his family, especially his grim sister Ulrike who slammed the door in his face, accusing him of disgracing his forefathers; and his deepest friendships usually ended in rancour, for Kleist was neither conciliating nor sympathetic. He was most comfortable in the company of sophisticated women of the Berlin *salons*, like Rahel Levin and his married cousin Marie von Kleist, who presented no sexual challenge. And when he gave up completely, another married woman was there to make the final noble gesture with him.

In September 1811, believing that Prussia was about to launch a full-scale attack on Napoleon, Kleist tried to get a commission in the army. 'His sole and entire wish,' wrote Marie von Kleist in a letter of reference, 'is to die for his country.' For various reasons, the commission was not forthcoming, and Kleist looked for some other means of meeting his end. Ever since his youth, he had pestered people to join him in a suicide pact, and he had already fixed on the bleak wooded shores of a lake near Berlin, the Kleiner Wannsee, as a spot where the deed might be done. Now he had met up with Henriette Vogel, a plump and pock-marked woman of his Berlin circle who was dying inexorably of cancer of the uterus and was terrified of the pain that she knew she would have to endure. Kleist had at last found passionate love: he and Henriette were united not in sex (which in any case her condition prevented) but in their desperate death-wishes. By November they had made their secret rapturous decision and exchanged letters—thus Kleist to Henriette: 'O sun of my life, sun, moon and stars, heaven and earth, my past and my future ... my tragic drama, my posthumous fame! Ah, you are my other, better self, my virtues, my merits, my hope ...'

The preparations were gruesomely elaborate and punctilious, as though the event was being turned into material for one of Kleist's short stories. They composed a series of florid and somehow meaningless letters of farewell, Kleist talking of 'the paean of triumph my soul has struck up in this hour of death', which were put into sealed boxes. Then, on 20 November, they took a cab to an inn called the New Jug, near the lake on the Berlin–Potsdam high road. Having put their luggage into two adjoining rooms, they went for an early evening walk, ate supper, and apparently spent most of the night drinking wine and writing last missives tying up the details of their financial affairs. The next morning they breakfasted on coffee and soup and sent a letter to a friend summoning him to the inn and their dead bodies. In the early afternoon, they asked for some rum and coffee to be brought down to the lakeside, where they planned to sit for a while. The innkeeper thought this odd, given the cold and foggy weather, but duly complied. Arriving at the lake with a covered basket containing three pistols, they asked for a table, two chairs, and the bill. The servants made their way back to the inn and noticed the misty outlines of Kleist and Henriette frolicking about merrily on the shore, skipping from stone to stone in the shallow water. When the servant returned, Henriette handed her some money in a cup and asked her to wash it and bring it back. As she trudged grumpily back yet again she heard two shots, then complete silence: 'So they're playing around with guns too,' was her only thought, she claimed at the inquest.

The corpses were soon discovered. Henriette lay flat on her back, with a smile on her face and hands neatly folded over her chest: a small, perfectly placed bullet-hole led cleanly to her heart. Kleist knelt at her feet, his teeth so tightly clenched that a jemmy had to be used to prise open his jaw. Apart from some reddish saliva around his mouth, there was no sign of blood, for the bullet had lodged in his brain. The letter sent to Berlin was at first assumed to be some sort of joke, but Henriette's kindly accountant husband (who seems to have been well aware of her relationship with Kleist) rushed horror-struck to the inn. The bodies were identified, the sealed boxes opened. The subsequent inquest concluded, in a strange mixture of old and new psychological terminology, that Kleist 'was of the temperament *sanguino cholericus in summo gradu** and undoubtedly suffered severe attacks of hypochondria ... If it is true that this eccentric temperament was accompanied by religious extravagance, it may be inferred that the deceased von Kleist was suffering from mental illness.'

The double suicide of Berlin caused enormous interest throughout Europe and was still vividly remembered eighty-odd years later when Crown Prince Rudolf and Baroness Marie Vetsera were discovered in the scandalous Mayerling death pact. The gossip writers

* lit. combining 'choleric with sanguine to the highest degree', after the medieval system of classification according to 'temperament'. 'Cholerics' were congenitally melancholy.

immediately rewrote the incident to cast Kleist and Henrietta in terms of a sentimental novel of the *Werther* type, with the theme of free love thwarted by bourgeois marriage. Even when something closer to the truth was established, the moralists remained scandalized, and Madame de Staël, in her 'Réflexions sur le suicide' decided that Kleist had only done it as a means to the fame that had previously eluded him.

Nothing that we know about Kleist—although the evidence is not always easy to fathom—suggests that this was the case. Nor can he usefully be described as mad: his suicide was more an act of premeditated choice, a test of his honour and free will prefiguring the *hara-kiri* carried out by the Japanese writer Yukio Mishima, whom he resembles in several ways. The Germany Kleist saw was a land of fantasists, cowards, and fools who wanted neither reality, liberty, nor art. He tried to disabuse himself of every illusion about the world and human nature, but went on being disappointed until death was the only uncrumbled monument on his horizon. Like the Prince of Homburg, he wanted, finally, to be noble and alone. It is not surprising that both Nietzsche and Kafka admired him profoundly.

Kleist presents a world in which humankind can see nothing but the misleading surface of things beneath which invisible forces wantonly work to make a nonsense of every assumption. The poetry of his slightly older contemporary Friedrich Hölderlin (1770–1843), on the other hand, is full of the dream of seeing beyond and through the surface to discover that everything makes ultimate sense.

At the centre of Hölderlin's vision is a dream of the Ancient Greeks. For Chénier, the Greeks suggested warm sensuality; but for Hölderlin, as for Shelley, they were something else again, embodying an era where man was whole, at one with nature and the spiritual world, the rites and mysteries of its religion animating the universe with joy. In his wonderful short novel *Hyperion*, written over the last years of the eighteenth century, this vision of Greece is seen anew through the eyes of a modern Greek youth who has lost his childhood sense of oneness and comes among the Germans, a race sour, divided, and alienated. 'I cannot imagine a people more mangled than the Germans,' Hyperion complains. 'You see artisans, but no human beings, thinkers, but no human beings, masters and servants, young and elderly people, but no human beings.' Through a long maturing process of experience and education, Hyperion recovers a fuller intuition of true humanity and 'blessed unity'. 'O spirit, spirit!' the book concludes rapturously:

... Beauty of the world! Indestructible enchanting spirit! You exist, and your eternal youth! What then is death, and all the griefs of men? ...

As the quarrels of lovers, so are the dissonances of the world. In the midst of strife there is reconciliation, and all that is parted reunites.

In the heart the arteries part and return, and all is harmonious, eternal, glowing life ...

The poet here becomes a sort of priest, a *seer*, whose task is to communicate to the benighted those deeper intimations of 'blessed unity' which emerge in the ancient mythologies and the utterances of the Old Testament prophets: Wordsworth and Coleridge saw their mission in a comparable light. But what happened when one no longer heard the divine voices? Or when they became confused and mutually contradictory? Such questions preyed on Hölderlin's psyche like maggots, feeding on his sanity.

As a bored theology student at the seminary in Tübingen in the early 1790s, he had joined a *Dichterbund*, a brotherhood of poets which met together once a week over a bottle of wine to recite the week's compositions. A 'Tree of Liberty' was consecrated in a nearby meadow round which the brotherhood solemnly danced, chanting the *Marseillaise* and Schiller's ode *An die Freude*, 'To Joy', later used by Beethoven in his Ninth Symphony:

> *Alle Menschen werden Brüder*
> *Wo dein sanfter Flügel weilt ...*

(All Men will be brothers when your gentle wing covers them ...)

His room-mates at the seminary were two precociously brilliant young philosophers, Schelling and Hegel: when the latter left to take up a post in Switzerland, they parted with the words '*Reich Gottes!*', 'To the coming of God's kingdom!' Come it would, they believed, in a Germany soon to be greened over with French political and social idealism. 'I love the race of the coming centuries,' Hölderlin wrote in 1793. 'For this is my blessedest hope, the faith which keeps me strong and active—our descendants will be better than ourselves, freedom must come at last, and virtue will thrive better in the holy warming light of freedom than under the ice-cold sky of despotism. We live in a period where everything is working for the better.'

Yet, as we have already seen, all that faith and optimism was sadly fragile stuff. Hölderlin's exact contemporary Wordsworth was at that very time in Paris, buckling under the bloody evidence of his own eyes. From a greater distance, Hölderlin could go on dreaming of liberty for longer—but he also shared with Wordsworth the problem of wriggling away from family pressure to join the Church and subscribe his life to a rigid Protestant ethic for which he felt little sympathy. To them both the true priest was the Poet, not the pastor; and when Hölderlin passed out of the seminary he approached his idol Schiller, whose odes he had been assiduously imitating, in the hope that the great man would take him under his wing. In the event Schiller was guarded: Hölderlin, he felt, may have had unusual talent and ardour, but he suffered from excessive intensity, 'subjectivity', and 'one-sidedness'; he should think more about the present, less about the future. So Schiller recommended him for a tutoring job (which ended in dismissal) and over the next few years both he and Goethe tried to calm Hölderlin down and round him out, suggesting that he concentrate on writing small-scale works on simple subjects drawn directly from his own experience. The advice was eminently sensible, but useless. Hölderlin's visions and ambitions were not just vulgar careerism, which needed tempering. Poetry was his destiny, and in *Hyperion*, which was then being drafted, he expressed the restless grandeur of his aspirations. 'No action, no thought can reach the extent of your desire,' he claims. 'This is the glory of man, that nothing ever suffices.'

In 1796 Hölderlin took up another tutorship, in the Frankfurt house of one Gontard, a Swiss banker, and his wife Susette. She was a woman slightly older than Hölderlin, a devoted mother as good as she was beautiful, thirsting for some spiritual and intellectual stimulation in the wealthy but barren and philistine environment to which her loveless marriage had consigned her. In her Hölderlin found all the fantasies he had of the sublimity of ancient Greece made flesh. Susette resembled some exquisite piece of classical statuary, her features sharply chiselled, her skin alabaster white, her raven-dark hair swept chastely back, demure yet enigmatic. He called her his Diotima, after the priestess who initiated Socrates into the mysteries of the ladder on which profane sensual love ascends and refines itself into absolute divine love. Their passion grew, like that of Paolo and Francesca in Dante's *Inferno*, as they read to each other over long dull evenings, and through their relationship Hölderlin experienced the profound joy which washes over pages of *Hyperion*.

Gontard, meanwhile, so the story goes, would arrive home every night from the bank or his club, hand his hat to the housekeeper and ask her the same question—'Is my wife at home?'—to which the reply came—'She is upstairs, reading with Herr Hölderlin.' For months Gontard suspected nothing, pleased only that his wife had found some outlet for her literary nonsense; until, that is, the housekeeper herself fell in love with Hölderlin, whose own unearthly Aryan beauty led his friends to call him Apollo. When he rebuffed her advances, she took revenge by insinuating innuendo into her nightly answer. This precipitated the inevitable scene and Hölderlin left for Homburg. He was in any case sickened by the contemptuous way in which Gontard treated him, but Susette he could not simply abandon. They met in secret whenever he could get back to Frankfurt—and when it became dangerous to meet even at the theatre, Hölderlin promised her that he would walk slowly past her bedroom window on the evening of the first Thursday of every month.

To the world, he was just another over-qualified arts graduate adrift in a slumping society. Life as an independent man of letters was not feasible. The second volume of *Hyperion* was published in 1799 and noticed only as an oddity; a letter to Schiller inquiring about the possibility of a university post was not even answered; a project for a new literary journal came to nothing. Given his repugnance for the Church, tutoring was the only means he had of earning any sort of living.

Recent scholarship has suggested that there was another aspect to Hölderlin's problem as well. Ever since Tübingen and the Tree of Liberty, the authorities had kept his activities on file and under surveillance. For one thing, he had been educated at the state's expense, on the condition of his entering the priesthood; this he refused to do, and he was constantly evading summonses to present himself before the appropriate board. For another, he had kept up links with various 'Jacobinical' secret societies, which were now being ruthlessly suppressed. Although he seems to have been a friend to a revolution 'in attitudes and conceptions' rather than one of armed insurrection, he would still have been marked out as a conspirator. His other insistent problem was his mother, to whom he was very close. At a time when he had little energy to resist, she hectored and needled him to renounce his 'paganism', take up the Church, and find content in her own narrow pietistic views. This Hölderlin could not, or would not, do; but in poems such as 'Bread and Wine' he tried to bring Apollo and Jesus, Greek and Christian, together, by relating all oriental religions to the same source—a thesis which fascinated advanced German theologians of the day—and showing the parallels between them. But where was this 'blessed unity' of contraries, except in the Poet's mind? And was not reality a world of fragments and confusion, abandoned by the gods who once had invested it with meaning?

> *Aber Freund! wir kommen zu spät. Zwar leben die Götter,*
> *Aber über dem Haupt droben in anderer Welt.*
> *Endlos wirken sie da und scheinen wenig zu achten,*
> *Ob wir leben . . .*

(But, friends, we come too late. Indeed, the Gods do live, but over our heads, above in another world. There they act eternally and seem to care very little whether or not we exist . . .)

In January 1802, with much foreboding, he left Germany altogether to take up a tutorship to a German family living in Bordeaux. What happened to him during the next few months is not clear. We know that he visited the new Musée Napoléon in Paris where he was deeply moved by the Greek sculpture; we know that he wrote home speaking warmly of his new charges; and we know that he wandered into the Auvergne and went through some obscure but intense visionary revelations. We know, above all, that by the time he returned to Germany in June of that year, his despondency had apparently turned to madness.

There is also a remarkable (though unverifiable) story, purportedly dating from this time and related by a teenage girl who lived in a château near Blois. Over some days she had observed a raggedly dressed but strangely impressive man, walking aimlessly round her father's grounds. She had assumed him to be one of the many foreign political refugees tramping round France at the time, and paid him no special attention until he became involved in a tussle with one of the park-keepers, who was trying to get rid of him. The girl and her father went out to resolve the matter and discovered the stranger, speaking awkward French, to be obsessed by their ornamental pond, surrounded by twenty-four statues of the classical deities, to each one of which he paid elaborate obeisance. 'The water should be as clean as the water of Cephisus or the spring of Erechtheus on the Acropolis,' he announced. 'The gods are no man's property. They belong to the world, and when they smile at us we are theirs.'

'Perhaps you are a Greek?' he was asked politely.

'No—on the contrary. I am a German,' he sighed.

'Is a German the contrary of Greek?'

'Yes,' he replied. 'We are all the contrary. You the Frenchman are too, the Englishman, your enemy, is too—we are all the contrary.'

The stranger was evidently a distressed gentleman and was consequently invited in to take refreshment. His manner, however, remained bizarre. Once in the house he laid himself out on a chaise-longue and fell peremptorily off to sleep. Later in the day he revived and was quizzed at length by the girl's elderly aunt, who had a taste for discussing *la philosophie*: she found his answers hard to fathom, but agreed that he was '*un vrai original*'.

'What is your name?' the girl asked shyly at dinner.

He buried his face in his hands and groaned. 'I will tell you tomorrow. Believe me, I sometimes find it difficult to remember.'

At about one o'clock in the morning, the household was awoken by terrified screams. Rushing into the hall, the girl discovered a servant writhing in terror at the feet of their guest, who was standing with a white sheet draped toga-like over his naked body, holding a light in one hand, a sword in the other, and striking a classical pose. He allowed himself to be led back to his room and gently put to bed. In the morning he vanished.

Some weeks later he arrived at his mother's house, 'pale as a corpse, emaciated, with hollow wild eyes, long hair and beard, and dressed like a beggar'. He was raving incoherently, lashing out on all sides and showing no clear idea where he was. Only when his mother handed him his copy of Homer did he calm down. Soon after came a letter from a friend reporting some devastating news—Susette Gontard had died from German measles.

Over the next couple of years he lived at his mother's in a tremulously delicate state, making idiosyncratic translations from the Greek—which Goethe and Schiller found ludicrous—and writing much of his most rhapsodic and magnificent poetry' 'Patmos', for instance, which meditates on the Aegean island where St John witnessed the Apocalypse described in the Book of Revelation, as well as some poignant short lyrics reflecting his solitude and the darkness encroaching on the dazzling light of his earlier visions:

> *Weh mir, wo nehm' ich, wenn*
> *Es Winter ist, die Blumen, und wo*
> *Den Sonnenschein*
> *Und Schatten der Erde?*
> *Die Mauern stehn*
> *Sprachlos und kalt, im Winde*
> *Klirren die Fahnen.*

(Alas, where shall I find flowers when winter comes, and where sunshine and shadows of earth? The walls stand speechless and cold, weathercocks creak in the wind.)

Much of this poetry survives only as fragments, phrases jotted down on a page, waiting isolated for a structure to bind them into song. In the stark concentrated power of the imagery and the absence of any obvious coherent meaning, they read uncannily like the verse of Pound or Eliot, a hundred and twenty years later.

No sooner had Hölderlin's condition improved enough for him to take up an undemanding job as librarian to the Landgrave of Homburg (to whom 'Patmos' is dedicated), than another troubling series of events arose to unsettle him. In 1805 a number of arrests were made among Hölderlin's political contacts, and charges of high treason were preferred against them, on the grounds that there had been a conspiracy to assassinate the conservative Elector of Württemberg. Hölderlin himself was implicated, but the Landgrave decently pleaded that his mental state precluded him standing trial.*

Hölderlin's condition now deteriorated swiftly. He smashed up his piano and started talking a gibberish made up of Greek, German, and Latin. By September 1806 his behaviour in public had become so offensive that there was no alternative but to commit him forcibly to a clinic—one, incidentally, following the modern principles of treatment by 'moral rehabilitation'. An eye-witness recorded the struggle to take him away: 'He did everything he could to throw himself out of the vehicle, but the attendant in charge pushed him back in again. Screaming that he was being abducted by military

---

* In his controversial biography of Hölderlin (1978) which has unfortunately not yet been translated into English, Pierre Bertaux claims that Hölderlin's madness was largely a matter of 'playing Hamlet', that is, of feigning madness to cover up for his secret revolutionary activities. This thesis has been angrily disputed and largely disproved, but the accompanying question—how far is the extreme obscurity of much of Hölderlin's poetry attributable to its function as concealed political allegory?—remains wide open.

Bertaux's ideas are symptomatic of a school of literary critics and biographers which matured in the heady days of 1968 and sought allies and images, heroes and martyrs, among the poets of a previous revolutionary age, unsullied by the dreary old clichés of hard-line Stalinism. In Peter Weiss' play *Hölderlin* (1971) the last scene symbolically (and quite fictitiously) brings the young Karl Marx to Hölderlin's tower room to receive the holy fire of revolution from the sublimely mad old Jacobin. In England, Blake and Shelley were similarly seen afresh as political activists: see, for instance, Paul Foot's *Red Shelley* (1978) or Adrian Mitchell's *Tyger* (1971).

guards and redoubling his efforts to escape [Hölderlin] scratched at the attendant with his enormously long fingernails until the man was completely bloodied.' The clinic diagnosed him as a victim of *dementia praecox*, but could do little for him. Today he would probably be treated as some sort of schizophrenic. He himself believed that he had been driven mad by his exposure to the sacred fire of ancient mystery rites. 'He who has seen God must die,' he wrote. '*Wie Feuer sind Stimmen Gottes*,' 'Like fire is the voice of God.'

In 1807 he was billeted in Tübingen on a master-carpenter named Ernst Zimmer, and given at most three years to live. Yet here, in a tower room overlooking river, forest, and valley, he was to live out another thirty-six years of mostly good-humoured insanity, receiving a great deal of kindness and respect from everyone around him. But who knows what terrible bewilderment festered beneath his mild exterior, or what anguish he was articulating through his mad piano-playing:

> He follows one thought, which is childishly simple, and can play it over many hundreds of times and wear it out to such a degree that it is quite unbearable. To this one must add the quick convulsion or cramp, which sometimes obliges him to pass up and down the keys like lightning, and the unpleasant rattling of his over-grown finger-nails. For he strongly dislikes having them cut ... When he has played for some time, and when his soul is moved, he suddenly shuts his eyes, raises his head, as if about to languish and pass away, and begins to sing. I could never find out in what language he sang, often as I heard him; but he did so with exuberant pathos, and it made one shudder in every nerve to see him and to hear him ...

In the 1820s Hölderlin became quite fashionable. A selection of his poetry was published, and now that there was a quaint story, an explanation to attach to his obscure outpourings, the literary ladies came to stare at him. The room he lived in was bare and whitewashed. A copy of *Hyperion* lay open on a table; he enjoyed reciting from it and wrote an unintelligible continuation. His characteristic form of greeting was 'Your Majesty' or 'Your Holiness', with much bowing and scraping. He obligingly penned spontaneous little ditties, occasionally hitting on something hauntingly beautiful, for his visitors' autograph books—which he signed Scardanelli or Scaliger Rosa, or Buonarotti, or Killalusimeno. 'Look, gracious sir, a *comma*!' he would proudly announce. When left to himself, he would take morning-long walks, compulsively plucking blades of grass and filling his pockets with stones gathered along the way. He talked to himself constantly, sometimes in his polyglot gibberish, and often as two clearly defined personalities, answering each other's questions. A friend once found 'a terrible, mysterious phrase' among his scattered papers: 'Only now do I understand human beings, since I have been living far from them and in solitude.'

For all the differences between the psychological dramas of Coleridge, Kleist, and Hölderlin, one specific common factor unites them: the betrayal or loss of an early vision of life that might be whole and pure. Coleridge lost pantisocracy and Asra but clung to a reconstituted Christianity; Kleist lost his *Lebensplan*, his country's honour, and his certainty about reality; Hölderlin his sense of 'blessed unity'. None of them could live with the thought that existence might be nothing more than a chaos of fragments; all of them reached out for the light of an ordering inclusive system and fell back into darkness.

It would be a mistake, however, to think of the era as one which gave itself over willingly to despondency and madness, as part of a craving for wild and weird experience. No one indulged in insanity as they did in the 1960s of R. D. Laing and Doris Lessing. It was the ache for wholeness, what Coleridge called the ache 'to know something *great—something one and indivisible*', that haunted the poets. Coleridge wrote this in 1797, a few months after his first visit to Racedown, and it was in Wordsworth that he believed himself to have found someone who *did* know 'something *one and indivisible*'. Wordsworth was the whole man, strong in his solitude, and for all the subsequent disillusion, Coleridge went on believing that until the end. 'He is all man,' he says of Wordsworth in *Table Talk*, 'a man of whom it might have been said "it is good for him to be alone".' A younger generation was less awestruck and his long-awaited epic poem *The Excursion* provoked much controversy when it appeared in 1814. 'It is rain upon rocks ... who can understand him?' Byron asked Leigh Hunt. It was easy to be irritated into seeing him as a solemn old fogey—Keats and Shelley both had to scratch at that itch. None the less, by the 1820s, there were few intellectuals in England who disputed that his was the most powerful voice of the era with the grandest idea—the interpenetration of the human mind with the soul of nature—and that, like Milton, his poetry embodied the spirit and destiny of the age.

Yet Wordsworth was an English phenomenon, whose appeal elsewhere was (and remains) minimal. If we look to Europe for wholeness and sanity, a poet who guided men to wisdom, it is Johann Wolfgang von Goethe (1749–1832) whose image comes into focus. 'Listen to Goethe,' wrote the great *salon* hostess Rahel Levin to a friend, 'Read him as one reads the Bible.'

Goethe presented his life as a constant process of maturing growth, a self-education which he called *Bildung*. Man, he thought, should aspire outward and upward, like a plant reaching for the light: too much doubt and introspection was withering. 'Avoid as you would the plague those whose heads are bowed down in woe,' he wrote. 'Live always as if life was just beginning.' He himself moved ever onward. There were no barren patches in his long life, and from every point, through every phase, he garnered some value or meaning which contributed to his greater sense of the whole. He overcame *Werther* and his suicidal tendencies, as well as the rantings of the *Sturm und Drang* period; he left his busy life as an active administrator at the court of the petty state of Weimar to take a liberating trip to Italy, where for two years he drank in the pleasures and beauties of the South; he found inspiration in pure classical forms for masterpieces like *Hermann und Dorothea* and *Iphigenie auf Tauris*, and from German folk-culture for the long-gestating *Faust*. His creativity as a poet went parallel to his scientific exploration of the principles of botany and optics—or of growth and light, as he preferred it. He loved many women uninhibitedly and was still happily falling in love in his seventies. His politics were unflappable and the vicissitudes of the French Revolution caused him little moral distress. Nature was his guide, not philosophical or political theory. What he lived, it has been said, was even more beautiful than what he wrote.

Not surprisingly there have also been those ready to look for feet of clay: any résumé of Goethe's career makes him sound too good to be true, and even among his contemporaries there were plenty who were gleefully irritated by what they saw as his smug detachment from the run of human problems and weaknesses. The novelist Jean Paul sneeringly referred to him simply as 'God', while others like Kleist smirked at the 'irregularities' in his sexual conduct. Goethe himself parried with a good deal of cool distaste for the extremer reaches of German culture. He found the Romantic school 'artificial, recherché, heightened, exaggerated, bizarre to the point of travesty' (although, characteristically, he learnt a lot from its techniques and materials), and his memory of Kleist was pitiless—'I was always filled with horror and disgust by this writer, as though by a body well-intentioned by nature, but in the grip of an incurable disease,' he announced. When

Hegel came to Weimar in 1827, Goethe gave a tea party at which the guest explained his philosophy of dialectics:

> 'Let us hope,' interposed Goethe, 'that these intellectual arts and dexterities are not frequently misused, and employed to make the false true and the true false.'
>
> 'That certainly happens,' said Hegel; 'but only with people who are mentally diseased.'
>
> 'I therefore congratulate myself,' said Goethe, 'upon the study of nature, which preserves me from such a disease. For here we have to deal with the infinitely and eternally true, which throws off as incapable everyone who does not proceed purely and honestly with the treatment and observation of his subject. I am also certain that many a dialectic disease would find a wholesome remedy in the study of nature.'

It was this sort of pronouncement that gave Goethe his status as an oracle for troubled times.

Although out of his enormous *oeuvre* only *Werther* and the first part of *Faust* (1806) were at all well known outside Germany, his last years at Weimar were punctuated by a stream of pilgrims, all hoping to hear wise words such as those spoken to Hegel. One young Englishman who prostrated himself at the shrine was Henry Crabb Robinson. 'I was so awed & oppressed by the "manly grace" of his figure ... that I believe I sho^d have forgotten my German had I attempted to speak,' he wrote in a letter home. 'He sat—wo^d you believe it?—precisely in the posture in which Kemble seats himself in Measure for Measure ... bent fist on his knees & with his burning Eyes fixed on the person he was speaking to.' On a later visit, Crabb Robinson was calm enough to notice that 'He is distinguished by an habitual manliness, consistency, vigour, truth, & health of Opinion & Sentiment ... he respects all things, and despises nothing but frivolity.'

A later translator and propagator of the Goethean gospel was the impassioned young Scot Thomas Carlyle, whom we previously encountered in the less salubrious surroundings of Coleridge's Highgate *salon*. To Carlyle Goethe really was something like God, bringing a code of values and meaning into a world shattered by politics, materialism, and unbelief: truly, a Man whom men might follow. Carlyle never met his hero face to face, but they held an elaborate correspondence and exchanged gifts (Carlyle reports the receipt of 'the daintiest boxie you ever saw'); and in 1831 he wrote to Goethe that to him he owed 'the all-precious knowledge and experience that

Reverence for our fellow-man, as a true emblem of the Highest, even in these perturbed, chaotic times ... [you] carry such life-giving light into many a soul, wandering bewildered in the eclipse of doubt.'

When Goethe died, Carlyle wrote an obituary which stated simply 'Our Greatest has departed'; Crabb Robinson talked of 'the mightiest spirit that has lived for many centuries'. In Weimar, Johann Ecker-mann, Goethe's long-suffering unpaid secretary, diarist, and post-humous editor took a last sad look at the eighty-two-year-old body which even in death seemed to embody a fullness of human beauty and moral sanity:

His faithful servant Friedrich opened for me the chamber in which he was laid out. Stretched upon his back, he reposed as if asleep; profound peace and security reigned in the features of his sublimely noble countenance. The mighty brow seemed yet to harbour thoughts. I wished for a lock of his hair; but reverence prevented me from cutting it off. The body lay naked, only wrapped in a white sheet, and I was astonished at the divine magnificence of the limbs. The breast was powerful, broad, and arched; the arms and thighs were full, and softly muscular; the feet were elegant, and of the most perfect shape; nowhere, on the whole body, was there a trace either of fat or of leanness and decay. A perfect man lay in great beauty before me; and the rapture the sight caused made me forget for a moment that the immortal spirit had left such an abode. I laid my hand on his heart—there was a deep silence—and I turned away to give free vent to my suppressed tears.

Chapter 3

'Woman's Whole Existence'

> Man's love is of man's life a thing apart,
> 'Tis woman's whole existence;
>
> Byron, Don Juan, 1, cxciv

Here is one of the most overworked clichés of 'Romantic' poetry, quoted as an immutable truth by worldly-wise (male) experts of the sex war, wherever Byron is read. Like so many such quotations, it is abused. In *Don Juan* itself, the epigram is uttered by a married woman, Juan's first lover Julia, who had been confined to a convent after being discovered *in flagrante*—and she speaks in despair rather than cynicism:

> . . . man may range
> The court, camp, church, the vessel, and the mart;
> Sword, gown, gain, glory, offer in exchange
> Pride, fame, ambition, to fill up his heart.
> And few there are whom these cannot estrange;
> Men have all these resources, we but one,
> To love again, and be again undone.

Was this in fact the case? What were women's resources in the Revolutionary and post-Revolutionary period? Was their destiny as bleak as Julia's lament implies? How did women see themselves, and how did the poets and intellectuals, the finest consciousnesses of the time, see them?

First, an important qualification: the number of women in the history of Europe who have sat about with nothing better to do than contemplate their emotional navels is extremely small. The majority of women slaved, and their labour formed an important part of the pre-industrial economy not only in the drudgery of farming, but in shop- and tavern-keeping, dentistry and midwifery, and in the trades of bakery, brewing, watch- and toy-making, and above all the processing of textiles (a spinster was originally a female spinner). Towards the end of the eighteenth century, however, with the impetus of mechanization, women's jobs, so often domestically based, began to be supplanted by large-scale centralized manufacture. Simultaneously there came the elimination of various epidemic diseases, an improvement in diet, and a consequent rise in life expectancy, fertility, and population. Accompanied by the depredations and taxations of the Revolutionary and Napoleonic wars, all this created an alarming new 'poverty gap'.

It was difficult for women to better themselves or even to escape. The laws of Church and State combined to enforce their subjugation. Their rights to property and inheritance were minimal; they had no political or voting powers; and perhaps most crucially of all, they had no access to professional training and apprenticeship. The early stages of the French Revolution brought some reform and more agitation—the lists of grievances, the *cahiers de doléances*, gathered from all sections of society in 1789, included a plea that men 'should not be allowed, under any pretext, to exercise trades that are the prerogative of women'—but by 1800 the position of working women who wanted to make an independent living was probably worse than it had been for centuries. The theatre and opera offered women an exciting chance to change their position in society through their own talents, but the stage was blackened by its low moral reputation; and it was only in the novel that women—as writers, readers, and fictionally represented characters (though not, of course, as controlling publishers)—in any sense dominated. The dreary and humiliating round of governessing remained the most realistic horizon for any woman who needed to work and remain respectable.

But there was also a movement towards what might be described as an emotional liberation for middle- and upper-class women that began in the middle of the eighteenth century. Its best remembered representative is Marianne Dashwood, one of the central figures of Jane Austen's early novel *Sense and Sensibility* (mostly written in 1797). Marianne follows—unwisely and unhappily, Jane Austen insists—the philosophy of Sentimentalism, which was based on the principle that, if allowed to follow its instincts, humankind was full of 'pity, tenderness, and benevolence'. To a Sentimentalist what consequently mattered in human relations was sincerity and candour, the refusal to kowtow to the conventions and compromises of so-called civilized life. These beliefs were sensationalized in two immensely influential didactic novels by Rousseau, *Julie, ou La Nouvelle Héloïse* (1761) and *Émile* (1762) which further proposed that natural feeling could only flourish in natural surroundings, away from the corruptions of cities, with their spirit of emulation and greed. The beauties and peaceful co-existence of trees, lakes, and mountains taught lessons of 'pity, tenderness, and benevolence' to those prepared to open their hearts and minds to their influence. 'She had obeyed the single impulse of her own heart; where that led her, there she followed,' wrote Thomas De Quincey of Dorothy Wordsworth, whose journals are perhaps the most pure and touching example of the Sentimental temperament, informed by gentleness rather than judgement, intuition rather than science, and a patient compassion for the victims and outcasts of a rapacious society.

To more conservative thinkers—for Sentimentalists were invariably liberal in their political views—there were many pitfalls and delusions in this outlook. It ignored the Christian doctrine of original sin and blurred the distinction between virtue and vice in a mist of forgiveness and sympathy; it encouraged an unself-critical wallowing in feeling which could lead (as in the case of Marianne Dashwood) to nervous illness; and it ignored all the structures of authority, especially that of the Established Church, on which social order and morality depended. Someone like Dr Johnson took this grimmer line: life was not a matter of walking through the countryside and feeling vaguely charitable, but a desperate struggle against a world of temptations. 'Teach us to understand the sinfulness of our own hearts,' wrote Jane Austen in a prayer that Johnson would have approved, 'and save us from deceiving ourselves by pride or vanity.'

The Sentimentalist was more hopeful, though hardly more cheerful, and had a rich literary diet on which to feed. The poetry of such as Thomson, Young, Gray, Goldsmith, and Cowper travelled Europe providing lengthy and melancholy meditations on change, decay, solitude, and the glories of nature. The Sentimental novel, of which Henry Mackenzie's *The Man of Feeling* (1771) is a famous example, presented high-minded dreamy personages tangled up in dilemmas of human relationships which call forth their utmost nobility, often with tragic results, and invariably a good deal of weeping and fainting. Such novels show a radical breakdown of the idea of 'active masculine' and 'passive feminine' personalities in the general welter of feeling common to both sexes, and were deliberately designed to squeeze the maximum emotional response out of the reader. They could also seem pretty ludicrous, as the teenage Jane Austen, knocking down their clichés like skittles in her satirical tale 'Frederic and Elfrida', makes plain: here Charlotte, unable 'to make anyone miserable', enters into a double engagement and drowns herself as the only solution:

She floated to Crankhumdunberry, where she was picked up and buried; the following epitaph ... was placed on her tomb.

EPITAPH
Here lies our friend who having promis-ed
That unto two she would be marri-ed
Threw her sweet Body & her lovely Face
Into the Stream that runs thro' Portland Place.

These sweet lines, as pathetic as beautifull were never read by any one who passed that way, without a shower of tears, which if they should fail in exciting in you, Reader, your mind must be unworthy to peruse them.

Yet to many women of the time such fiction did not seem trivial. As Philip Larkin could write, with a poet's licence, that 'sexual intercourse began in nineteen sixty-three', so it could be said that Romantic love—more properly, Sentimental love—began between 1762 and 1774: the years in which Rousseau's *La Nouvelle Héloïse* and Goethe's *Werther* were published.* In these two novels, Europe first found the myths that still make up one of the most potent fantasies of the Western world. It grew out of this new sensitivity—the capacity to register and show emotion, and the desire to cultivate it for its own sake. The norm of eighteenth-century relations between the sexes was based on the contract of marriage and a parallel trade in the betrayal of it through unashamed promiscuity—taking what could be got, for what it was worth, when it could be got. In England marriage partners were advertised for in newspapers, in an era which saw a marked surplus of women over men. Love was a matter of a shilling for a whore, or a game of flirtation played for the prize of swift carnal gratification. The stake was not a broken heart, but a dose of the pox. The libertine James Boswell records over twenty visitations from 'Signor Gonorrhoea' in his journals. Hogarth's paintings *Marriage à la mode*, John Cleland's *Memoirs of a Woman of Pleasure*, and Laclos' *Les*

---

* The novels of Samuel Richardson—*Pamela* (1740–1), *Clarissa Harlowe* (1747–8), and *Sir Charles Grandison* (1753–4)—were a significant formative element in Sentimentalism. Written in the form of letters exchanged between various parties, they made fashionable the exploration of the intimate oscillations of human consciousness. Where they differ from the later Sentimental novel is in their endorsement of a strict Protestant morality, the values of middle-class family life, and the proper subordination of the female. See Ian Watt, *The Rise of the Novel* (1957) and Margaret Doody, *A Natural Passion* (1974).

Liaisons Dangereuses further chronicle the refinements and squalors of the situation.

The new Romantic love did away with rakes, whores, bawdy talk, powder and patches. It etherealized sex and made it into an affair of the soul rather than the body, a secular equivalent to the love a religious devotee feels towards the godhead. It burgeoned in rural simplicity rather than panelled drawing-rooms, seeking—and failing—to transcend all social restrictions and conventions. It gloried in the pain as well as the exaltation of love and thought in terms of the commitment of a lifetime—Jane Austen's Marianne Dashwood is typical in her disapproval of 'second attachments'. Most significantly, it believed that man and woman in love could be free and equal— equally noble, equally passionate.

So ingrained are such assumptions in our culture that it is difficult to imagine a time when they seemed revolutionary. But Sentimentalism was not just a literary vogue, and one strange relic gives us peculiar insight into the way that real people took the sensibility of Julie and Saint-Preux, Charlotte and Werther into their own lives. In 1777 the seventeen-year-old Mary Hays, later to be well known as a champion of women's rights and a novelist, fell in love with one John Eccles, who reciprocated her feelings. Their love letters survive to chart, in pages of unremitting earnestness and tedium, a copybook Sentimental passion. Being too young and penniless to marry without the consent of their parents, they were forced into secrecy and an elaborate correspondence in which they rehearse every minute pang, doubt, and nuance that pass through their over-heated little brains. Miss Hays is particularly concerned with 'delicacy', that scrupulous self-restraint which precludes the gross and vulgar business of sexual contact. So delicate, in fact, is Miss Hays, that she addresses her love as 'Mr Eccles' and can only bring herself to notate certain sacred words by their initials, such as 'l—' and 'k—s'. The certainty that they are on the side of the angels keeps them going. 'Half the world have no souls,' Miss Hays writes categorically: 'I envy them not their dull insipid calmness—rather would I suffer all those heart-rending, exquisite distresses, which too often flow from sensibility.'

None of it brought the wretched pair any happiness, and the affair ended as Sentimentally as possible, with Eccles dying in 1780 shortly after parental consent for marriage had been won. Mary Hays spent the next ten years in a state of absolute mourning—of which one can only be thankful no details remain.

Sentimentalism also put strong emphasis on 'natural' family ties, particularly that of mother and child, and explored the mystique of child-rearing. New thinking was stimulated by the educational pro-gramme set out by Rousseau in *Émile*, which emphasized the child's innocence and argued that schooling should not be a matter of forced book-learning imposed from without, but a natural development inculcating morality, social utility, and undoctrinaire religion. People began to think of 'childhood' as a special condition to be cherished and to see children as having qualities of personality which as adults they had lost. Middle-class women began to suckle their own babies again rather than farm them out to wet-nurses, thus nurturing the maternal bond. Children's sweet little remarks were recorded in diaries and letters, and their sweet little acts of natural innocence tearfully recorded. It became the fashion to indulge children's whims and demands, and to do nothing to inhibit their natural tendency to run riot. Children were no longer expected just to fit into the adult world as best they could: they now had their own styles of clothes, their own 'learning-can-be-fun' picture books, their educational toys (the years of the French Revolution saw a roaring trade in miniature guillotines), all designed, often by *Rousseauistes*, exclusively for them.

But Sentimentalism was not an unmixed blessing to women with mind and will. There was a definite tendency in Rousseau's writings to endorse the notion that women's 'natural' roles were those of helpmeet and mother, and that their education should be delimited accordingly. Men continued to tell women that they were intrinsically inferior intellectually and that their aspirations to learn, think, and write were ridiculous and even repulsive. Women should not 'unsex' themselves by emulating male qualities. It was an old story, which all the Enlightenment of the eighteenth century failed to carry much further. The term 'bluestocking'* was bandied about contemptuously and the circles of literate women, denied any other academic commu-nity, who met in the *salons* and drawing-rooms of London, Paris, and Berlin were the butt of constant petty abuse. Even Keats, the least sceptical of men, could not resist a tirade: 'The world, and especially our England, has within the last thirty years been vexed and teased by a set of Devils,' he wrote in 1817, 'a set of women, who having taken a snack or luncheon, set themselves up for Towers of Babel in lan-

---

* The derivation, ironically, refers to the colour of male, rather than female stockings. In 1750 Mrs Elizabeth Montagu started evening conversation parties at which wit and learning were more important than fashion and etiquette, and where gentlemen were welcome to attend in everyday blue worsted stockings rather than the formal black silk normally required for visiting.

guage, Sapphos in poetry—Euclids in Geometry—and everything in nothing'; one of his ambitions, he adds, was to 'upset the drawling of the bluestocking world'. Byron bantered too, tossing off a feeble squib called 'The Blues' and proposing, with typical Byronic cheek, a reactionary solution to women's discontents:

> They ought to mind home—and be well fed and clothed—but not mixed in society. Well educated too, in religion—but to read neither poetry nor politics—nothing but books of piety and cookery. Music—drawing—dancing—also a little gardening and ploughing now and then. I have seen them mending the roads in Epirus with good success. Why not, as well as haymaking and milking?

It must be admitted that the bluestockings were not an immediately attractive lot. Pious and priggish, with time and money on their hands, they had no animus against men, did not chain themselves to railings, wear trousers, or have interesting love affairs. Spiritually and intellectually they were stuck somewhere between the drawing-room and the library. Their business was strictly moral, literary, philosophical, and historical: outstanding among their scholarly achievements was the translation of a Greek Stoic philosopher Epictetus, by the virtuous Miss Elizabeth Carter, mistress of eleven languages. Miss Hannah More wrote a historical drama for Garrick which sold four thousand copies in two weeks; she also ended up the sour and narrow champion of Sunday schools.

It is significant that the most successful woman intellectual of the pre-Revolutionary era wanted nothing to do with such a prickly crowd and openly preferred the company of men. Kitty Macaulay (1731–91) took, uniquely, the longer view. The centre of her activities was an eight-volume history of England since the seventeenth century, fully documented and unashamedly biased towards progressive and republican positions, which she planned to follow up with a history of the War of American Independence. Liberty was her passion and she called, among other things, for the abolition of hereditary titles, the redistribution of property, electoral reform, and the introduction of a copyright law. She also saw further than any of her contemporaries into the situation of her sex—as D. M. Stenton has noted, 'She was the first woman to draw attention to the "absolute and total exclusion from every political right" suffered by all women.' In her *Letters on Education* (1790) she firmly denied any inherent differences between male and female intelligence.

Dr Johnson, from his opposing conservatism, found her tiresome, and lost no opportunity of picking at what he considered her pretensions. While living in Bath, she won a reputation for flamboyance bordering on elegance, and when Boswell passed on the gossip that 'she had of late become very fond of dress, sat together hours at her toilet, and even put on rouge', Johnson replied tartly, 'It is better she should be reddening her own cheeks, than blackening other people's characters.' Her second marriage, to a Scots doctor twenty years her junior, doubtless caused further ribaldry—but then she was evidently a woman who could give as good as she got.

Her American history was never written, although she did brave the rough Atlantic crossing in 1784 to visit the new-born republic, where she spent ten days inspiring George Washington with tales of his predecessors among the Ancients. As a historian, she was not of lasting importance: others covered the same ground with less bias and more sensitivity. What really mattered was that she was fearless, respected, and prominent, a woman whom men could not patronizingly pigeonhole. To the next generation of women intellectuals in France and England she provided an enviable model.

'*Je veux être la Macaulay de mon pays*,' wrote the imprisoned Madame Roland, wife of the Minister of the Interior, in 1793, as she embarked on her memoirs, written against the deadline of her trial and the guillotine; Mary Wollstonecraft thought her 'the woman of the greatest abilities ... that this country has ever produced', and when she began in 1791 on her *Vindication of the Rights of Woman*, she 'anticipated Mrs Macaulay's approbation ... but soon heard with a sickly qualm of disappointed hope' and the still seriousness of regret—that she was no more'. Kitty Macaulay was dead, and all her Whiggish optimism about future liberty would soon die too, on the streets of Paris. The doors to the arenas of political participation would shut fast for women in the summer of 1793, after the assassination of Marat by Charlotte Corday. This, proclaimed a Jacobin newspaper, is what comes of women leaving the family hearth and renouncing the natural docility of their sex:

Charlotte Corday was twenty-five; in terms of our customs, that makes her almost an old maid, and one with a mannish demeanour ... this woman had utterly thrown off her sex; when nature recalled it to her, she felt only distaste and tedium; sentimental love and its sweet emotions came nowhere near the heart of a woman with pretensions to learning, wit, free thought, politics, who has a passion for philosophy and longs for public acclaim. Kind and decent men do not like women of this sort ...

Months earlier, in a more hopeful atmosphere, the ideas of the Marquis de Condorcet on the subject of women's suffrage and rights had at least been debated. Marriage had been made into a civil contract, with divorce obtainable by mutual consent. There was a clamp-down on prostitution and libertinism and an insistence on the egalitarian *tutoiement* and the appellations of *citoyen* and *citoyenne*. Official emulation of the styles and principles of republican Rome gave women a grave dignity; the severe classical lines of the tunic and toga took over from frills and ornament; loyal *citoyennes* named their daughters Cérès, Civilisation, even Phytogneâtropé ('giving birth to warriors'). The heroic part played by women in some of the great events of the Revolution, like the 1789 Versailles bread march (described by Carlyle as 'ludicro-terrific and most unmanageable'!), was publicly honoured.

Women also began organizing themselves. The patriotic women's clubs may often have provided only the sort of soup-kitchen and bandages support we associate today with women's voluntary work, but many of them had a campaigning edge too. Most remarkable was the short-lived Society of Revolutionary Republican Women, led by one Pauline Léon. Angry, anarchic, and to the left of the Jacobins, their chief concern was not political rights for women but cheap food, and they paraded noisily in the streets to argue their case, often wearing trousers and spoiling for a fight. A Dutch émigré Etta Palm d'Aelders put the more conventional case for women, and the Amazonian playwright Olympe de Gouges made a magnificent nuisance of herself in public assemblies: once she challenged Robespierre, whom she detested, to swim with her across the Seine. She composed pamphlets proposing a national theatre for women and state *ateliers* for the unemployed, as well as a seventeen-article Declaration of the Rights of Woman, which argued for complete legal and political equality of the sexes. If women had the right to mount the scaffold, she announced, then they also had the right to mount the rostrum to speak in the Assembly.

It was into this ferment of possibilities that the English woman writer Mary Wollstonecraft came in December 1792. Paris must have sounded like a good place for a woman to be then, especially if she was the author of the celebrated *Vindication of the Rights of Woman*, published early that same year and already disseminated across Europe. But her motives were not simply professional or ideological: she was also escaping from a hopeless passion for a married man, the painter Henry Fuseli. Among the possibilities of Paris, Mary half-jokingly suggested to a friend before she left, might be 'a husband for the time being'.

Mary Wollstonecraft grew up, like Shelley, with a sense of personal grievance and deprivation that turned her into that type of revolutionary which finds it difficult to join clubs and march in a straight line, but is fuelled by a bottomless fund of undirected resentment. She was born in 1759 to a middle-class family of above-average unhappiness—her father was drunken and irresponsible and Mary observed bitterly the attention and education lavished on her elder brother. Various intense relationships with members of her own sex watered her emotional growth, which was to be an angry and troubled one. In 1784, with two of her sisters (one of whom she had firmly dragged away from an unsatisfactory husband) and her closest friend, she set up a school on Newington Green, a centre of free thought and radicalism in East London. This soon collapsed, partly because Mary did not have her heart in infant teaching, even if it was *au* Rousseau, and after tossing off a pot-boiling pamphlet on female education, she spent another disastrous period as governess to the children of some Irish aristocrats. Impatience, self-pity and a sense of her own neglected worth had left her a bad candidate for the ordinary run of female careers.

Her next move was audacious, and it paid off. She presented herself penniless at the door of her publisher Joseph Johnson with nothing to offer except the manuscript of her first novel and her future services. She meant business, and to his credit Johnson took her seriously, agreeing not only to provide her with a house, a maid, and all expenses, but also to give her a job as 'in-house' writer, editor, and translator. It was a remarkable bargain—on rather better terms than Virginia Woolf's room of her own with £100 a year—in that although women writers were a common enough phenomenon in London, their work was invariably contracted *ad hoc*: Johnson was in effect making Mary a salaried professional, then the rarest of all female statuses. He was not trying to be kind to her: Johnson was a sharp and successful operator, publishing a list which spread wide over all areas of social and political reform, as well as fiction and children's books. He wanted not so much creative genius as someone who could quickly translate important new books from the Continent, cast a sharp critical eye over new manuscripts, and write hard-hitting book reviews for the monthly journal he published. Mary worked flat out, could never be accused of being mealy-mouthed, and gave him a good return on his investment.

The Johnson stable included Godwin, Cowper, and Blake, and he had contacts with all the London and provincial intelligentsia; later he would publish some of the polemical pamphlets of the young Wordsworth and Coleridge. The open house he kept for his authors provided Mary with the means to that first-hand education in the new ideas previously denied her, and she was soon a familiar and respected figure in radical circles, burning with the blunt argumentative forcefulness that women so often have to use to make themselves heard in a man's world. At Johnson's she learnt the revolutionary value of Reason, and like the Godwinian Wordsworth, she dragged 'all passions, notions, shapes of faith / Like culprits to the bar', questioning every inherited piety and assumption. She criticized, for instance, the clever way in which the Tory politician Edmund Burke capitalized on the tones and tears of Sentimentalism in his *Reflections on the Revolution in France* to appeal to instinctive feelings of patriotism against the logic-mongers of France. Pity and tenderness, wrote Mary in her highly successful riposte *A Vindication of the Rights of Man*, were not enough; an inflamed imagination 'drained off nourishment' from the vital faculties of thinking and doing. The point was to change the world, which was what the French were doing:

> Sensibility is the mania of the day, and compassion the virtue which is to cover a multitude of vices, whilst justice is left to mourn in sullen silence, and balance truth in vain ... Quitting the flowers of rhetoric, let us, Sir, reason together ...

One can picture her standing in front of Burke and staring him firmly in the eye: the portrait of her painted in 1791 (*see plate 7*) confirms the image.

Reason, however, was not Mary Wollstonecraft's real talent. She thought in short, explosive bursts, jumping back and forward, emphatic and berating. At its worst her style was turgid and repetitive. Even *A Vindication of the Rights of Woman* verges in parts on the incomprehensible, and even one of her greatest admirers, Godwin, had to admit that it was 'eminently deficient in method and arrangement'. To call it, in Claire Tomalin's word, 'an extravaganza' is to imply a sparkle and variety that it conspicuously lacks. Lumpish and chaotic would be nearer the mark.

She wrote it at great speed, in six weeks of the autumn of 1791, urged on by Johnson to follow up the success of the previous year's *A Vindication of the Rights of Man*. It was a brilliant piece of publishing, which caught both the crest of the wave of interest in 'rights' and broadened the dimensions of the issues. It is not a book of lucid argument or considered research; it is not even a book of desperate, starving outrage. What makes it so modern (which is not to imply that it is easily readable) is that it shares with the feminism of the early 1970s an intense irritation with the whole pointless and condescending rigmarole of relating to men sexually. Women treated as men's playthings and reduced to responding with wiles and flirtation—'from the tyranny of men, I firmly believe, the greater number of female follies proceed'; 'femininity' an idea invented by men; marriage as legalized prostitution, with women regarded as men's property rather than as full human beings—this will be of familiar stuff to any reader of Betty Friedan or Germaine Greer, but in 1792 Mary Wollstonecraft was hitting an invisible raw nerve with a hammer blow. It is this directness that made the *Vindication* important. Earlier appeals for women's education and so on had been precisely that—appealing. But the *Vindication* does not ask favours or map out rational programmes of reform: far more original, it dares to be outspoken, cross, and rude. Women must learn to rationalize and theorize their situation; to do so involved a difficult break with male-dominated forms and areas of expression which kept women in their subordinate place. It is this which causes its deficiencies of method, arrangement, and style. But it is difficult to live with that sort of discontent curdling one's psyche. In her early thirties, with friends, fame, books, and her own earned money, she stood proud and alone. 'Every obligation we receive from our fellow creatures is a new shackle,' she claimed, 'takes from our native freedom, and debases the mind'. This championing of women's independence was brave and necessary, yet it also left Mary without any channel for her strong capacities for love and compassion. Her crazy pursuit of an impossible object, the painter Fuseli, only confused her further. Fuseli was nearly fifty, vain and flattered by Mary's attentions—but he did not actually like her very much: besides, he had only recently married. For her part, Mary did not quite know what it was she wanted from him. The affair culminated with Mary asking his wife point-blank to accept a *ménage à trois*, in which she, Mary, would take over the spiritual and intellectual side of things, leaving the wife all legal and fleshly rights. It was, Mary declared in a telling phrase, 'a rational desire'—but the door was slammed in her face, and she left for Paris, as she grimly wrote, 'neck or nothing'.

She lodged in an attic in the Marais, from which there was a fine view of the ruined Bastille; but Paris was not welcoming. Johnson had asked her to send back some 'foreign correspondent' reports, but at first she stayed indoors all day, feeling frightened and isolated. Her best French phrases came out stammering and clumsy; in a letter home she wished she had her London cat with her. One day she saw from her eyrie Louis XVI being driven under heavy escort down the rue du Temple to his trial, the streets chillingly silent except for the occasional roll of a drum. That night, 'for the first time in my life', she could not blow out her candle: death was in the air. Wordsworth had just left Paris for England when Mary arrived. In the tenth book of *The Prelude*, he recalls experiencing a similar fear only a few weeks previously, after walking through an empty square which had recently witnessed the funeral pyre of a mass of slaughtered corpses:

> ... that night
> When on my bed I lay, I was most moved
> And felt most deeply in what world I was;
> My room was high and lonely, near the roof
> Of a large mansion or Hotel, a spot
> That would have pleased me in more quiet times,
> Nor was it wholly without pleasure then.
> With unextinguished taper I kept watch,
> Reading at intervals. The fear gone by
> Pressed on me almost like a fear to come.

Again like Wordsworth, Mary made contact with the group of English and American expatriates who met at White's Hotel near the Palais-Royal. They were all sympathetic to the Revolution, most of them fellow-travellers with the republican or 'Girondiste' wing of the Revolution then arriving at the peak of its influence. At the centre of the White's circle was the pretty, affected, and not over-intelligent English poet and journalist Helen Maria Williams (1762–1827), who had more than a touch of what in our time has been called radical chic. Her Sentimental ballads had been all the rage in the 1780s (Wordsworth was a fervent admirer of them), but she was now settled as a rather fanciful and inaccurate foreign correspondent in Paris, where she had a *salon* and an enjoyable sex life. In London, Mary would probably have found her trivial—one of the women she criticized in the *Vindication* 'for ever trying to make themselves *agreeable* to men'—but in Paris she needed friends, and Helen was an easy woman to be fond of, despite her sillinesses.

Through her new acquaintance, Mary came near to the heart of revolutionary power. She was commissioned by the Committee for Public Instruction to write a report on women's education in the new

French republic, and she also became friendly with the extraordinary Madame Roland, who without any official post or public writing had become one of the major influences on French politics.

Manon Roland, born Jeanne-Marie Phlipon in 1754, had been brought up in Paris, the daughter of a *petit-bourgeois* engraver. She was a precociously bookish child whose intense reading of Plutarch and Tacitus inspired her to seek 'a noble destiny' for herself. As a girl of ten, she begged her parents to let her prepare for her first communion in the solitude of a convent; at twenty-one, she was so deeply moved by the candour of Rousseau's *Confessions* that she turned down a decent run of suitors, on the grounds that they could offer her no more than bourgeois comforts. Throughout her youth she had prepared herself by a rigorous programme of self-education, embracing algebra, physics, and botany, as well as history and literature. Dedicated to the betterment of humanity and the Roman spirit of self-sacrifice and *gravitas*, she was, in the words of Stendhal, 'too passionate to be a coquette and too opinionated to be a diplomatic *salon* hostess'. In 1780 she finally married a slow and serious middle-aged civil servant, Roland de la Platière, who worked as an inspector of industry in the brief but Enlightened ministry of Turgot. Their relationship recalls that of the idealistic Dorothea and the withered biblical scholar Casaubon in George Eliot's *Middlemarch*; and like Mary Hays, Manon made a meal of it in a series of sexlessly ardent letters, full of the Rousseauan glories of wife submitting to her natural master:

> My path is in your footsteps. Direct, order, wish! My prize is your regard; it is by your merit that I am worth anything, it is for you alone that I mean to exist.

Bound by the Higher Friendship, their marriage would be calm and severe in style, directed towards Liberty, Truth, and Justice: 'We must sweat like galley-slaves to be worth anything, let us conjoin our strengths and tire the malignity of fate by our constancy.' Even poor Roland, no shirker, seems to have been a little daunted by all this: could she not turn her mind to the domestic arrangements a moment?

The years before the outbreak of revolution were spent in the environs of Lyons, where Roland diligently continued to build a career of quiet distinction, promoting free trade and new technology. Madame Roland however felt the ennui of the provinces. Looking after her baby daughter with one hand, with the other she researched and copied for an immense dictionary of trades and manufactures which Roland had been commissioned to assemble. It was the galley-slave drudgery she had anticipated, but although she submitted to it heroically, it could not satisfy her. Nor was she much of a success as a provincial official's wife, for she was too aggressive to waste her time making small talk to the wives of local dignitaries. Far more involving was her correspondence with her husband's colleagues and friends, many of them lawyers and journalists in the forefront of Enlightenment reform, from whom she could hear news of the latest books and controversies.

With the events of 1789, she sensed at last the approach of her noble destiny. The Revolution made Roland a coming man, and his wife was behind him, determined not to lose a trick. When in 1790 he was sent back to Paris to plead the case for grants to the ailing industries of Lyons, she used every opportunity to attend public sessions in the parliamentary assembly and debates in the various political clubs; her simple and spartan *salon* brought together some of the best of the rising young minds, including that of Robespierre. She herself talked very little; instead, she listened—everywhere, to everything and everybody, gathering the unique range of knowledge about opinions, personalities, and shifting loyalties on which over the next three years she would build her power. Already she felt disgust at the empty rhetoric and vacillation flourishing around her at a time when firm leadership, decisive policy, and united action were needed to stop the Revolution falling to a royalist coup. No one seemed to agree on what they wanted; no one seemed able to consolidate.

All this she thought and wrote in private. A noble destiny, not a career, was her aim. She did not believe it to be the glory of a wife and mother to stand up and shout in public like Olympe de Gouges, nor did she concern herself with the rights of Woman. As 'Wife of Roland', she saw herself as a Roman matron, exerting influence from the family hearth by force of her incorruptible virtue and straight-backed personality. But in effect, as her husband became older and more befuddled by power, she became the reality of the command behind the name—the brains, energy, organization, and policy of Roland.

By 1792, when Roland had risen to become Minister of Home Affairs, sharper party lines had drawn up in the chaotic talking-shops of Paris. Madame Roland and her husband stood with the 'Girondiste' or 'Brissotin' tendency, which leant towards the idea that France should become a federal republic on the American model, with similar civil liberties and, it was hoped, a similarly high moral tone. The Gironde also generally supported the idea of a crusading war to be waged by France on behalf of the liberties of enslaved Europe. In Madame Roland's view, this would be a character-forming exercise for the French, since, 'adversity makes nations as it makes individuals'. From the same distance of nearly ten years and an ocean, she thought of the happy outcome of the War of American Independence, establishing a quiet and sober nation of hard-working, property-owning farmers and traders living in equity and equality under the guarantees of a constitution. To fight and win a war on ideals was her fatal dream.

Meanwhile, she worked tirelessly as her husband's private secretary, writing his letters, editing and even composing his speeches and pamphlets. She sat in on meetings, gave private interviews, and acted as a discreet channel of confidential information. Her judgements of personality were ruthless. Those she liked and trusted could expect their cases to be seen to: a word in Madame Roland's ear could lead an issue to be raised at cabinet level. Equally, her enmities were scorching. It was she who in June 1792 devised the ferocious letter to the King, charging him with failure to abide by the Constitution. 'I know that the austere language of truth is rarely well received near a throne,' it sneered. The King was enraged, and dismissed Roland; two months later France dismissed the King, Roland was reinstated, and with the establishment of that magic word, 'republic', the star of the Gironde should have been at its height.

But the consolidating unity for which Madame Roland hoped did not follow. Robespierre was antagonized. The character-forming war against the King's ally Austria was not going the way of liberty and bad news from the front precipitated the panic which led to the September Massacres in the Paris prisons. The blood-curdling rhetoric of Danton and Marat, both of whom loathed Madame Roland as much as she loathed them, had reached the people of Paris in ways that made the exhortations of the Girondins look politically naïve. The Girondins had the sentiments, but the Jacobins had the electricity.

For Madame Roland there was a further complication of a more delicately intangible kind. Over the years of the Revolution, she had come to realize that throughout her marriage she had been the driving force behind her husband, a man who had the soul and abilities of an administrator, a civil servant, no more: without her vision and intellect, he would have remained a competent provincial nobody. Now, under pressure of high office, she saw him dither and bang his fist like the rest of the mediocrities; she saw him weary of the constant battle which to her was the only path to glory. What she had intended to be a collaboration of soul-mates was turning into the pathetic spectacle of a grey-haired and irritable old man, clinging desperately to a woman nearly twenty years his junior.

Such thoughts became insistent for the obvious reason: at the age of thirty-eight she had discovered real sexual love for the first time, an experience which put her past in a new perspective and made her marriage look like an emotional sham. In her memoirs she recalled the flatness of her wedding night: 'I wonder whether anyone with so much capacity for sensual pleasure could have tasted it so little,' she wrote, with the hindsight of fulfilment. Her lover's name was François-Leonard Buzot, a startlingly handsome Girondin deputy, whom she had known for some time as a regular visitor to her *salon* and study. Her feelings for him were acute and absolute, and true Rousseauan that she was, she had to live by them. Like the heroine of *La Nouvelle Héloïse* confessing her affair with Saint-Preux to her elderly husband, she went straight to Roland and sincerely told him all. Of course, she would stay with him, for she lacked nothing in honour, and Buzot too had his wife—but he could no longer call her heart his. For Roland, increasingly unpopular, haunted by his inability to control the murderous street riots, barracked and slandered in the press and the Assembly despite his total administrative integrity, it must have been a blackly isolating blow.

There was another woman in Paris, a new friend of Madame Roland's also in her thirties, who was discovering for the first time the force of a sexual love: this was Mary Wollstonecraft.

Through the first troubled months of 1793, she had grown closer to one particular member of the White's Hotel circle, the thirty-nine-year-old American Gilbert Imlay. The champion of the Rights of Woman might well have disliked him. He had a reputation for dallying with women and was currently rumoured to be involved with Helen Maria Williams. His past as an adventurer, man of the world, and occasional writer was mysterious, his future doubtful. He talked of leaving France to set up a farming community in the United States and of joining a French expedition against the Spanish in Louisiana; meanwhile, Paris presented him with plenty of opportunities for various shades of wheeling and dealing. Imlay was a man to grab at the main chance, ever ready to drop his scruples; he was probably a liar too. But he had rangy charms that Mary found very attractive and he gave her a sort of attention, flattering and seductive, that she had never before received. So she plunged into love and found it delicious.

Around them was turmoil. In January the King was executed, an event which multiplied political divisions. Roland resigned, the public and personal strain having taken its toll, and he and his wife went back to their dictionary of manufactures. In February, there was looting and rioting in Paris, caused by inflation and food shortages, and the start of a serious counter-revolutionary campaign in the Vendée. By March, war had been declared against Britain, Holland, and Spain. Following defeats on the north-east front Dumouriez, a general with strong Girondin connections, deserted to the Austrians, and all Girondin ministers became the objects of paranoid suspicion. Roland's letters and papers were seized; wild accusations of treachery and conspiracy redoubled.

But for Mary and Imlay it was a time of perversely blossoming joy. War—and we must not forget that Paris was a walled city at war with itself—screws up the pitch of emotion and heightens the sense of relationship, of what is valued and might at any moment be lost. It breeds that heady supercharged emotion that survivors of the London blitz lyrically recall, and its victims know the ultimate alternative—that, as W. H. Auden expressed it, 'we must love one another or die'. To love becomes more urgent as the world fills up with death.

The history of the Revolution is full of fragile idylls—Chénier in Versailles that same summer was gathering baskets of fruit for Madame Lecoulteulx—and the cottage that Mary and Imlay rented in Neuilly makes the setting for one of the most poignant. By the beginning of June, most of the leading Girondins had been imprisoned. Roland managed to escape to Rouen, evading his warrant through some bold delaying tactics of his wife, who was herself illegally arrested shortly after. Feelings against enemy aliens ran high, and mass arrest or deportation looked imminent. It was obviously safer and easier for Mary to live outside the city walls, inside which various curfews and restrictions applied: Imlay, as citizen of a nation officially friendly to the French, had less to worry about. The Neuilly cottage was tiny and quaint, surrounded by forest through which she could—and once did—walk to Versailles and its eerily empty palace halls. A gardener attended to her needs, gave fatherly advice, and brought her grapes. She worked, in a desultory way, on what was to be her most desultory book, the *Historical and Moral View of the French Revolution* (she must have been inhibited by the fear that the authorities would catch her with a treasonable manuscript). Her mind was elsewhere, contemplating the triumph of that inner revolution of heart and soul which so many would cherish through the years of disillusion. Imlay's love had transformed her—'like a serpent upon a rock that casts its slough and appears again with the brilliancy, the sleekness, and the elastic activity of its happiest age', suggested her first biographer.

Much of the time she was alone. Imlay came to her from Paris whenever he could, and she went to meet him at the Longchamp toll-gate, *la barrière*, that became their private lovers' joke. As they walked home, he would have catalogued the news of a long, hot summer—of Charlotte Corday's assassination of Marat in defence of the wronged Girondins; of Robespierre's inexorable rise to power through the Committee of Public Safety and a conception of national unity far more perfect and terrible than anything envisaged by Madame Roland.

In September she was pregnant and moved back to Paris. Imlay registered her as his wife at the American Embassy, but then went and spoilt things by spending an increasing amount of time at the port of Le Havre, or Havre-Marat, as it had been renamed, where he had business interests. Mary began, fatal sign, to feel slighted and her letters take on a mildly hectoring tone. 'Of late, we are always separating . . . I do not wish to be loved like a goddess;' she wrote, 'but I wish to be necessary to you.' The dreamy isolation of the summer became a gnawing loneliness. In October all her English friends were arrested under the new machinery of the Terror. Mary escaped by virtue of her *bona fide* American status, but she might well have been happier in the Luxembourg prison, alongside Helen Maria Williams, who spent much of her time there doling out bracing cups of tea to those summoned to trial and execution. It was a bad season for women: Marie Antoinette was guillotined, as was Olympe de Gouges, breathing hell-fire defiance; another campaigner, Théroigne de Méricourt, having been publicly whipped by a posse of Jacobin wives, was confined to a madhouse. On 31 October, the same day that twenty-one Girondin heads fell in a record thirty-eight minutes, the women's clubs were abolished, signifying an official suppression of the agitation for women's rights. A few days later it was the turn of the unbowed Madame Roland.

During her months in prison she had found a spiritual peace she had never known before, despite worries about the fate of her colleagues and the scurrilous attacks of a satirical magazine, *Père Duchesne*, which pictured her as the toothless hag Madame Coco, plotting with royalist English against the people of France. Against this, she had two great strengths to draw on. One was her passion for

Buzot, still at large in the provinces, which imprisonment purified and exalted; the other was the writing of her *Mémoires*, a superb piece of self-justification, inevitably unfinished, but vivid, witty, acutely analytic, and perhaps the prose masterwork of the first revolutionary years.* Both the letters to Buzot and her manuscripts were smuggled out by her loyal friend and visitor Sophie Grandchamp.

Towards the end of her first month of incarceration, she was dramatically released, only to be immediately re-arrested and 'properly' charged with 'suspicion of complicity', 'notorious liaisons', and 'the public uproar against her'. Lack of substantial evidence did not inhibit the Revolutionary Tribunal, but there was still disappointment when scrutiny of the Roland accounts revealed meticulous probity. Madame Roland was now sent to the prison of Sainte-Pélagie. It was dirty and rowdy: the carousing obscenities of the prostitutes and actresses offended her sensibilities, but she had learnt indifference to externals. Madame Roland went on telling herself her own story, living and feeding off her rich store of memory: like Rousseau in his *Confessions*, she reviewed the tiny but significant incidents of childhood, the animosities, humiliations, and absurdities as well as the aspirations and achievements. Prison, as so many have found, is paradoxically a place of mental freedom. 'How I cherish fetters in which I am free to love you and think of you without end,' she wrote to Buzot.

> If Heaven accords me no more, may it keep me in this situation until my ultimate deliverance from a world abandoned to injustice and misfortune. You have made beautiful this sad resort, you have diffused into this place all the happiness that those who dwell in palaces sometimes long for in vain.

On the evening of 30 October Sophie Grandchamp came to her cell to describe the guillotining of the twenty-one Girondin leaders. The two women stood and wept. Then Madame Roland controlled herself. Her own end could not be far off, and she had come to terms with it, all thoughts of suicide banished. 'I shed these tears for my country,' she told Sophie. 'My friends have died martyrs for liberty ... Now my fate is sealed; there is no more uncertainty. I shall join them soon, and show myself worthy of following them.' She shed no more tears, but begged that Sophie should stand on the parapet of the Pont-Neuf as her tumbril passed, and give her a last farewell.

---

* It is scandalous that, at the time of writing, it is unavailable in a modern English translation.

As expected, she was duly called for trial. At the Conciergerie next to the court she was thrown in alongside a duchess, a pickpocket, a nun, a prostitute, and a lunatic, but her inner calm was not broken. She would practise what she preached: 'Anyone who puts their life before everything else, or indeed anyone who counts it for anything at all in times of revolution, will never attach much value to virtue, honour, or country.'

The Tribunal had little difficulty in bringing a trumpery conviction against her for being part of a 'horrible conspiracy against the unity, the indivisibility of the Republic, the liberty and safety of the French people'. Dressed in white, her hair flowing loose to her waist, Madame Roland grimly made the Roman thumbs-down sign as she was escorted from the courtroom. A few hours later, on the thundery afternoon of 8 November, Sophie clung to the parapet of the Pont-Neuf, making the supreme effort to answer her friend's ghastly request. When she saw the composed and smiling figure in the tumbril, hair shorn and hands tied, she could scarcely contain herself—but she met and acknowledged those martyr's eyes, shining with the ecstasy of self-righteousness.

At the guillotine in the Place de la Révolution, Madame Roland asked the executioner to take a trembling old man before her and put him out of his misery. As her turn came to mount the scaffold, she fixed her gaze on David's newly erected clay statue of Liberty and cried out, '*O liberté, comme on t'a jouée!*', 'O Liberty, what a fool they have made of you!'* The rain poured down as Madame Roland died a Roman death and met her noble destiny.

Her husband, a fugitive in Rouen, killed himself on hearing the news; Buzot was found some months later, dead in a field near Bordeaux, his body half-eaten by wolves. The *Mémoires* were published in 1795, and an English translation under the imprint of Joseph Johnson came out in the same year.†

Mary Wollstonecraft's life followed a more muddled course. In January 1794 she left Paris to join Imlay in Havre-Marat. There was still a deep tenderness between them and the spring brought the arrival of their baby daughter Fanny, but their relationship was eroding inexorably. Imlay was feckless, harassed, and in chronic

* Another version of this, '*O liberté, que de crimes on commet en ton nom,*' 'O Liberty, what crimes are committed in your name,' is not generally considered authentic.
† Claire Tomalin, in her *The Life and Death of Mary Wollstonecraft*, has plausibly suggested that Mary may have been the anonymous editor of a revised second edition.

debt—a fact of which he had not previously informed her. His interest
in matters of social and political reform proved superficial compared
to his interest in trading soap and alum, in customs embargoes and
tariffs. He wanted to be left alone at times, and he wanted worldly
prosperity: 'The secondary pleasures of life are very necessary to my
comfort,' he admitted. He did not like scenes; Mary, for all her efforts
to make excuses for him, could not avoid them. As she became more
petulant, he tried to calm her down and conciliate, offering her
everything except the loyalty and devotion she wanted and was so
ready to reciprocate. It is a familiar situation and they responded in
familiar ways.

Imlay slithered out of the impasse by decamping to London for
'business reasons', telling Mary that he would send for her and the
baby soon. There was no good reason for her to go, inasmuch as
France was still the place where she had first tasted happiness and
England a country for which she now felt 'repugnance that almost
amounts to horror', but she clung to the dregs of her memories of
Neuilly, and so when he finally did call, she dragged herself back,
'dead to hope'—only to discover, after various prevarications, that he
had set up with another woman, that he still regarded her as his best
friend, would help her with the baby, thought that she was a wonderful
person, etc. She presented him with an ultimatum: either they should
live together or they should make a clean break. Imlay dithered. For
the author of the *Vindication of the Rights of Woman* there must have
been the humiliating realization that she had fallen dupe to the very
male tyranny she had warned against.

Later that year she made a serious suicide attempt. Imlay had
charged her with a business commission and sent her on a trip to
Scandinavia. Probably he presented it as a nice holiday for her,
secretly hoping for a little breathing-space and the time to see to his
new mistress. Mary was intrigued by Sweden and Norway (and later
published a travel diary of her impressions), but her bitterness against
Imlay was unassuaged: 'You tell me that my letters torture you,' she
wrote him. 'You are right; our minds are not congenial. I have lived in
the ideal world, and fostered sentiments that you do not
comprehend—or you would not treat me thus. I am not, will not be,
merely an object of compassion ...'

When she came back to London and found him set up with an
actress, no amount of reason and theory, not even the claims of her
baby, could hold her back. She took a boat down the Thames to
Putney Bridge and waited for an opportunity to jump off unobserved.

It turned out a horrible botch: her clothes buoyed her up in the water and would not let her drown. The agony of choking finally sent her unconscious, but she was fished out by some boatmen and deposited in a rough riverside inn, where she came round. This was not quite the end of the dismal affair. As a last-ditch compromise, Mary proposed to Imlay, as she had to Fuseli, a *ménage à trois*. When he refused and went back to Paris, never to be heard of again, she seems to have shaken herself into surviving. It was time to pick up the pieces and recover some self-respect. But she could never afterwards bear to hear ill spoken of her first lover.

Some months later, Mary Hays, author of the Sentimental love letters and now a notorious novel, *Memoirs of Emma Courtnay*, which shockingly presented its heroine in active sexual pursuit of a male, brought Mary together with William Godwin. Mary Hays herself was in a bad state, writing further interminable screeds to a man who had no interest in her and using Godwin as an 'agony-uncle' in yet more letters, which she also incorporated into *Emma Courtnay*.* Mary Wollstonecraft was back working on a novel called, somewhat predictably, *The Wrongs of Woman*, and, more surprisingly, a comedy based on her French experiences which unfortunately does not survive. Godwin was at the height of his reputation, as the author of *Political Justice* and the novel *Caleb Williams*. The two of them had plenty in common, not least that they were both looking for practical and lasting companionship. Their affair started slowly and somewhat cagily, but it was adult, sceptical, realistic: they soon learnt to be honest with each other. 'It grew with equal advances in the mind of each,' Godwin remembered. 'It would have been impossible for the most minute observer to have said who was before and who was after.' Mary's wry deprecating wit asserted itself. She could keep her head over Godwin's shortcomings, balancing reason and feeling as she had failed to do over Imlay. They teased each other and often argued, but the general tenor of things is embodied in Godwin's remark: 'It is best that we should be friends.' When she became pregnant, the two anti-matrimonialists swallowed their principles and married: their friends laughed, sometimes sardonically, but Mary was unrepentant. 'A husband is a convenient part of the furniture of a house,' she

---

* Mary Hays's correspondence had quite a reputation in her lifetime: in 1800 Coleridge reports, much to his distaste, that his acquaintance Charles Lloyd was reading out to friends her 'ranting, sentimental' letters to him as 'a subject for *laughter*', then answering them 'quite *à la Rousseau*'.

admitted. She did not want to be loved like a goddess, but convenience, if not necessity, would do very well.

Mary Wollstonecraft died in September 1797 from an infection contracted while giving birth to the baby who was to become Mary Shelley. Godwin was shattered by his wife's death, but in idolizing her memory he did it more harm than he could appreciate. His hastily assembled *Memoirs of the Author of 'A Vindication of the Rights of Woman'* aimed to tell the whole unadulterated truth, Imlay and all, in the fond belief that his picture of an Idealist, 'a Female Werter', defeated by a cruel world, her soul 'almost too fine a texture to encounter the vicissitudes of human affairs', would speak to every Sentimental heart.

This was to misjudge the *fin de siècle* cultural climate, which was becoming ever more firmly antipathetic to anything which hinted at Revolutionary ideology—especially after news of the disgraceful French invasion of neutral Switzerland. Godwin's book amounted to further titillating evidence of the scandalous life-style of the radicals, and Mary's death in childbirth was simply divine retribution. The 'Rights of Woman' debate, such as it had been, was fading: the conservative campaigner and bluestocking Hannah More wrote contemptuously of 'Female Politicians'; the Reverend Richard Polwhele's pamphlet *The Unsex'd Females* was one of many deploring the small band of women who sought independence and manly prerogatives. Novels featured caricatured Wollstonecrafts: Maria Edgeworth's *Belinda* (1801), for example, comes up with Mrs Harriot Freke, who hunts, shoots, swears like a trooper, and pours scorn on all notions of feminine 'delicacy'.

The qualities so admired by Jane Austen—submission to discipline, educated common sense, the distrust of restlessness—became the consensus, and it is significant that not a single copy of Mary Hays's *Appeal to the Men of Great Britain in Behalf of the Women*, published by Johnson in 1798, is known to have been preserved. By 1810 a feminist like Shelley's unfortunate soul-sister Elizabeth Hitchener, described by Shelley's biographer Hogg as 'a tower-proof, fire-proof, bomb-proof blue', was indeed a 'freke'.

Mary Wollstonecraft's daughters Fanny Imlay and Mary Godwin grew up, however, in the powerful shadow of their dead mother's image. Godwin had declined into relative obscurity as his ideas fell out of fashion, and the family moved to the genteel poverty of an apartment above his educational publishing and bookselling business in Holborn. He was idolized by the two girls, but proved a distant and reticent father, dominated by his brisk second wife, a Mrs Jane Clairmont, who brought her own two children, Charles and Jane, with her. The family psychology had something of a fairy-tale figuration to it, with Mary and Fanny playing orphaned Cinderella to Mrs Clairmont's wicked stepmother, usurping their position and putting her own children first.

From an early age, Mary was determined and clever, but fundamentally a melancholic: being the product of such an extraordinary marriage gave her an alienating sense of having been singled out, which later manifested itself as priggishness; perhaps she also had a deep unconscious guilt at being the 'cause' of her mother's death. The other running tension in her life was her relationship with her stepsister Jane or, as she preferred to call herself on grounds of allure, Claire. Dark and pretty, vivacious sometimes to the point of silliness, Claire had thwarted ambitions in the theatrical line which she sublimated into her emotional involvements. Throughout the most important years of their lives Claire would dog Mary, at best an irritating companion, at worst her insidious enemy.

Thus in brief stood Godwin's uneasy household in 1814, ready for the catalyst of Percy Bysshe Shelley and the promise he brought of love, money, liberty, and excitement.

In the spring of that year, Shelley was living in Bracknell, Berkshire, panicking at the collapse of his marriage to Harriet. The dagger of blame was plunged into his machinating sister-in-law Eliza, who had been skulking around in the background making trouble since their elopement and was now interfering with the nursing of his and Harriet's baby Ianthe. 'I certainly hate her with all my heart and soul,' he snapped in one of his terrifying bursts of invective, 'she is no more than a blind and loathsome worm that cannot see to sting.' But this was only a way of squaring his conscience with the sad simple truth that he was bound to a woman he did not love and could not decently rid himself of. On other fronts, things were no better. Negotiations with his father at Field Place scarcely advanced, reducing him to taking out loans at 300 per cent interest; and he was writing nothing beyond the odd hysterical letter. His only stability was Madame Boinville, a wealthy and cultivated widow of liberal views, whose French husband, a one-time friend of André Chénier's, had recently died in the retreat from Moscow. Apart from the opportunity her *salon* provided for meeting a fascinating collection of radicals, atheists, and vegetarians, Shelley considered Madame Boinville 'the most admirable specimen of human being I had ever seen', while the tea, sympathy, and Italian lessons dispensed by her pretty daughter Cornelia gave further comfort. Perhaps he was half in love with her: Hogg certainly remembered seeing him at the Boinvilles' 'trembling with emotion' and spilling the contents of his cup 'into his bosom, upon his knees, and into his shoes', with Cornelia standing patiently by, mopping up the mess with her handkerchief. But the answer lay elsewhere, as a premonition, while he 'wandered in the fields alone', had told him:

> A train of visionary events arranged themselves in my imagination till ideas almost acquired the intensity of sensations. Already I had met the female who was destined to be mine, already had she replied to my exulting recognition, already were the difficulties surmounted that opposed our entire union. I had even proceeded so far as to compose a letter to Harriet on the subject of my passion for another. Thus was my walk beguiled ...

A few weeks later, on a visit to Godwin, he noticed the sixteen-year-old Mary and the vision was realized. Here was a pure young creature, ready for love and Shelley's conception of chivalric gallantry, who could 'feel poetry' and 'understand philosophy'. What followed in the ensuing whirlwind weeks is well known—the hours of talk sitting up against Mary Wollstonecraft's gravestone in Old St Pancras Yard; the copy of *Queen Mab* inscribed 'I am thine, exclusively thine'; Godwin, with one eye on the possibility of Shelley's money, the other firmly and conventionally disapproving; the letters to the wretched Harriet, with Shelley's protestations that 'our connection was not one of passion & impulse ... I shall ever be a friend affectionate and sincere'; the tales of mad outbursts and slamming doors, of which Mrs Clairmont's is the most lurid:

> [Shelley] pushed me aside with extreme violence, and entering, walked straight to Mary. 'They wish to separate us, my beloved; but Death shall unite us,' and offered her a bottle of laudanum. 'By this you can escape from tyranny; and this,' taking a small pistol from his pocket, 'shall re-unite me to you.' Poor Mary turned as pale as a ghost, and my poor silly [Claire] who is so timid even at trifles, at the sight of the pistol filled the room with shrieks ... With tears streaming down her cheeks [Mary] entreated him to calm himself and go home ...

It all culminated in a dawn escape to France on what must rank as the most bizarre honeymoon in literary history.

They made for Dover with the appendage of Claire, whose ostensible motive for playing gooseberry on Mary's great adventure was the opportunity to improve her French. Their idea seems to have been to trace the footsteps of Fleetwood, the eponymous hero of one of Godwin's novels, who is pursued over the Alps to the Swiss lakes; but what they failed perhaps to appreciate fully was that this would also entail passing through countryside devastated by the last stages of the Napoleonic Wars, in which memories of the ravaging Allied Armies were still raw and bitter. Because of the hostilities France had been 'closed' to English tourists for the best part of twenty years, and they could hardly expect a warm welcome: it was like deciding to take a holiday in Germany's zero hour of 1945.

Mary was badly seasick on the all-night channel crossing and collapsed at Calais half-dead with exhaustion; Claire remained pert, which was fortunate, because her mother almost immediately caught up with her and begged that she should dissociate herself from a scandalous elopement: with Mary, already beyond the pale of redemption, she was not concerned.

Claire vacillated but Shelley parried, and she decided to throw in her lot with social ruin and a life, as she thought, of freedom and fun. Mrs Clairmont returned to England in high dudgeon as the little party, Shelley not quite twenty-two, the two girls only sixteen, set off for Paris, marvelling in Mary's words 'at the strange costume of the French women' and looking 'with curiosity on every *plât*, fancying that the fried-leaves of artichokes were frogs'.

They arrived in the capital in dire need of money and spent a frustrating time trying to negotiate credit notes, coin, and passports through Claire's schoolgirl French. Paris made Mary think of her mother, and, touchingly, she opened a small casket which she had hitherto kept secret, to show Shelley Mary Wollstonecraft's love letters to Godwin and other relics. They also made vain efforts to contact Helen Maria Williams, who would doubtless have been intrigued to hear of the latest posthumous twist in the saga of her old friend of the White's Hotel days.

Having raised £60, they bought an ass and set off again, covering thirty miles a day and reaching Troyes within a week. It was not an easy trip. The ass went lame and Shelley ended up slinging the poor creature over his shoulders. Then Shelley sprained his ankle, and they had to trade the ass for a mule, who proved intransigent after his kind; so that went, and they bought a little cart instead. At one inn Claire had to fight off both rats and the innkeeper from her bed. The little food they could get was repulsive, and not surprisingly the natives proved 'unamiable, inhospitable & unaccommodating'. Worst of all was the trail of desolation left by the war. 'Village after village entirely ruined & burned,' wrote Shelley, 'the white ruins towering in innumerable forms of destruction among the beautiful trees. The inhabitants were famished; families once perfectly independent now beg their bread ... filth, misery & famine everywhere.'

From Troyes, Shelley wrote to Harriet, suggesting as her 'firm & constant friend' that she should come with the baby and join them all in 'a sweet retreat I will procure for you in the mountains'. Her anguish was never real to him: he staved off guilt by proposing a number of airy solutions, none of which ever acknowledged her feelings of helplessness and betrayal.

Still toying with the fantasy of establishing an open commune of like spirits, Shelley conceived of a novel for which over the next few weeks, with Mary's help, he wrote some four chapters. *The Assassins* tells of an idyllic little republic of primitive Christians living in conditions of Rousseauan purity and behaving with Godwinian benevolence. It is typical of Shelley that he should be thinking along such lines, even at a time when one might expect him to be penning rapturous lyrics to Mary and settling for the companionship of his beloved alone. But the visions of *Queen Mab* were not fading: Claire's journal records a lunchtime conversation on the road from Troyes which artlessly captures the true note of Shelleyan idealism.

> We got some bread and got into the woods by climbing through a retired glen which ascends, and the pines hang so thickly over it that a deep shade was formed. Here we sat and eat [sic] our bread. Shelley said there would come a time when no where on earth, would there be a dirty cottage to be found—Mary asked what time would elapse before that time would come—he said perhaps in a thousand years—we said perhaps it would never come, as it was so difficult to persuade the poor to be clean. But he said it must infallibly arrive, for society was progressive and was evidently moving forwards towards perfectibility—and then he described the career made by man—I wish I could remember the whole—but half has slipped out of my memory ...

There were ominous moments of resistance too, when Mary's primness and caution sank like a stone through the Shelleyan ether. She was outraged when Shelley, bathing naked in a stream, called for her to join him. And Claire noted, 'Shelley asked her why she of a sudden look so sad—and she answered I was thinking of my father—and wondering what he was now feeling. He then said "Do you mean that as a reproach to me"—and she answered "Oh! No! Don't let us think more about it."' In later years there would be more of this side of Mary.

Meanwhile their spirits rose as they left the war zone and approached the Alps, despite a cart driver who much to their annoyance was only capable of responding to the sublime grandeur of the landscape in terms 'of butter and cheese—how good the pasturage was for the cows'. Shelley, however, greeted it like a poet. 'Shelley in an ecstasy and declared how great was his joy,' wrote Claire. 'How great is my rapture he said, I a fiery man with my heart full of youth and with my beloved at my side, I behold these lordly immeasurable Alps ...'

After a pause to sell the cart and raise more money in Neufchâtel, they hurried to their chosen destination of Lake Lucerne. It was not the paradise for which they had been hoping. They spent a total of three days there, unable to find satisfactory lodgings and dismayed that the mountains were covered with cottages and populated by people 'most immoderately stupid & ugly almost to deformity'. On the third day, as the rain fell hard and the stove smoked horribly, they took stock and decided to return to London. Travel had not broadened Claire's mind at least: she decided that 'after having travelled & viewed the follies of other nations my own country appears the most reasonable & the most enlightened'.

They made their way back up the Rhine on a series of water-buses, and once again appreciation of the splendours of Nature was marred by the encroachments of others. Rousseauan and Godwinian he may have been, a prophet of the millennium, but Shelley had the utmost contempt for present vulgarity, knocking down one man who took their seats while they were away and frightening off a bore who wanted to practise his English by talking about royal executions. Mary opined that her fellow-passengers were 'horribly disgusting' and that it would be best 'to absolutely annihilate such animals'; while Claire was appalled at the spectacle of men sociably kissing each other and the 'drinking, smoking, singing and cracking jokes of a *risqué* nature', concluding, 'Never was a more disgraceful set than the Common order of People of Germany.' Waiting for a passage from Rotterdam, Mary began a novel, 'Hate', Claire another, 'The Ideot': the titles comically sum up their feelings. They were penniless, hungry, and fractious: suddenly children desperate to get home.

'What a set! What a world!' lamented the Victorian critic Matthew

Arnold, throwing up his hands in despair at the revelations of the first full biography of Shelley, published some seventy years later: where in all these adolescent shenanigans might be the morals, bearing, and dignity appropriate to the poetic calling? Certainly for months after the return from Switzerland, Shelley's energies were consumed in a frenzy of apparently futile activity. The world had caught him like a rat in a box, and he was scuttling from corner to corner in a vain attempt to break out. Access to his money was denied him. Harriet, prompted throughout by her sister Eliza, instigated legal action, having accepted that her husband was not going to return shamefaced and begging for forgiveness: Mary remarked laconically in her journal that she was 'an odd character'. Godwin remained intransigent and even the liberal-minded Boinvilles, with whom he had freely discussed his marital problems, were furious at his behaviour. It was, as Richard Holmes has thought, 'ironic that the result of all his efforts to liberate himself and those around him from the trammels of morality and society seemed so far to be an almost total entrapment in the complications of his own daily existence'.

In their cramped lodgings in St Pancras, Shelley, Mary, and Claire lived close to the edge. The bailiffs were in pursuit; Mary was pregnant; Shelley plotted to kidnap his two younger sisters from their school in Hackney and continued dreaming of an 'Association of Philosophical People'. There were darker fantasies too, in which Shelley and Claire drew dangerously close to each other, sitting up far into 'the witching time of night' discussing things 'passing strange' and 'hardly daring to breathe'. The vision of a politically reformed society ruled by reason did not satisfy him imaginatively; he also cherished the underworld of powers and sensations, where science dissolved into magic.

Mary, meanwhile, kept her detachment and went to bed early. One thing she never suffered from was hysteria, and she had had long and exasperating experience of Claire's self-dramatization. Equally, she was not one to sit by meekly submissive, and during the last months of her pregnancy she was diverted by the pressing attentions of Shelley's Oxford friend and partner in atheism Hogg. Quite what went on between these two we can only guess, since pages have significantly been torn out of the surviving journal and the relevant letters are ambivalent. But we do know that her baby died ten days after birth, that the death of Shelley's grandfather improved his financial standing, and that by the late summer of 1815 Shelley and Mary had left London for Buckinghamshire, to live alone together for the first time.

'One feels sickened forever on the subject of irregular relations,' confessed Matthew Arnold on contemplating Shelley and his *ménage*. Today, on the other hand, it is all too easy to over-dramatize him as an apostle of sexual liberation as the 1960s discovered it. The evidence is actually rather disappointing. By average Western standards, Shelley was bodily chaste. It is perfectly possible that he never had physical sex with anyone except his two wives, though probable that he also had an experience with a prostitute while a schoolboy at Eton, and some brief involvement with Claire. This scarcely adds up to the career of a libertine. Like so many of his 'progressive' contemporaries, Shelley regarded the promiscuous sexual activity of the pre-Revolutionary generation as gross and decadent. What his philosophy of free love championed was not the uninhibited release of instinctual desire between two individuals, but Love itself, the *spirit* of love, existing outside the social institutions of marriage and family, and spreading through the universe, all-embracing and infinitely inclusive. Love was as sacred a word to him as it was to the Sentimentalists, and one to be approached at all times with extreme 'delicacy' and respect. He detested any hint of obscenity or flippancy ('Thy voice is dearest / To those who mock at truth and Innocency', he wrote in a recently discovered sonnet, 'To Laughter'), and neither his poetry nor his letters show a trace of the lip-licking sensuality that can be found in Goethe and Byron. The vulgar pass that Elizabeth Hitchener made at him or that Hogg made at Harriet filled him with raging disgust: it was not what he meant at all.

To put it bluntly, Shelley's was a case not so much of what D. H. Lawrence called 'sex in the head' as of 'sex in the clouds'. When he 'fell in love' late in his young life with Emilia Viviani and Jane Williams, he was worshipping an ideal, incidentally framed by a human form. 'I think one is always in love with something or other;' he wrote, 'the error, and I confess it is not easy for spirits cased in flesh and blood to avoid it, consists in seeking in a mortal image the likeness of what is perhaps eternal.' His poem 'Epipsychidion', a sort of emotional autobiography, culminates in a fantasy of sailing off with Emilia Viviani to a magic island where 'We shall become the same, we shall be one / Spirit within two frames.' But Emilia is not an identifiable human personality, only 'the Vision veiled from me / So many years'. The real woman—a friend of Claire's, trapped in a convent while waiting for her parents to arrange a suitable marriage—does not figure. 'As to real flesh and blood, you know that I do not deal in those articles,' he admitted wryly. 'You might as well go to a ginshop for a leg of mutton as expect anything human or earthly from me.'

Against all this Shelley faced a tragedy of love that could not be resolved by mingling and melting into the ether: the decline of his relationship with Mary.

In August 1819, still only twenty-one, Mary wrote in her journal: 'We have now lived five years together; and if all the events of the five years were blotted out, I might be happy; but to have won and then cruelly to have lost, the associations of four years, is not an accident to which the human mind can blend without much suffering.' The great concentrating grief among these associations was the death of her two children Clara and William, whose existence had seemed the justification for all the other privations and miseries she and Shelley had endured. But there was also the horror of the suicides of her half-sister Fanny Imlay and, following pell-mell, that of Harriet Shelley; the continual problem of her father, who scrounged and pestered Shelley for money without providing any real moral support in return; and the more immediate irritation of Claire and whatever intimacy she had with Shelley. 'Heigh ho the Claire and the Ma / Find something to fight about every day,' wrote Claire in her journal; but Mary endured silently, through gritted teeth, as she endured Shelley's other infatuations and what she drily called his 'Italian Platonics'. Beyond this was their exile from England and the years of wandering through Italy without a proper home, hounded from the distance of a thousand miles by the scandal and gossip that had attached itself to the name of Shelley.

Her depression set in hard and deep, successfully masked from friends and acquaintance, but painfully communicated to Shelley, struggling to preserve his poet's sense of joy. He wrote inertly of his helplessness before her gloom:

> My dearest Mary, wherefore hast thou gone,
> And left me in this dreary world alone?
> Thy form is here indeed—a lovely one—
> But thou art fled, gone down the dreary road
> That leads to Sorrow's most obscure abode;
> Thou sittest on the hearth of pale despair,
> Where
> For thine own sake I cannot follow thee.

Like Henry James's Isabel Archer, they ended up 'ground in the mill of the conventional', confronting each other as if from opposite ends of a long breakfast-table with nothing to say that had not already been said. And so Shelley learnt the narrowness of his anti-matrimonialist principles; learnt that just to knock down any law which binds husband and wife 'for one moment after the decay of their affection' as 'a most intolerable tyranny' did not wipe away the loyalties and responsibilities involved in any close relationship; learnt the painful adult acceptance of guilt: 'The ghosts of our dead associations rise & haunt us in revenge, for our having let them starve, & abandoned them to perish,' he wrote bitterly to Peacock; learnt what Keats knew so terribly, that 'There are impossibilities in the world.'

Shelley made many practical attempts to help Mary up from 'the hearth of pale despair', not least in trying to find her some congenial company. In a revealing letter of 1820, only published in 1980, he begs Mary's friend Maria Gisborne to pay them a visit in Pisa, describing a situation ironically unlike any vision of Shelleyan love:

> Mary has resigned herself, especially since the death of her child, to a train of thoughts, which if not cut off, cannot but conduct to some fatal end. Ill temper and irritation at the familiar events of life are among the external marks of this inward change, and by being freely yielded to, they exasperate the spirit, of which they are expressions. Unfortunately I, though not ill tempered, am irritable, and the effect produced on me, awakens the instinct of the power which annoys me in her, and which exists independently of her strong understanding, and of her better feelings, for Mary is certainly capable of the most exalted goodness ... It needs a slight weight to turn the scale to good or evil. Mary considers me as a portion of herself, and feels no more remorse in torturing me than in torturing her own mind—Could she suddenly know a person in every way my equal, and hold close and perpetual communion with him, as a distinct being from herself; as a friend instead of a husband, she would obtain empire over herself that she might not make him miserable—In seeking to make another happy, she would find her own happiness ...

In another letter to Mary herself, written in 1821, Shelley suggests, not altogether sincerely, the solution of an escape to a desert island— to which in 'Epipsychidion' a few months previously he had mag- icked Emilia Viviani!

> My greatest content would be utterly to desert all human society. I would retire with you & our child to a solitary island in the sea, would build a boat, & shut upon my retreat the floodgates of the world—I would read no reviews & talk with no authors ...

'The other side of the alternative' was Shelley's old dream of 'an Association of Philosophical People', 'a society of our own class, as much as possible, in intellect or in feeling'. The option is there in 'Epipsychidion' too

> I never was attached to that great sect,
> Whose doctrine is that each one should select
> Out of the crowd a mistress or a friend,
> And all the rest, though fair and wise, commend
> To cold oblivion ...
> True love in this differs from gold and clay
> That to divide is not to take away.
> Love is like understanding, that grows bright,
> Gazing on many truths;

although the all-consuming Two-into-One sexual merger at the climax of the poem contradicts it.

But Mary was not to be rallied with doses of the Shelleyan: only the birth of another child, Percy Florence, briefly consoled her. Then came the last hammer-blow—in June 1822, as if the ghost of Harriet had risen up from the waters of her own death to claim him in revenge, Shelley was drowned in the Gulf of Spezia. From then until her death in 1851, Mary was haunted by the feeling that she had failed him, and in penance she turned herself into a prototype of the Victorian widow, protecting and marbling his memory. 'Methinks my calling is high,' she wrote. 'I am to justify his ways. I am to make him beloved to all posterity.' Even her handwriting unconsciously became like his. In the preface to her carefully censored edition of his poetry, published in 1839, she proclaimed, 'Whatever faults he had ought to find extenuation among his fellows, since they prove him to be human: without them, the exalted nature of his soul would have raised him into something divine.'

A sense of humour and proportion was not characteristic of the Shelley circle, Mary least of all. 'You have a tendency,' Leigh Hunt suggested tactfully, 'to look over-intensely at the dark side of human things.' Time hardened rather than mellowed her. None of her subsequent admirers, whose number included Prosper Mérimée, ever got beyond the front parlour. In one important respect, she did betray Shelley: her views became blandly conservative. She wrote off the Radicals of the 1830s as 'dull, envious, and insolent'; and when a friend advised her to send her son to a school 'where they will teach him to think for himself', she is said to have retorted, 'Teach him to think for himself? Oh my God, teach him rather to think like other people!' Her wish was fulfilled, in that Percy Florence Shelley grew up stolid, kindly, and enthusiastic only about his hobbies of sailing and amateur theatricals—an unlikely last product of his extraordinary ancestry. The circle turned in another direction. At the death of Shelley's father, Percy Florence inherited the baronetcy and Field Place. His wife Lady Jane Shelley consecrated a sanctum to Shelley in one of their later homes. Under a ceiling painted with stars stood a life-size statue; on the wall was the famous portrait; glass cabinets displayed locks of hair, letters, fragments of bone; and heavy mahogany chests held the precious manuscripts.

Mary's own literary career continued energetically if unenthusiastically, as she churned out novels, short stories, travel writing, and over half a million words of historical biography for the *Cabinet Cyclopaedia*. Her fiction is not compelling, although both *Mathilda* and *The Last Man* present intriguing parallels to her life with Godwin and Shelley. Certainly nothing came near the success, either popular or aesthetic, of her first published work *Frankenstein*, conceived in 1816 while she, Claire, and Shelley were staying with Byron on Lake Geneva, and published anonymously in 1818. The germ of the novel seems to have been the discussions that Shelley had with Byron's doctor companion John Polidori about some recent experiments in what we might call bio-technology, and Shelley gave her advice and editorial help throughout: none the less it is substantially her achievement. This needs to be said only because did we not know Mary was to be the author, *Frankenstein* would fall neatly enough into Shelley's own developing *oeuvre*. The scribbler of two teenage Gothic novels, fascinated by chemistry and electricity, the disciple of Godwin and his ideas about the perversion of natural benevolence, the poet of *Alastor* with its mysterious quest through sublime landscapes, might well have gone on to bring forth *Frankenstein*. That it was Mary who took up and re-forged the available themes is a measure of the closeness of their intellectual sympathy, not an indication of Mary's 'dependence'.

By one of those strange passages to which public reputation is subject, Mary Shelley has become the most widely read of all writers of her era, inasmuch as Frankenstein and his monster has proved the most potent of all Romantic mythical images. Donald F. Glut's remarkable *'Frankenstein' Catalogue* (1984) lists over three thousand offspring: from translations, film and theatrical adaptations (of which Mary herself saw the first, in 1823) to the detritus of plastic toys and comic strips. A teenage novel has thus remained familiar, albeit in bastard shapes, to those who have never heard of Werther or Childe Harold.

But to Mary Shelley's contemporaries the most famous woman in Europe outside royalty and the theatre was Germaine, Madame la Baronne de Staël, known to the newspaper-reading world of her day as the apotheosis of the blue-stocking, a critic, novelist, and hostess, the formidable opponent of Napoleon, and a 'star' personality whose thoughts and doings were reported from Edinburgh to Naples, Lisbon to St Petersburg. At her death the *Edinburgh Review* called her 'the most powerful writer that her country has produced since the time of Voltaire and Rousseau—and the greatest writer, of a woman, that any time or any country has produced'. This pre-eminence was not attained without a long head-start which puts her beyond comparison with other celebrated women of her time; but if being born rich, wilful, intelligent, and prominent minimized the disadvantages of being female, there was nothing that could save her from what her biographer J. Christopher Herold aptly described as a 'superb emotional muddle'.

Her father was the millionaire Swiss banker Jacques Necker, her mother Suzanne Curchod, a severely moral pastor's daughter with whom the historian Gibbon had once disastrously tried his luck. Germaine, their only child, was born in 1766 and brought up in an environment where there was a good deal more wealth and worldliness than common family affection. Her parents hoped that she would make a dynastic marriage which would bring the name of Necker further *éclat*—at seventeen, for instance, they were vainly trying to pair her off with the prodigious William Pitt, who at twenty-three was pausing between appointments as Britain's Chancellor of the Exchequer and Prime Minister. In the event she ended up with a relatively anonymous Swedish diplomat, Baron Staël von Holstein, whose suit had been first filed when Germaine was twelve. Their union was more in the nature of a treaty than a love-match, and Madame de Staël rarely paid her husband more than the minimum of attention. She was not one to retreat into the role of dutiful wife.

The Necker family were accustomed to life in the eye of the storm. In 1776 Necker himself had been brought to Versailles by Louis XVI, to act as a wonder-working financial consultant whose genius for raising enormous loans and guaranteed credit would paper over the French monarchy's incurable bankruptcy without the disagreeable necessity of raising taxes. Although it was the sort of policy which could only work for so long (and which between 1781 and 1788 put him firmly out of political favour), it made him a crucial figure at the beginning of the Revolution, when he attempted compromise between the crown and the Third Estate. When this failed and Necker returned to Switzerland, his daughter stayed behind in Paris, sufficiently well established in her own right to weather her father's disgrace. She had begun to write—a Sentimental play and some reflections on Rousseau—but she was more talked about as the *salon* hostess of the rue du Bac, who followed the custom of receiving morning visitors in bed, provocatively revealing her Rubensesque flesh and form and conversing more challengingly than any woman in France. Lacking in neither confidence nor means, she had no difficulty in making her voice heard.

In the alignments of the Revolution, she showed none of Madame Roland's high ethical austerity, and the social and political emancipation of women did not preoccupy her. Her area of manoeuvre was the middle ground of opinion: she was, broadly speaking, a liberal and a rationalist who hoped that France could follow the example of the British Constitution. As Necker's daughter, she was also a focal point for intrigue, and she managed one decisive backstairs coup, in pushing into the Ministry of War her lover, the King's mysterious cousin, the Vicomte de Narbonne, who fathered two of her sons. But come the rise of the Jacobins and the September Massacres to which she almost fell victim, exile seemed the only way to keep her head, and she spent much of the Terror in Switzerland, organizing passports and escape routes for stranded friends for whom France now meant death.

It was while she was drumming her fingers with impatience to return to the excitements of Paris that she fell in with a scion of a distinguished Swiss military family, Benjamin Constant (1767–1830). He was twenty-seven, gangling and pot-bellied, with a nervous twitch, bloodshot, bespectacled gimlet eyes, and violent red hair. He was working, as he would sporadically until his death, on a vast history of comparative religion; he had political ambitions; and above all, he was persistently interesting, which for Madame de Staël was paramount. They began talking and did not stop, as it were, for seventeen years—although for the last five the conversation was conducted largely at screaming pitch.

It is not easy to regard two such assertive egotists with much sympathy, especially when all they could plead in mitigation was the deprived background of riches and privilege. Nevertheless Constant in particular had a psyche that was doomed from the start. His mother had died giving birth to him and he spent most of the remainder of his life trying to recover a mother-figure; his father, a shrivelled-up cynic, pushed him through a series of tutors, and stood back coldly to await the results. Thus at seven the young Benjamin, already fluent in Greek, was in the charge of a fanatic atheist who tried to rape the music-master's daughter and then took his charge to live with him in a brothel; later there was a defrocked monk who went mad and killed himself. At thirteen he was attached to the University of Oxford; at fifteen he set up his first mistress; at sixteen, he moved to Edinburgh, where he studied in the midst of the glories of the Scottish Enlightenment; and at seventeen he contracted the incurable disease of compulsive gambling.

Constant developed two further destructive hobbies in the course of this eventful education. One was quarrelling—he fought over twenty duels, one over the honour of his dog and another, when he could scarcely move, from an armchair. The other was older women. By the time he met Madame de Staël he had already married and divorced a woman five years older than himself and been painfully involved with the extraordinary Madame de Charrière, twenty-seven years his senior. He approached maturity bored and aimless, molten iron ripe for the forge of Madame de Staël.

An undated document signed by Constant survives from the first years of their relationship:

> We promise to consecrate our lives to each other; we declare that we regard ourselves as indissolubly bound to each other, that we will share forever and in every respect a common destiny, that we will never enter into any other bond, and that we shall strengthen the bonds now uniting us as soon as lies within our power....

This is more like the tone of a legal contract than an amorous outpouring, and it suggests how very little trust there was between the two parties concerned. It was not sexual or marital love that held them. In fact, Constant only briefly conquered Madame de Staël's 'invincible antipathy' to his repulsive physique by pretending to be dying from a suicidal overdose of opium. There was no pleasant domestic dimension to their involvement. Both of them needed the light refreshment of other lovers—usually of the beautiful, sweet-natured, and compliant variety—but it was impossible for an outsider to loosen that primary knot of conversation, of mind and idea, that tied the primary commitment. As one observer put it, 'One knows nothing of Madame de Staël until one has seen her with Benjamin Constant. He alone had the power ... to awaken an eloquence, a profundity of soul and thought, which she only ever showed in all its glory when he provoked it in her.' At the centre of their dialogue was the master-plan that Constant, through Madame de Staël's patronage and collaboration, should rise to political power in France. The results were disappointing, and Constant failed to establish himself in either the vacuum of the Directory regime or in the Consulate. Nevertheless by 1803 Napoleon had become so exasperated by the criticism emanating from the de Staël *salon* in Faubourg Saint-Germain that he exiled 'that appalling woman' from France. 'They say she talks about neither politics nor myself,' he growled, 'but somehow it happens that everyone comes away liking me that much less.' Not to be in Paris was torture for her. She was born to be at the centre of power, and Napoleon was sharp enough not to underestimate her corrosive influence.

Now a widow and permanently restless, she travelled round Europe, often with Constant, picking up writers and intellectuals for the chaotic house parties she held in the château which she inherited from her father at Coppet on Lake Geneva. Coppet was no haven of contemplative Rousseauan tranquillity. Madame de Staël had little respect for either the surrounding natural splendour or normal quotas of sleep. Fat, blowsy, and addicted to what became known as the 'Coppet dose' of opium, she would lurch from room to room at any hour of day or night, fantastically dolled up in purple and orange shawls and turbans, carrying a morocco-bound notebook in which she would scribble down highlights of her conversations. To do her justice, she was not, like Coleridge, simply a monologist. What she needed was regular injections of mental stimulation, and, as insistent as a Circe or Calypso, she forced her enchantees to oblige. Her lair was a political, literary, and sexual hotbed, and most of the time tension ran so intolerably high that when their captor was absent even for a few hours, those left behind would, out of sheer relief, prance around giggling like schoolchildren. In comparison with Coppet, every Shelley *ménage* comes to look positively monastic.

It was in this giddying atmosphere that Constant realized that he was being eaten alive by a woman whose demands and moods were becoming increasingly irrational. 'One's whole life (every minute, every hour, every year) must be at her disposal,' he wrote in his journal. 'When she gets into one of her rages, then follows a tumult of all the earthquakes and typhoons.' That he had recently met up again with an old flame, Charlotte von Hardenberg, who seemed to offer him the straightforward advantages of married life, only made his enslavement to Madame de Staël the more agonizing. 'She is hateful, hideous, unsupportable,' his journal continued, 'I must break with her or die ... her impetuosity, her egotism, her unceasing self-preoccupation make Charlotte's sweet, calm, humble, and modest demeanour a thousand times more attractive. I am tired of the man-woman who has had me in handcuffs for the last ten years.' But a promise he had once made never to marry anyone else and the terms of their original contract was held to his head like a pistol. Nor did Madame de Staël show any inhibitions about resorting to the tactics of humiliating public scenes. Once he braved the announcement that he was leaving: she summoned her children, denounced the traitor, and made as if to strangle herself with a cambric handkerchief, her screams echoing through every corner of the château. He had lied, cheated, and dishonoured her. No, she would not marry him, but if he left she would kill herself, and the world would know why.

On another less squalid occasion the house party mounted a performance of Racine's tragedy *Andromaque*, in which the impropriety of the casting recalls, times ten, the production of *Lovers' Vows* in Jane Austen's *Mansfield Park*. Madame de Staël played Hermione, betrothed to Pyrrhus, played by Constant. In one transcendently embarrassing scene, Hermione rails at him over his passion for the Trojan Andromaque:

> *Perfide, je le vois,*
> *Tu comptes les moments que tu perds avec moi.*
> *Ton coeur, impatient de revoir ta Troyenne*
> *Ne souffre qu' à regret qu' un autre l'entretienne.*
> *Tu lui parles du coeur, tu la cherches des yeux.*
> *Je ne te retiens plus ...*

(Traitor, I see you count the seconds that you waste with me. Your heart, impatient to see your Trojan again, suffers only from having to address another. You speak to her of love, your eyes seek her out. I hold you back no longer ...)

But holding him back was precisely what she managed to do. He married Charlotte in 1807, but did not dare tell Madame de Staël. For most of the following months, he lived on in Coppet in fear and trembling of discovery, while poor Charlotte was put up at a nearby hotel. *Andromaque* ends with Hermione ordering Pyrrhus' death, and

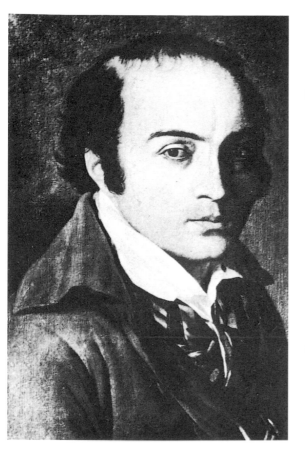

1 André Chénier, painted by Suvée, in the prison of Saint-Lazare, July 1794.

2 'The Summons of the Last Victims of the Terror': a dramatization of the scene painted by Müller in the mid-nineteenth century. Chénier sits on the chair, pen still in hand, as a Jacobin reads out the list of those called to trial – and almost certain death.

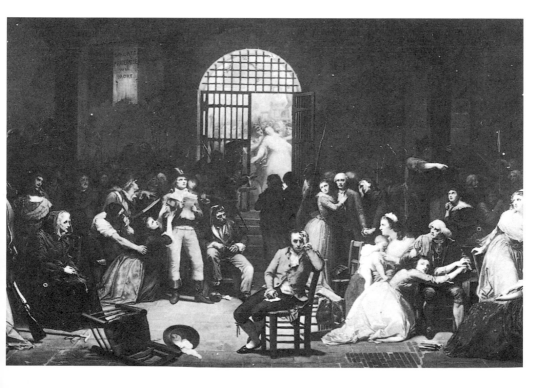

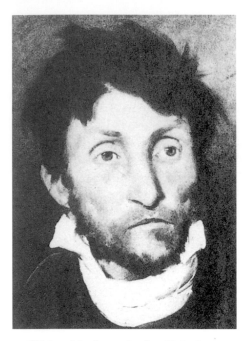

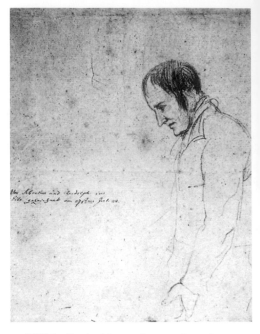

3 Géricault's hauntingly clinical representation of a kleptomaniac, painted *c.* 1822

4 Hölderlin in his madness, 1823, drawn by J. G. Schreiner and Rudolf Lohtauer.

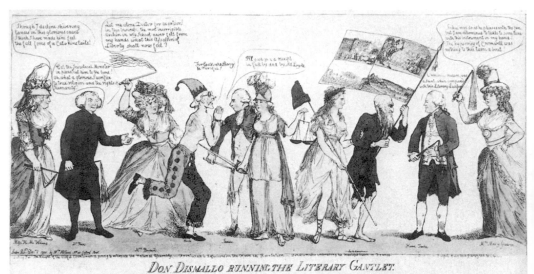

DON DISMALLO RUNNING THE LITERARY GANTLET.

5 'Don Dismallo running the literary gauntlet.' An anonymous satire of 1790, depicting Edmund Burke stripped to the waist and attacked by, among others, Helen Maria Williams (*extreme left*) and Mrs Macaulay (*extreme right*) – liberal-minded opponents to his *Reflections on the French Revolution*.

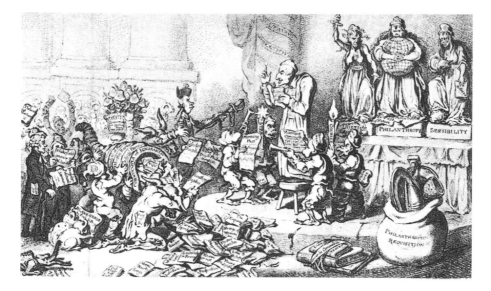

6 Detail from Gillray's satire, 'The New Morality', published by *The Anti-Jacobin Review* in 1798. So-called radicals (Coleridge with an ass's head, Southey holding the sword) are shown presenting their revolutionary case to an altar presided over by perversions of Justice, Philanthropy, and Sensibility. Among the books disgorged on the floor are works by Godwin and Mary Wollstonecraft.

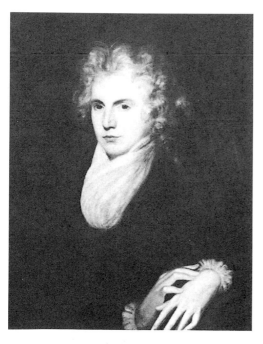

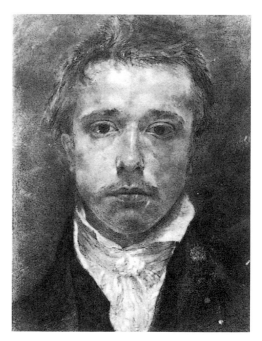

7 *Left* An impressively Amazonian portrait of Mary Wollstonecraft by James Roscoe, *c.* 1790, showing her in all her severely rational grandeur.

8 *Right* A self-portrait of the young Samuel Palmer, *c.* 1826. Palmer was strongly under the influence of William Blake; the intense nervous concentration of the facial expression demonstrates the fascination with which artists at the time scrutinized and confronted their own psyches.

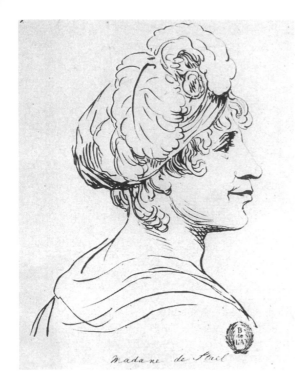

9 A vivid anonymous sketch of Madame de Staël, *c.* 1810.

10 A vignette illustration from an early nineteenth-century edition of Bernardin de Saint-Pierre's *Paul et Virginie*, a charming Rousseauan novel extolling the values of sentimentalism.

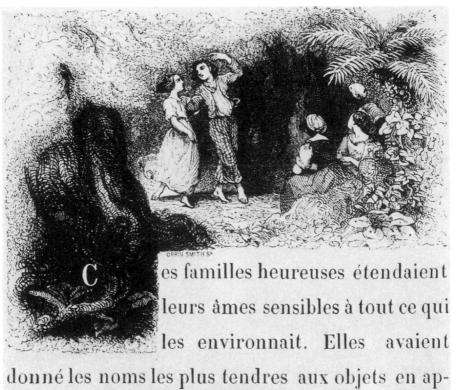

Ces familles heureuses étendaient leurs âmes sensibles à tout ce qui les environnait. Elles avaient donné les noms les plus tendres aux objets en apparence les plus indifférents. Un cercle d'orangers,

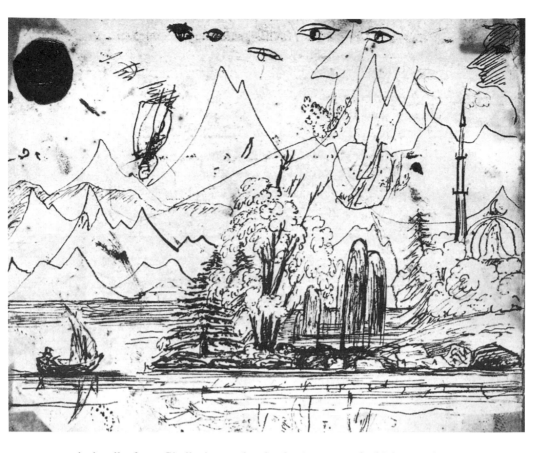

11 A doodle from Shelley's notebook, the imagery of which reveals many of the preoccupations of his time at Marlow, while he was writing *The Revolt of Islam*. Note the mosque and minaret; the skiff on the water; the alpine landscape; the aerial boat and other flying objects; and the ghostly disembodied eyes.

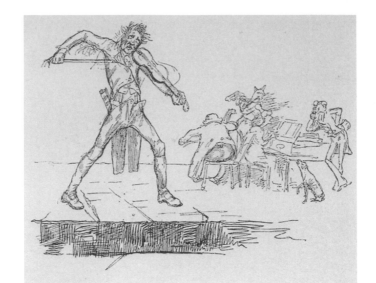

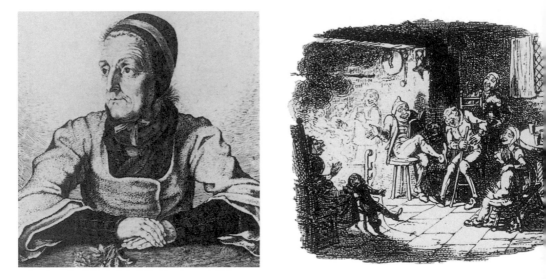

12 *Top* One of Hoffmann's own sketched illustrations for *Kreisleriana*: note the animal-like appearance of the figures in the background.

13 *Left* Katharina Weitmann, a tailor's wife, was one of the sources from whom the Brothers Grimm drew their famous folk-tales, published in Germany 1812–22. The Grimms liked to claim that what they transcribed from peasants like Frau Weitmann was completely authentic and verbatim. Recent scholarship, however, strongly suggests that they silently put the raw material through a considerable amount of re-touching and editing, in order to make the tales more coherent and acceptable to the middle-class reading public.

14 *Right* Foreign texts were translated into English with extraordinary speed during the early nineteenth century. The first English translation of the Grimms' tales, for instance, appeared in 1823. The above was its frontis-piece, engraved by George Cruikshank, whose drawings would later grace the novels of Dickens.

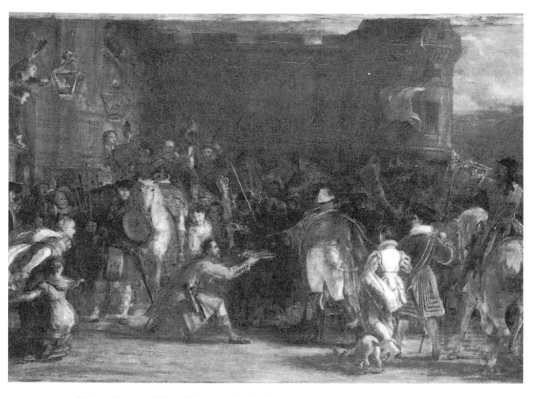

15 'King George IV at Holyrood, 1822', painted in 1828 by Sir David Wilkie. The King's state visit to Scotland provided a marvellous excuse for a pageant of Scottish history and culture, as presented in the poetry and novels of Sir Walter Scott. Here he receives the keys to the Palace of Holyrood from the kneeling Duke of Hamilton.

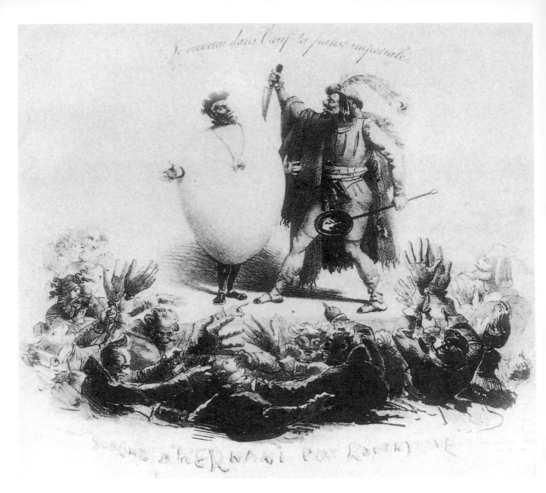

16 One of the many caricatures on the subject of Hugo's *Hernani* and its tumultuous reception. The egg will be cracked for use in a '*plat romantique*'; the audience jeers and applauds the spectacle hysterically.

then killing herself from remorse; but at Coppet the situation only dragged on for years in a widening spiral of sordid revelations, reprisals, melodramatic gestures, hopeless compromises and confrontations, culminating in Madame de Staël's suing of Constant for the money spent in their years together. Fortunately, in 1811, she found a consuming object of desire in young John Rocca, a stunningly good-looking wounded soldier, who reciprocated with the proverbial canine devotion. At the age of forty-five, Madame de Staël had Rocca's child and in 1816, the year before her death, she married him. Constant, uncharacteristically, twice refused Rocca's challenge to a duel, and returned to his original state of ennui, gambling away thousands in a night, sullenly ploughing on with his *magnum opus*, and confiding to his journal that his wife was 'the most boring creature the earth has ever borne ... How I regret Madame de Staël!' During Napoleon's hundred days' return from Elba, he entered into negotiations over a new constitution and a post in a future government—an action which laid him open to accusations of duplicity; but he ended his life in Paris as a respected spokesman for the Liberal persuasion, won through to some sort of stability, and died a national hero in the midst of the 1830 'Liberal' Revolution.

Yet Constant is best remembered today for his short novel *Adolphe*, written in 1806–7 at the height of his problems with Madame de Staël, but only published in 1816, in London. It is a book remarkable for the way it explodes the Sentimental idea that Love was Love, pure and simple, and in so doing, both looks back to the psychology of Laclos' *Les Liaisons Dangereuses* and forward to Proust: Byron was one of the earliest admirers of its candour. *Adolphe* charts the ironies of wanting someone only until the chase is over, of cowardice masking as kindness and consideration, of the blackmail and inertia that poison affection. Adolphe himself is a projection of Constant to the extent that he physically vomited while writing the book, but the deceptively pathetic character of Ellénore must have been drawn more on his experience with the sad Irish courtesan Anna Lindsay than on the overtly rapacious Madame de Staël (or so the latter preferred to believe). *Adolphe* lives whatever its sources: in the way that it starkly details a relationship reducing two people to hopeless misery, without moral certainties or the consolations of guilt and innocence, it remains chillingly modern.

Madame de Staël's writing has weathered less well. Her once famous novels of passionate victimized women, *Delphine* (1802) and *Corinne* (1807), now seem turgid and contrived compared with the masterly economy of *Adolphe*. More interesting, albeit only academically, are her long essays *De la littérature* and *De l'Allemagne*. These are both pioneering and speculative essays in the sociology of culture—why, she asks, do particular artistic and intellectual trends emerge in particular societies at particular times? To answer these questions for *De l'Allemagne*, she went to Germany herself, on a trip which illustrates her bold individuality of spirit.

Polite society in eighteenth-century France and England regarded Germany as a land of beer-swilling peasants with mud on their boots, and German was considered a barbarously ugly language unworthy of any civilized person's attention—as late as 1823 it was said that only two Fellows of Oxford University could read it even competently. The fact that from the 1760s onwards there had been a remarkable renaissance of German literature and thought was generally unknown, even though isolated texts such as *Werther*, Klopstock's religious epic *Messias*, and Bürger's spook ballad 'Lenore' had made their mark in translation. The process by which a new image of German culture as a whole was mediated to Western Europe makes an important chapter in the literary history of the age, and one for which Madame de Staël must take a large portion of credit.

She began her study by taking some rather desultory German lessons from her sons' tutor, but neither spoke nor read the language comfortably when the time came in 1803, during one of her periods of exile from France, to make the field-trip. This did not inhibit her research since the Germans were only too happy to show her round and interpret. As the author of *Delphine*, which had already sold out through three editions, she was a glamorous international celebrity, the likes of whom had rarely been seen in the land, and everywhere along her royal progress she was received with something like awe.

One of her first stops was Frankfurt, then as now a city of banks and businesses. Madame de Staël made straight for Goethe's elderly mother, who was thoroughly intimidated by this over-dressed creature with her morocco notebook. 'What does this woman want from me?' she asked her son. 'I never wrote so much as an ABC in my life.' Madame de Staël feared at first that her most vulgar prejudices might be confirmed: everything seemed so ugly and uncomfortable, rooms were chokingly full of smoke, and the Germans slow-witted and crude. But she also decided that there was 'deep, poetic feeling' beneath the 'vulgarity of the external forms'—and she was greatly taken with the mouth-organ, an instrument unknown in France which she learned how to play.

At Christmas she made her way through four feet of snow to the duchy of Weimar, the 'new Athens' of Germany, where she was determined to quiz the great Goethe. He, however, had fled from her advance and gone into hiding in nearby Jena so as to escape the fuss and bustle attendant on her arrival. When she showed no sign of moving on, he shuffled reluctantly back in the company of Schiller, whose lack of French caused him acute shyness in the great presence. Privately they agreed in finding her clever but shallow, with no real feeling for poetry and a shocking capacity to reduce the deepest philosophical issues to the level of drawing-room chat: nothing, apparently, was sacred to her. She for her part was amused to find no Werther in a blue jacket and yellow waistcoat, but a corpulent and rather unsophisticated *Bürger* whose mistress was the housekeeper and whose head 'was filled with the most bizarre metaphysics imaginable'. Later their relations improved, and there were some stirring dinner-table arguments, but she remained at a loss when it came to the Goethean philosophy, so alien to her measuring and rationalizing way of thinking. In an effort to understand what was not written to be understood, she hired Henry Crabb Robinson, a young Englishman resident in Weimar, to explain some of the more recondite texts to her. It was a hopeless assignment. At one point Crabb Robinson, an ardent Goethean, lost his temper. 'Madame,' he shouted, 'you don't understand Goethe, and what is more you never will.' 'Sir,' she replied firmly, 'I understand everything worth understanding, and what I don't understand simply doesn't matter.' Undaunted, she later gave Fichte 'about quarter of an hour' to explain his philosophy to her. 'He looked at me as though I were a housewife,' she noted drily.

Her major find when she moved on to Berlin was August Wilhelm Schlegel, a member of the *Athenäum* circle of Romantics with aspirations to becoming a mincing French gentleman.* Madame de Staël grabbed him. He became the most abject of all her admirers, following her around for years, and infuriating Constant by his fawning behaviour at Coppet. More important, he served her as a ready source of information for *De l'Allemagne*, which continued to gestate until

---

* The catty Heinrich Heine in his book *The Romantic School*, written expressly to correct and advance on *De l'Allemagne*, recalls meeting Schlegel in Paris in 1831, his pate covered with a blond wig and his chest festooned with medals, decorations, and ribbons. 'He was dressed in the height of the fashion of the year Madame de Staël died [1817]. With a senile saccharine smile like that of a faded belle sucking a sweet, he tripped along coquettishly ... he seemed to be enjoying, as it were, a comical second edition of his youth.'

1810. Ostensibly designed as an introduction to German society, history, and culture for non-German speakers, it was also covertly a counterblast against Napoleonic ideas of French supremacy—and the censors duly destroyed all the plates and pulped the entire first edition. The book reached publication only in London, in 1813, but its moment came with a vengeance. Napoleon's empire was crumbling and the *salons* of Europe wanted new ideals, new fashions to replace the discredited pretensions of France. *De l'Allemagne* was not a scholarly tome so much as a vivid first-hand report from a new frontier, pointing to a panorama of Christian mysticism, poetry and feeling, of Black Forests and tales of chivalry. The fact that her accounts of the philosophy behind it all were unbalanced and often inaccurate scarcely mattered. It stands as a superb example of the higher journalism which, as we would say, put Germany 'into perspective', stimulated further study, and made complex information accessible to the ordinary reading public.

But in Germany there were some shaking heads. 'Poor woman,' wrote Rahel Varnhagen, after reading the book and remembering her meeting with Madame de Staël in Berlin a decade earlier, 'she saw nothing, understood nothing, heard nothing': all sound and fury, without 'a listening soul, reflecting in solitude'. Rahel spoke as one with all these qualities of inner wisdom. Carlyle once called her 'the spiritual queen of Germany', and in her lifetime, 1771 to 1833, she had something of the aura that fifty years later was to hang round George Eliot, who herself knew of Rahel as 'the greatest of German women'. Yet she wrote nothing except letters to family and friends, played no part in public life, and had no great wealth or beauty to glamorize her. Today we would call her a guru.

We have met her briefly before, as Rahel Levin, a friend of Kleist. Typically, she refused to condemn his suicide: it was, she earnestly believed, an act of free choice, an attempt to be true to his own most profound moral prompting; and for Rahel (as she was always known), such a following of the truth within the Self was fundamental.

As part of the first generation of German Jews to live outside the restrictions of the ghetto, she stood apart from orthodoxies, renouncing the religion of her fathers to marry a *goy* and braving all the pain and guilt that haunts the alienated Jew. She looked sceptically at the turbulent intellectualizing of her age 'mirroring itself to infinity, even to vertigo' and was among the first to appreciate Goethe as not just a great poet, but the exemplar of clarity and wholeness of vision. Later in her life, she became convinced that the socialism of the

Saint-Simonians pointed the way forward for humankind. Fichte, Beethoven, Mendelssohn, Heine, Hegel, Goethe himself, were all witnesses to her radiant quietness and warmth; her incorruptible goodness was undisputed. In a chapter so full of striving, thwarted wilfulness, of panic and defeat, it is salutary to contemplate for a moment the image of a woman who was both strong and still.

How, then, would these women have responded to Byron's epigram that love was their whole existence? Might they not have regarded it somewhat ambivalently, aware that if it was not their basic driving motivation, their engine, it had none the less proved the element that set the pace? One hears their voices. Mary Wollstonecraft: 'Love is the only existence that men allow me. What can I allow myself? It is the men who are obsessed with us as inert objects of desire. We want to be rational, useful creatures.' Rahel: 'Yet love is existence, in that it is the essential channel of our intimate connection with other human beings.' And Madame Roland: 'You talk of the private life, of individual loves: what about the love of Virtue, of Justice, of *la patrie*? The love that shows itself in active compassion for the poor?'

What would the men answer? They, after all, were the ones who made the ideals and generalizations which defined love, whether Shelley's 'Italian Platonics' or the Marquis de Sade's orgies of instinct and pleasure. How did they match their theories to their actual experience?

Somewhere between Shelley and Sade lies that magnificent confusion of a man and writer Friedrich Schlegel, whose exploration of the nature of sexual love, in his novel *Lucinde* published in 1799, had something of the same effect on German culture that D. H. Lawrence's *The Rainbow* would have in England over a century later. The situation—for there is no discernible plot or even narrative continuity—draws deep on Schlegel's own passion for a married woman, Dorothea Veit, whom he met in Berlin in 1797, while consorting with Rahel and her circle. Later they married and converted to Catholicism, but the first flood of their passion was torrential and absolute, a catastrophic breaking of all conventional bonds. Bluntly, *Lucinde* put the sex back into Sentimentalism. Even though never pornographically blatant, it is full of a charged, suggestive, and obsessive eroticism, more earthy and inward-looking than Shelley's, heralding the over-heated solipsism of Wagner's *Tristan und Isolde*: 'I can no longer say *my* love or *your* love,' writes Julius/Schlegel to Lucinde/Dorothea, 'both are identical and perfectly united, as much love on one side as on the other. This is marriage, the timeless union

and conjunction of our spirits, not simply for what we call this world or
the world beyond death, but for the one, true, indivisible, nameless,
unending world, for our whole eternal life and being.'

Stendhal was another who wrote at length on the subject of love, but
with the stated intention of coming to 'an exact and scientific descrip-
tion' of the phenomenon. *De l'Amour* (1822) proposes four types of love
(*amour passion, amour physique, amour goût, amour vanité*) interacting
with six temperaments (sanguine, bilious, melancholic, phlegmatic,
nervous, athletic) and six political conditions (eastern despotism,
absolute monarchy, veiled oligarchy, federal republic, constitutional
monarchy, and the state of revolution). Love develops through seven
stages—two degrees of admiration, hope of reciprocation, the actual
birth, a crystallization or 'the impulse of folly that makes us see all
beauties and perfections in the woman we love', a period of doubt,
followed by a second, stronger crystallization. Half way through, he
falters: 'I have just re-read a hundred pages of this essay; I seem to have
given a very meagre idea of real love, of the love which takes over the soul.'

De l'Amour was an attempt to exorcize the irrationality of just such
an emotion, as if mapping a history and geography of love might tidy
up the mess in which his feelings for Mathilde Viscontini Dembowski,
the book's invisible, unheard muse, had left him. He had met Mathilde in 1818, when he was living in Milan: she was a twenty-eight-year-
old beauty, recently separated from her Polish soldier-of-fortune
husband and now mysteriously involved with the *carbonari* freedom-
fighters. Stendhal, who has been called 'the most docile of Don
Juans', hoped and admired from afar, then bashfully edged a little
closer. 'Women are hungry for emotion, anywhere and at any time,' he
writes hopefully in *De l'Amour*. Mathilde seems to have been the
unfortunate exception. Apparently all she could see in her worshipper
was a short, fat and excitable eccentric, who refused to be discouraged
by her obvious lack of interest in him. Nor, suspecting him to be an
agent for the French spying on her underground activities, did she
trust him. All this served to fan the flames: Stendhal followed her
around in the disguise of dark glasses and an overcoat; sometimes he
was openly ardent and full of fine speeches, sometimes gloomy and
silent. The germ of *De l'Amour* was a (refused) offer to write for her
alone a novel which would explain his behaviour. Denied her society,
he wrote abjectly that he 'would give the rest of his life to talk to you
for a quarter of an hour on the most innocuous matters'. But Mathilde
just wanted to see the back of him—a wish that was granted in 1821
when politics forced him to leave Milan.

He never saw Mathilde again, never spoke of her, and never forgot her. The day of her death was marked in the margin of his copy of the book she had inspired: '1 May 1825—death of the author.'

Another woman central to Stendhal's life was one he never met or even set eyes on. This was Madame Roland, whose *Mémoires* he had revered since his provincial youth. In her he saw all the pride and heroism that France had lost after Napoleon, and it must have been the drama of her trial that he remembered when he came to the scene of Julien Sorel's defence in *Le rouge et le noir*. It is she who in *De l'Amour* is presented as the sort of person for whom he is writing. 'The woman whom I respect most in the world,' he calls her, '*cette femme sublime, la divine Madame Roland*.' It was someone like her that he was looking for through his years of clumsy Don Juanery—a woman he could talk to, with a temperament both feminine and forceful, serious yet witty, who could understand what he was driving at. Stendhal had no use for Italian platonics or *belles dames sans merci*. What he ultimately wanted, from Mathilde as from all the others, was intellectual companionship, and along with all its nonsense *De l'Amour* contains a delightfully self-interested plea for the education of women, on the grounds that an intolerably bored woman is intolerably boring. The book incidentally was a complete flop, selling, Stendhal claimed, only seventeen copies in thirteen years.

The great Russian poet Pushkin was another who managed to pass beyond platonics: further than that, he ordained no philosophy of love nor a policy on the matter of women at all. In 1821 he read Constant's *Adolphe* and was deeply impressed by its analysis of the egotism of modern man—but morbid self-consciousness was not his problem. He could enjoy promiscuous sex without agonizing about it, because he could love a different woman every night without 'a waste of spirit in an expense of shame'. Pleasure, not guilt, was his motivation. He also knew what so many of his contemporaries did not: that desire and seduction can be very *funny*. In his *Liber Amoris*, Hazlitt clinically records the degradation he suffered over his infatuation with his landlord's two-faced, two-timing daughter: Pushkin would have made a brilliant comedy out of it. In a letter to a friend he delights in relating how a peasant girl he was pursuing gave him a bowl of disgusting soup and ended up banging him over the head with her balalaika; his glorious poem 'Count Nulin' is a modern version of the Rape of Lucretia, in which the crisis is averted by a sharp slap on the face; 'The Gavriliad' naughtily reflects on the blasphemous possibility that the Immaculate Conception might have been a very enjoyable occasion. For Pushkin, sexual love was an appetite and an energy, not a soul-search.

But most of the writers we call Romantic felt it as a problem. The ideals attached to it from Rousseau onwards worked so powerfully on the imagination—'Love is my religion,' cried Keats in his agony over Fanny Brawne—that the human realities involved could scarcely compete. We have seen the gnawing ordinariness of Shelley's problems with Mary, side by side with his flight to fantasy in 'Epipsychidion'; and poor Coleridge, tied legally to Sara's 'ill-tempered speeches' and 'freezing looks', but spiritually wrapped round Asra. For the German Friedrich von Hardenberg, alias Novalis, the 'rejuvenating stream of death', '*des Todes/Verjüngende Flut*', brought a sort of resolution. Mourning over the grave of his adored child fiancée Sophie, he turns her, like Dante's Beatrice, into an emanation of divine otherness, beckoning him on towards the light, away from a world dissolved into dream.

To those left below, daily life could not so easily be ignored, and there were pains that could not be made into poetry. The mass of women were not *belles dames* either *sans* or *avec merci*, but domestic slaves. Dorothy Wordsworth is today associated with pressed flowers and long walks, but without the dubious privilege of having a great poet as her brother and close companion, her existence was bleakly typical. To quote Norman Fruman:

> In her Grasmere journal for May 31, 1802, Dorothy Wordsworth wrote: 'My tooth broke today. They will soon be gone. Let that pass, I shall be loved—I want no more.' She was then thirty years old, plain, barely five feet tall, weighed less than one hundred pounds, ate so poorly and worked so hard that her prematurely aged appearance regularly shocked friends and relatives who had not seen her for some years. She suffered constantly from headaches, raging toothaches, bowel complaints, vomiting and assorted bodily ills, and yet never had anything resembling proper medical or dental attention until many years later. Her toil was unremitting: cleaning, cooking, mending, gardening, sewing clothes and curtains, shirts and nightcaps, brewing beer, making wine, boiling preserves and jelly, and always, the copying of William's manuscripts.

Overflowing with what De Quincey called 'excessive organic sensibility' and sympathetic emotion, her self-image was that of the willing handmaid to her brother's poetic mission. She refused even to consider the possibility that she herself might have a cultivable literary talent: 'I have not those powers which Coleridge thinks I have—I know it—my only merits are my devotedness to those I love, and I hope a charity towards all mankind.' Her journals are full of gaps and silences, mirroring events and feelings without any assertion of will or opinion, as intriguing for what they leave out as for what they record.

And yet she claimed to be happy. 'I shall be loved—I want no more.' When she declined into senility, or, as some think, psychotic madness, falling into violent rages, screaming obscenities, and making what Crabb Robinson called 'the most unseemly noises', those she loved did not fail her. She was one woman who might have agreed that love had been her whole existence; but it was not the love that leads to self-sacrifice, devoted drudgery, and pushing a wheel-chair around that the poet had in mind.

Chapter 4

'Lovely Shapes and Sounds Intelligible'

Jean-Jacques Rousseau writes to his friend M. de Malesherbes in 1762:

When my troubles force me to count away the long hours of the night, and feverish agitation prevents me from savouring even a moment's sleep, then do I often seek distraction from my present state in musing on the various events of my life—and the regrets, the sweet recollections, the sorrows, the tenderness together work to make me forget my sufferings. And what period of my life, monsieur, do you think I recall most happily in my dreams? Not the pleasures of my youth; they were too rare, too mingled with bitterness, and are now lost in the past. No, I recall the pleasures of my retreat, my solitary walks, those swiftly passing but delicious days that I spent alone with my good and simple housekeeper, my beloved dog, my old cat, with the birds of the countryside and the deer of the forest—with the whole of Nature and its unknowable Creator.

Rising from my bed before the sun, so as to contemplate its own rising in my garden, my first wish whenever I saw a fine day dawning, would be that neither letters nor visitors appear to disturb its charm. Having given over the morning to various duties, all of which I would fulfil with pleasure, since I could always put them off to another time, I hastened to dine, so as to escape nuisances and provide myself with a longer afternoon. So, before one o'clock, even on the most blazing hot days, I set off into the midday sun with my faithful dog as companion, my pace quickening for fear that someone should come and demand my attention before I could slip off; but once past a certain corner, how my heart palpitated, how joyfully I breathed, knowing myself safe and repeating 'Here I am, my own master for the rest of the day.' I continued at a more leisurely pace, seeking out some wild spot in the forest, some deserted area in which nothing showed the hand of man or proclaimed his servitude and domination, some retreat which I could believe myself to have been the first to penetrate, and in which no

144

unwelcome third party would interpose between Nature and myself. It is in such a situation that, she, Nature, seems to assume in my eyes an ever fresh magnificence. The gold of the broom and the purple of the heather struck my heart with their splendour; the majesty of the trees covering me with their shade, the delicacy of the surrounding shrubbery, the astonishing variety of plants and flowers underfoot, kept my mind continually vacillating between observation and wonder: the gathering-together of so many interesting phenomena jostling for my attention drew me unceasingly from one state to another, nurturing my dreamy and indolent mood and making me repeat to myself: 'No, not Solomon in all his glory was ever arrayed like one of these.'

My imagination would not leave such a richly apparelled landscape empty for long. I soon peopled it with those close to my heart; and banishing opinion, prejudice, all artificial passions, I bring into the havens of nature men worthy to live there. I create for myself a delightful society, of which I think myself not unworthy. I would build a golden age of my fancies, filling those fine days with all the scenes of my life that have left sweet memories, and with those that my heart still desired. I was moved to tears at the thought of the true pleasures of humanity, pleasures so delicious, so pure—and yet, until now, so far from the hearts of men. Oh, if in such moments some thought of Paris, of my century, of my author's vanity came to trouble my reverie—with what disdain did I banish it, giving myself up without distraction to the exquisite feelings of which my heart is full. And yet in the middle of all this, I confess, the nothingness of my fancies sometimes suddenly saddened me. Even if all my dreams had become realities, they would still not satisfy me; I should go on imagining, dreaming, wanting. I found in myself an inexplicable emptiness which nothing could fill, some spring of the heart towards another sort of pleasure, which I could not articulate, but of which I still felt the need. Well, monsieur, this in itself was a pleasure, since it filled me with a feeling that I would not wish to have missed.

Soon, I raise my thoughts from the face of the earth to all the beings of Nature, to the universal system of things, to the incomprehensible being who embraces all. And so, my mind lost in this immensity, I was not thinking, or reasoning or philosophizing; I felt, with a sort of delight, overwhelmed by the force of this universe, I gave myself over with ecstasy to the welter of these great ideas, I loved to lose my imagination in infinity: my heart, too restricted by the limits of the earth, felt tied down. I stifled in the universe: I wanted to fling myself into the infinite. I believe that if I could have uncovered all the mysteries of Nature, I should have felt myself to be in a situation less delicious than this dizzying ecstasy to which my mind yielded uninhibitedly, and which, in all my emotional agitation, would sometimes make me cry out: 'O great Being, O great Being'—without being able to say or think anything else.

And so in a continual state of exaltation, the most delightful days that human creature has ever spent passed by; and when sunset made me think about returning, astonished at the swift passage of time, I would reflect that I hadn't taken full advantage of the day, that I could have enjoyed it still more; and to make up for lost time, I would say to myself: 'I shall come back tomorrow' . . .

From a letter of Coleridge:

Eskdale, Friday, Augt. 6th. [1802] at an Estate House called Toes
There is one sort of Gambling, to which I am much addicted; and that not of the least criminal kind for a man who has children & a Concern.—It is this. When I find it convenient to descend from a mountain, I am too confident & too indolent to look round about & wind about 'till I find a track or other symptom of safety; but I wander on, & where it is first *possible* to descend, there I go—relying upon fortune for how far down this possibility will continue. So it was yesterday afternoon. I passed down from Broadcrag, skirted the Precipices, and found myself cut off from a most sublime Crag-summit, that seemed to rival Sca' Fell Man in height & to undo it in fierceness. A Ridge of Hill lay low down, & divided this Crag (called Doe-crag) & Broad-crag—even as the Hyphen divides the words broad & crag. I determined to go thither; the first place I came to, that was not direct Rock, I slipped down, & went on for a while with tolerable ease—but now I came (it was midway down) to a smooth perpendicular Rock about 7 feet high—this was nothing—I put my hands on the Ledge, & dropped down / in a few yards came just such another / I *dropped* that too / and yet another, seemed not higher—I would not stand for a trifle / so I dropped that too / but the stretching of the muscle[s] of my hands & arms, & the jolt of the Fall on my Feet, put my whole Limbs in a *Tremble*, and I paused, & looking down, saw that I had little else to encounter but a succession of these little Precipices—it was in truth a Path that in a very hard Rain is, no doubt, the channel of a most splendid Waterfall.—So I began to suspect that I ought not to go on / but

then unfortunately tho' I could with ease drop down a smooth Rock 7 feet high, I could not *climb* it / so go on I must / and on I went / the next 3 drops were not half a Foot, at least not a foot more than my own height / but every Drop increased the Palsy of my Limbs—I shook all over, Heaven knows without the least influence of Fear / and now I had only two more to drop down / to return was impossible—but of these two the first was tremendous / it was twice my own height, & the Ledge at the bottom was [so] exceedingly narrow, that if I dropt down upon it I must of necessity have fallen backwards & of course killed myself. My Limbs were all in a tremble—I lay upon my Back to rest myself, & was beginning according to my Custom to laugh at myself for a Madman, when the sight of the Crags above me on each side, & the impetuous Clouds just over them, posting so luridly & so rapidly northward, overawed me / I lay in a state of almost prophetic Trance & Delight—& blessed God aloud, for the powers of Reason & the Will, which remaining no Danger can overpower us! O God, I exclaimed aloud—how calm, how blessed am I now / I know not how to proceed, how to return / but I am calm & fearless & confident / if this Reality were a Dream, if I were asleep, what agonies had I suffered! what screams!—When the Reason & the Will are away, what remain to us but Darkness & Dimness & a bewildering Shame, and Pain that is utterly Lord over us, or fantastic Pleasure, that draws the Soul along swimming through the air in many shapes, even as a Flight of Starlings in a Wind. I arose, and looking down saw at the bottom a heap of stones, which had fallen abroad and rendered the narrow ledge on which they had been piled doubly dangerous. At the bottom of the third Rock that I dropt from, I met a dead Sheep quite rotten. This heap of stones, I guessed, and have since found that I guessed right, had been piled up by the Shepherd to enable him to climb up and free the poor Creature whom he had observed to be crag-fast, but seeing nothing but rock over rock, he had desisted and gone for help and in the mean time the poor Creature had fallen down and killed itself. As I was looking at these I glanced my eye to my left, and observed that the Rock was rent from top to bottom. I measured the breadth of the Rent, and found that there was no danger of my being *wedged* in, so I put my knap-sack round to my side, and slipped down as between two walls, without any danger or difficulty. The next Drop brought me down to the Ridge called the How. I hunted out my Besom Stick, which I had flung before me when I first came to the Rocks, and wisely gave over all thought of ascending Doe-Crag, for now the Clouds were again coming in most tumultuously. So I began to descend, when I felt an odd sensation across my whole breast—not pain or itching—and putting my hand on it I found it all bumpy—and on looking saw the whole of my Breast from my Neck- to my Navel, exactly all that my Kamell-hair Breast-shield covers, filled with great red heat-bumps, so thick that no hair could lie between them.... startling proof to me of the violent exertions I had made.

A year or so later, Coleridge jots down some memories in his notebook:

Images. Shadow of the Tree in the ruffled water distinguishable from the Breeze on the water only by its stationariness.—In clear water over an uneven channel, as in the Greta behind my House, a huge *Boa* convolvulus—an enormous Adder /—at other times, the waving Sword of Fire of the Cherub over Paradise.—

Star (at Barnard Castle) bright, large, the only one, right over the Tower—now absolutely cresting it—& now as we came nearer, twinkling behind the motionless Fragment, a high wall *ruined* into a rude Obelisk.

Shootings of water threads down the Slope of the huge green Stone.—Varieties of this on the Clyde, in my Scotch Tour.

The *white rose* of Eddy-foam, where the stream ran into a scooped or scolloped hollow of the Rock in its channel—this shape, an exact white rose, was for ever overpowered by the Stream rushing down in upon it, and still obstinate in resurrection it spread up into the Scollop, by fits and starts, *blossoming* in a moment into full Flower.—Hung over the Bridge, & musing considering how much of this Scene of endless variety in Identity was Nature's—how much the living organ's!—What would it be if I had the eyes of a fly!—what if the blunt eye of a Brobdignag!—

Black round Ink-spots from 5 to 18 in the decaying Leaf of the Sycamore.

A circular glade in a forest of Birch Trees, and in the center of the circle, a stone standing upright, twice a tall man's Height—and by its side a stately Ash Tree umbrellaing it.—

A road on the breast of the mountain, all wooded save at the very Top where the steep naked Crag lorded it—this road seen only by a stream of white Cows, gleaming behind the Trees, in the Interspaces.

A Host of little winged Flies on the Snow mangled by the Hail Storm, near the Top of Helvellin. (1803)

Two men, of extraordinary intelligence and sensitivity, writing about comparable experiences but separated by a generation and an historical epoch: these passages tell us much about the way men and women thought of themselves and how they related to what they saw of the world.

Rousseau was writing in the midst of the most hectic period of his life. In the space of two years he had become lionized as the author of the novel *La Nouvelle Héloïse* and persecuted as the purveyor of the pernicious doctrines of *Émile*, which undermined the teachings and institutions of the Catholic Church. He addressed Malesherbes as his friend and ally, in an attempt to put the record straight: he was not the troublemaker that the press and gossip made him out to be, but a man of pure and simple heart, sincerely following the dictates of natural feeling. It was one of the great ironies of his reputation that this 'natural feeling' itself became the foundation of an artificial style, much cultivated by urbane ladies all over Europe. Thus Marie Antoinette played the milkmaid in a farmhouse built in the grounds of the palace of Versailles; and as late as 1847, in *Dombey and Son*, Dickens was satirizing the last gasp of the Rousseauan type in the figure of the withered old belle, Mrs Skewton. 'Cows are my passion,' she drawls. 'What I have ever sighed for, has been to retreat to a Swiss farm, and live entirely surrounded by cows—and china.... What I want, is frankness, confidence, less conventionality, and freer play of soul. We are so dreadfully artificial ... I want Nature everywhere. It would be so extremely charming.'

Yet Rousseau himself was also following established literary conventions. The fond recollection of past rural happiness was a popular theme of mid eighteenth-century English poetry, which was much read and widely imitated. James Thomson in his poem *The Seasons* (1726–30), for instance, talks about 'the haunts of meditation'—a phrase which could serve as an epigraph to this letter. We should also notice that Rousseau is not remembering a specific experience, but a series of experiences some years back, out of which he wants to create an image of himself; Coleridge, on the other hand, is describing what happened yesterday and aims to be detailed and factual, naming names and trying to convey each twist of his mind and turn of events.

Rousseau's walks are a passage into isolation and introspection, during which nature, untouched by the spoiling hand of man, purifies his mind with impressions and feelings which vacillate 'between observation and wonder'. He 'reads' the landscape like a book which reveals the handiwork of God, or rather of that unnamed 'great Being' whose presence is obscurely but powerfully sensed. Rousseau's imagination works transformations on the immediate realities of the scene. He does not stop at appreciating the beauty of trees and flowers. He imagines a community of the like-minded, inhabiting the woodland glades; he goes on to imagine infinity. This faculty—for imaginatively re-creating and elaborating raw visual impressions in the mind's eye—was another common theme of contemporary English poetry. Thus Edward Young wrote in his *Night Thoughts* (1746):

> Our senses, as our reason, are divine.
> But for the magic organ's powerful charm,
> Earth were a rude uncoloured chaos still.
> Objects are but the occasion; ours the exploit;
> Ours is the cloth, the pencil, and the paint
> Which nature's admirable picture draws ...

In other words, there was a creative interaction between mind and world, nature presenting an outline which the imagination coloured in with value and meaning. This idea had been mooted by the philosopher John Locke in his *Essay Concerning Human Understanding* as early as 1690 and over the next century and longer it became an increasingly problematic concept which could undermine all common-sense certainties about the division between the substantially 'real' and the 'imaginary'. The young Wordsworth, for instance, found himself 'often unable to think of external things as having external existence, and I communed with all I saw as something not apart from but inherent in my own immaterial nature. Many times while going to school have I grasped at a wall or tree to recall myself from this abyss of idealism to the reality.'

But for Rousseau, as for so many eighteenth-century English writers, the exercise of the imagination was primarily a source of pleasure, mingled with a melancholy awareness that what was imagined had to remain a dream, a fancy of nothingness. To imagine was to desire, and desire feeds on what it cannot have, not what it already possesses. And so Rousseau, in all his exclamations of inner content, sincerely admits to an 'inexplicable emptiness' at the moment of his highest delight.

Coleridge's experience is much more complex, partly because his capacity for self-analysis was much more sophisticated than Rousseau's. He presents his adventure raw and authentic, even to recording the unsavoury details of the rash of red heat-bumps on his chest:

they too become an integral part of the story, for Coleridge was always observing the operation of cause and effect in himself and asking, 'Why, if this happens, should that be the result?'

At the root of this letter, however, written to his beloved Asra (and surviving only in a manuscript copied out in her hand), is the confirmation of his belief that 'Nature ne'er deserts the wise and pure'. For Rousseau Nature was a source of pleasure and wonder, but Coleridge also felt that it had an actively benevolent intent towards humankind, if only we knew how to watch and wait—this was something he and Wordsworth had discussed. As he lies on the ledge of rock, at a loss 'how to proceed, how to return' and apparently in a horribly sticky situation, the implication is that his awe at the magnificence of the crags and clouds interacts with his own inner 'reason & the Will' to renew his strength and stop the shaking. The way out comes upon him almost like a biblical miracle, as though the rent in the rock was offering its services as a friend. Coleridge would have taken this idea quite seriously. He and Wordsworth both believed that every *thing* in the world—be it animal, vegetable, or mineral—was filled with spirit, alive and interconnected. The Ancient Greek poets sometimes fancied that trees, for instance, might be 'hollow statues', each inhabited by a tutelary 'godkin or goddessling', but Coleridge was not playing pretty: he was following a radical new body of scientific thought, then being pursued in both France and England, which acknowledged no barrier between body and spirit, mind and matter. Life was the energy, the vital force that rolled through all things like the wind, and made a human thought every bit as real and living a phenomenon as a stone or a blade of grass. 'Everything has a Life of its own,' he wrote in 1802, 'we are all *one Life*.' This is not a contradiction. The remembered images jotted down into the notebook are witness to what Coleridge calls 'endless variety in Identity', the same spirit passing into different forms and working out a mysterious and exquisite harmony of co-existence—as 'the *white rose* of Eddy-foam' is 'for ever overpowered by the Stream rushing down in upon it' and yet still 'obstinate in resurrection'; or the standing stone is silently umbrella'd by the 'stately Ash Tree'.

Coleridge's thinking was part of one of those broad changes which periodically alter the way in which we conceive the world and which slowly filters down from the higher reaches into the assumptions of ordinary uneducated people. In the middle of the eighteenth century the received view of the natural world had been drawn from the dissemination of the ideas of Sir Isaac Newton. Newton saw the universe as essentially an ordered and divinely planned phenomenon, functioning according to mathematically ascertainable laws of force and motion, whose actions and reactions could be scientifically proven: fifty years on, this conception was beginning to seem mechanical and reductive. All over Europe, in different ways, men like Baron d'Holbach in France, Goethe and Schelling in Germany, Wordsworth and Coleridge, as well as geologists and botanists, came to evolve another image of the world: not that of the intricate Newtonian clock, wound up by God and left to tick away by rote, but a plant whose life and growth cannot be rationally comprehended or measured.

Coleridge was also preoccupied with the matter that cropped up in relation to Rousseau's letter to Malesherbes. How, he wanted to know, does the mind make pictures? Hanging over the bridge, watching the white rose of eddy-foam, he considers, 'how much of this scene of . endless variety in Identity was Nature's—how much the living organ's—what would it be if I had the eyes of a fly!—what if the blunt eye of a Brobdignag!'* The 'living organ' of the eye does not register straight: the mind sees in the eddy-foam not just water, but a white rose, a scallop, blossoming into full flower. It creates images out of raw perception, selecting, associating, censoring, remembering, and transforming. Seeing becomes feeling. Nature acts on the human consciousness and the human consciousness acts on Nature, as a photosynthesizing plant feeds the atmosphere by which it has been fed. It was in some high degree of this power that lay the faculty of composing Poetry, and Coleridge coined the word 'esemplastic' to describe the Poet's ability to shape and order impressions into a meaningful unity. In the famous formulation of the critic M. H. Abrams, the Poet's mind was no longer a mirror reflecting Nature, but a lamp, illuminating it from within.

Yet life could not begin and end in Nature. As a young man Coleridge believed, like an ecologist today, that human beings are not simply masters of the planet with absolute rights to exploit or eliminate 'inferior creation'. 'I hail thee *Brother*,' he had written to a young tethered ass, in the excitement of planning his community on the banks of the Susquehanna,

> And fain would take thee with me, in the Dell
> Where high-soul'd Pantisocracy shall dwell! ...
> Where Rats shall mess with Terriers hand-in-glove
> And Mice with Pussy's whiskers sport in Love...

* The Giants in the Second Part of Swift's *Gulliver's Travels*.

But at the same time that he envisaged this complete harmony between all creation, he was concerned—increasingly so—to preserve a strong idea of a supreme creating God above the visible universe. This was a belief to which Wordsworth, at least until his orthodox middle age, was indifferent, and it made a point of contention between them. 'The vague misty, rather than mystic confusion of God with the world & the accompanying nature-worship,' wrote Coleridge towards the end of his life, is 'the trait in Wordsworth's poetic works I most dislike.'

This is fair criticism—except in so far as Coleridge was himself lost in the mists. His philosophical writings characteristically start off confidently, promising a definite destination. However, the first cross-roads in the argument both intrigues and confuses him. Forgetting about the map, he takes ten steps down one path to see what the view might be like, then hurries back and walks half a mile down another—which turns out to be a dead end. Anything spotted on the way sidetracks him; he does not look at the contours of the wood, so fascinated is he by the bark on the trees. Eventually, he draws to a halt quite capriciously, as though he has simply run out of breath or dropped off to sleep. When he recovers he has forgotten where he is or even where he was going, but what an interesting walk it has been for all that!

This is very much how *Biographia Literaria* (1817), Coleridge's frustrating attempt to account for his intellectual growth, proceeds. The silk handkerchiefs are only half pulled out of the magician's hat. It is a book, like Coleridge's life, of grand intentions and broken promises, diving into digressions, ambling into anecdotes, and plastering up the cracks with chunks of impenetrable philosophy secretly lifted straight from the writings of the German philosopher Schelling, Hölderlin's friend.

But then Coleridge could not have written a cut-and-dried manifesto, concluding with points one to ten, without having gone sharply against the grain of what he was saying. Like his sublime meditational poems 'This Lime-Tree Bower My Prison' and 'Frost at Midnight' or the notebooks, *Biographia Literaria* can be regarded as the result of an experiment in charting what comes out when the mind is allowed to wander freely and thus reveal the way it lives, develops, and changes as organically as anything else in Nature. (One might appropriately imagine at this point how Coleridge would have interpenetrated with Sigmund Freud: it is certainly easy to picture him delightedly participating in psychoanalysis and its search for Self through the dynamic conflicts of Ego, Superego, and Id.) For all its weakness in terms of logic and lucidity, Coleridge's thinking has one shining virtue: it responds intimately to personal feeling and experience, taking us closer to him than we can come to perhaps any of his contemporaries.

Thus far we have centred the discussion on visual perception and the connection between eye and mind. But hearing is an equally sensitive part of our awareness, and also one which, especially through the organized sounds of music, can have a profound and moulding effect on the emotions. The leaders of the French Revolution understood how to exploit this when they arranged for the great rallying *fête* on the Champ-de-Mars in 1790 to be preceded by 'a victorious overture' played by an orchestra of twelve hundred wind and brass instruments and twelve massive gongs. From the 1789 bread march to Versailles until the last days of the Terror, the *sans-culottes* paraded through the streets chanting the rough and insistent anthem of the Revolution, the '*Ça ira*', 'It's going to happen'; while the opera houses were packed with audiences cheering the thunderous new Revolutionary musicals (or operas with dialogue) on themes of imprisonment and rescue, heroic defiance and the collapse of tyranny. Throughout Europe every friend to Liberty was roused by the *Marseillaise*, composed in 1792 for the armies on the Rhine and immediately triumphant: 'Send me a thousand men and one copy of the *Marseillaise*, and victory will be my reply,' wrote a general on the front to the Assembly. This was music made public and political, after the principles of Plato's *Republic*, music designed specifically to rouse, inspire, and unite the French people in a spirit of militant patriotism, music based on the call of the trumpet and the roll of the drum.

But in German-speaking countries in particular, there were also those who cultivated a new and intensely private experience of music, making the attentive ear the central and primary aesthetic faculty. Here music gained a unique status as the one *abstract* art-form, untrammelled by common everyday associations. Other genres—painting, sculpture, poetry, the drama—all involved a greater or lesser degree of imitation or reflection of the surface appearances of the world: people, objects, the universal tool of language. But music spoke in a magic tongue beyond ordinary understanding, communicating only mysteries. It was *aussprechlich*, beyond speech, inexpressible. 'Music discloses to man an unknown realm,' wrote E. T. A. Hoffmann in an essay on Beethoven, 'a world that has nothing in common with the external sensual world that surrounds him, a world in which he leaves behind him all definite feelings, to surrender himself to inex-pressible longing.'

Such capacities made music a potential trouble-maker, dangerous to social order and reaching into parts of the psyche that otherwise lay dormant. A simple violin melody, an old ballad could draw up dark and strange forces. It was through this belief that music in the nineteenth century was so often regarded as the language of madness, the leaving-behind of normality. Hölderlin's long finger-nails careered up and down, up and down the keyboard of the piano in his attic chamber. 'Mad people sing,' wrote Hazlitt, and in Tieck's story 'Musical Joys and Sufferings', a pair of crazed Italian opera singers croon in their empty attic, filled only with 'societies of Angels, led by King David', who relish the dissonance. Even more chilling is Kleist's tale 'St Cecilia, or the Power of Music', in which the sound of a *Gloria* sung by some Catholic nuns drives four young Protestants, who had threatened to smash up their convent, into a permanent trance of piety, from which they only emerge every day at midnight, to intone the same *Gloria* in voices reminiscent of 'leopards and wolves howling at the sky in icy winter'. Kleist eerily counterpoints the innocence of the nuns and the beauty of their singing—apparently conducted by the ghost of the patron saint of music, St Cecilia herself—with the music's appalling demoniac influence. Later in the story, the young men's mother visits the convent in an attempt to find out what happened and notices the score of the fatal *Gloria* lying open on a music stand. Even the notes on the stave look like 'magical signs, with which some terrible spirit seemed to be marking out its mysterious sphere'. Easy enough to equate discord with madness: but Kleist suggests that the sweetest and holiest of harmonies can also be poisonous.

One of the keenest admirers of Kleist's tales, first published in book form in 1810–11, was Ernst Theodor Amadeus Hoffman (1776–1822: the 'Amadeus' was a name he substituted for 'Wilhelm', in homage to Wolfgang Amadeus Mozart), at that time an obscure composer writing operas and ballets to order for a provincial German opera house. His progress up to this point had been erratic: Hoff-mann's life was like a shaky walk along a tightrope, with the flames of Hell blazing below. As a child, he had heard the Devil's voice on the seashore, and felt a mixture of pity and terror at the agonized sound. It was an experience he could never quite laugh off.

He had been brought up by a muddle of eccentric and variously crippled relations, whose neuroses he uncomfortably inherited.

Despite prodigious musical abilities, he had followed family tradition and trained for the Law, of which he was always a diligent and methodical practitioner: but what he most wanted to be was a painter. On being dismissed from an official post when some insulting caricatures of his superiors were discovered, he was virtually exiled in 1802 to Plock, an eastern border town which proved as dreary as its name promised. There was not much to do, and Hoffmann improved the shining hour by studying musical composition, painting some gloomy Salvator Rosa-ish landscapes, and writing essays. In 1804 he and his mousy Polish wife Mikla were posted to Warsaw, where his range of activities was extraordinary. On top of legal and administrative duties, he conducted the orchestra of the Warsaw Academy of Music, redesigned their premises, and painted a series of murals to decorate them. In 1805 alone he also wrote two comic operas, a symphony, a piano sonata, and several other pieces of music. In 1806, when Napoleon occupied Warsaw, Hoffmann refused to take an oath of loyalty and forfeited his legal position. After a period of near-starvation scavenging for odd bits of work, he ended up a contract composer to the opera house of the South German town of Bamberg, supplementing his income by designing stage sets, producing plays, writing about music, and taking in pupils.

One of the latter was a fourteen-year-old daughter of the local aristocracy, with whom Hoffmann fell absurdly but desperately in love. Julia Marc was a pretty girl of whom little record survives, except in the form of Hoffmann's fantasy. She does, however, seem to have had a pure singing voice and genuine musicality, and it was certainly her gift in this direction that forged Hoffmann's infatuation. For months he tortured himself with dreams of his unattainable muse, almost gloating on the madness of the situation and confiding it only to his diary. Did she ever guess the poisoned obsession inside her scrawny and wizened music-master, with his strange piercing gaze, tiny hands, and hook nose? Hoffmann believed that she did, although he never told her in so many words. Matters came to a head when Julia's mother decided that the good family name needed the consolidation of bourgeois capital, and therefore sold her daughter into a marriage of convenience with a smug middle-aged merchant from Hamburg named Gröpel.

It was more than Hoffmann could bear to see the girl, barely sixteen, go to her fate like a lamb to the slaughter, and there was an embarrassing tea party during which in front of the ladies, both men became very drunk and mutually abusive. Gröpel finally fell flat on the drawing-room floor in a stupor and a scandal was narrowly avoided. Hoffmann never saw Julia Marc again. Eight years later, he heard the news of her divorce from Gröpel and noted sadly that it was said that experience had made her hard and cold: what became of her subsequently is a mystery. The sound of a girl's voice is a persistent feature of Hoffmann's fiction: in the doll Olympia, for example, the perfect facsimile of a human being whose singing is no more than clockwork and who drives poor Nathanael to madness and suicide ('The Sandman'); in the imprisoned Antonia who will die if she ever sings again ('Rat Krespel'). Always and over again, it is as though Julia Marc has been revisited and magicked into another and often sinister shape and sound.

Hoffmann left Bamberg in 1813, resigned to his loss but promised a job as a music director of an opera troupe which performed in both Dresden and Leipzig. By a delightful coincidence the very month that Hoffmann arrived in Leipzig, there was born in the city one greater composer: Richard Wagner. Hoffmann knew Wagner's uncle and father well, and one wonders whether he ever brought gifts to the Wagnerian cradle and cast his burning eye on the babe. Certainly the young Wagner was an enthusiastic reader of Hoffmann, and it is not often remembered that his opera *Tannhäuser* is closely modelled on one of his obscurer tales.

Despite the toil and hope invested in his last musical work *Undine*, an original attempt to make an opera out of German folklore first performed with some success in Berlin in 1816, Hoffmann's career as a practising musician never amounted to much, for all his efficiency in churning out competent sub-Mozartian pastiche. Driven out of Leipzig by an unscrupulous impresario, he resumed his career as a legal official in 1814, and for the next nine years acted out a bizarre double life. Novalis, the poet of transcendent darkness and the absolute nothingness of the material world, had also functioned from nine to five as Friedrich von Hardenberg, a conventionally ambitious mining engineer; Hoffmann now became the day-time arbitrator of Law and night-time arbitrator of Chaos, writing a string of tales of the weird and marvellous which are still popular today. The split is dramatized in the central character of 'Mademoiselle de Scudéry', a story of the celebrated goldsmith Cardillac who turns out to be a mass murderer, killing to save his artefacts from those he sells them to and yet despises. A split implies a double, and Hoffmann's tales also circle round the dilemmas and phenomena of doubleness: ghosts, mirrors, one person uncannily resembling another, mechanical dolls and automata. 'I see myself through a multiplying glass,' he wrote in his diary in 1809. 'All the forms which move around me are other Myselfs.' In the words of René Wellek, the double for Hoffmann is 'the question mark put to the concept of the human self, a symbol of the doubt we have of human identity and the stability of our world'.

With more than a touch of the gruesome irony of which his tales are full, Hoffmann's nemesis involved the collision of his own double self. Since 1819 day-time Hoffmann had sat, with some distinction, on an important committee which investigated subversive activities within the Prussian state. Although he had little interest in the politics of the angry young men who came before him, he became progressively more incensed at the underhand means the committee employed to press charges and convict. One drunken evening night-time Hoffmann admitted to his tavern friends that a new tale, 'Meister Floh', contained some indelicate satire of the committee and its doings. This fact found its way back to the desk of von Kamptz, the Minister of Police, who, on inspection, was outraged to discover himself, in the unmistakably ludicrous shape of 'Hofrat Knarrpanti', a chief target. Preparations were made to arraign Hoffmann and a prosecution could have resulted in his ultimate and complete disgrace. But Hoffmann was one step ahead of his judges. Not only was his liver rotten with alcohol, but he was also seized up with ataxia, a grotesque type of paralysis which leaves the victim staggering and tottering, limbs beyond control. The authorities realized that there would be no point in pursuing the matter: Hoffmann would soon be dead: which he was.

If Hoffmann's music had died even before he did, his tales have proved a continuing inspiration to musical posterity, providing the scenarios for operas (*Tannhäuser*, Hindemith's *Cardillac*, Offenbach's *Les Contes d'Hoffmann*), ballets (Delibes' *Coppélia*, Tchaikovsky's *Nutcracker*), and some of Schumann's finest descriptive piano music (*Kreisleriana*). It is not hard to understand why this should be so. No writer of the German Romantic period produces a more bold and garish theatricality: his characters are lit by footlights and daubed with greasepaint. Compared to Kleist's tales, with their eerie ambiguities and unnerving amorality, Hoffmann's seem obvious, sensational, superficial. Kleist's prose is as cold and alien as his subject-matter; Hoffmann's is often clumsily over-heated. The violence and madness in Kleist are integral to his disturbed vision of the world; in Hoffmann they are more macabre and voyeuristic—in Bamberg he paid regular visits to the local lunatic asylum, observing symptoms and methods of treatment.

None of this is to deny his unfailing readability and fertility of imagination. Considered as a writer who set out only to thrill and entertain, he succeeds magnificently; but like Scott and Byron, Hoffmann was victim of his own popularity, forced to produce to meet an enormous demand and thus denied the chance to develop according to the true artist's internal dynamic. On the subject of music alone did he rise above serving the market, actually educating public taste rather than pandering to it. His spooks, mechanical dolls, and cackling old scientists were not completely serious, but his love of Mozart and Beethoven was.

Hoffmann's first published story, 'Ritter Gluck', written during his Bamberg years, already combines the themes of music and the double self. Sitting in the palpably real and bustling context of a Berlin café in 1809, the narrator encounters a disgruntled composer who turns out to be rewriting the operas of Gluck, twenty-two years after the latter's death. In the final sentence he claims, with a flourish, that he *is* Gluck. Whether the man is mad or a genius, or indeed the ghost of Gluck is left unanswered.

In 'Don Juan' (1813), Hoffmann describes a strange hotel connected to an opera house. As the narrator witnesses a mysterious but potent performance of Mozart's *Don Giovanni*, he receives a visitation in his box from the singer of Donna Anna—or is it the ghost of Donna Anna herself, for the singer is still on the stage?—through which he comes to a revelation of the opera's inner meaning. Don Giovanni is no mere libertine, justly punished for his sins, but a man of intelligence and energy, driven to excess by his contempt for the meanness and mediocrity around him; while Donna Anna is fuelled not by the longing for revenge on her murdered father so much as by repressed desire for the man who introduced her to the excitements of sex. Mozart and his opera never sounded the same again to anyone who read Hoffmann, for 'Don Juan' turned a 'perfect' and 'charming' composer into a Romantic poet, touched by daemonic forces, and his Don Giovanni into a doomed Byronic hero.

Hoffmann was also one of the first to recognize Beethoven's genius, writing essay-fantasias on his instrumental music which pointed to the colossal and immeasurable struggles embodied in the Fifth Symphony and to the namelessly deep emotions evoked by the piano and chamber music. This is familiar enough to us: but in 1815, most of musical Europe still identified Beethoven with nasty senseless noise. It was Hoffmann who created a vocabulary of images which could turn the noise back into meaning.

Hoffmann's most successful musical creation was the fictional composer Johannes Kreisler, who appears in a number of tales, chiefly the two series of *Kreisleriana* sketches, and the novel *Kater Murr*. Kreisler is the nearest Hoffmann came to a self-portrait, and predictably it is a many-faceted, even fragmented one. But Kreisler also represents an interesting transition in the social history of music and the development of 'Romantic' ideas about the nature of an Artist. In the eighteenth century a composer in Central Europe lived by contracting himself to a court or church, where he would produce a large amount of music for specific occasions, as well as generally administering and conducting all musical affairs—the orchestra, choir, and so on. The usual term for such a post is *Kapellmeister* and Haydn's thirty years with the Esterházys are a shining example of how happily the system could work when the musician was ready to listen and the patron to hear. But with the decline of the great court establishments over the Revolutionary and Napoleonic periods, kapellmeistery went into decline. More musicians began to risk independence, asserting their right to pick and choose commissions, both relying on commercial appeal and despising its vulgarity. The essence of eighteenth-century kapellmeistery had been the ability to turn one's hand to anything pertaining to music and its performance. Now 'composing' became a more specialized activity, with a 'composer' regarding himself less as a nobleman's or bishop's servant, organizing entertainment in return for security, than as a 'creative artist' whose talent blew where it listeth. Mozart and Beethoven were both caught between the alternatives, being too wilful to make a compromise with kapellmeistery and too profligate to maintain a decent freelance living. Kreisler is caught in something of the same tangle, as Hoffmann was himself: Kreisler, we learn, was a court *Kapellmeister*, but was dismissed for insulting the resident prima donna and refusing to write music to a libretto by the hack resident poet. He can and must be loyal to his genius alone, even at the price of the sanity of ordinary life.

But freedom is no better. Kreisler scorns the alternative world of bourgeois Philistines* and their complete misunderstanding of art and the artist, as much as the old world of aristocratic service with its birthday cantatas and battle symphonies. In 'Kreisler's Musical Sorrows', Hoffmann draws on his experiences in Plock and Bamberg

---

* Hoffmann was the first to popularize this word, in the familiar sense of one 'whose interests are material and commonplace'. It was originally used by German students to describe anyone outside the university. The modern sense was taken into English by Carlyle and Matthew Arnold in *Culture and Anarchy* (1867).

to show his composer at a provincial aesthetic *soirée*, obliged to accompany the amateur lady singers: worst of all is the civic treasurer's wife, who 'squeaks, miaows, gurgles, moans, groans, wobbles, twitters' ('*quieke, miaue, gürgle, stöhne, ächze, tremuliere, quinkiliere*'). At the end of the evening, the host begs Herr Kreisler to improvise at the piano for his guests' delight. Kreisler cannot be bothered, so he slips out his score of Bach's Goldberg Variations and plays them instead. No one notices: indeed, his audience soon slips quietly out, bored stiff, leaving Kreisler alone with the divine Bach, whose music seems like a sublime enigma, a page of Sanskrit, something unfit for the ears of the Gröpels and civic treasurers of this world.

This is the ultimate reality of music—what Donna Anna in 'Don Juan' calls '*die Geheimnisvolle Sprache eines fernen Geisterreichs*', 'the secret-filled speech of a distant kingdom of the Spirit'. It is not necessarily comfortable or comforting. In the brief prose poem '*Ombra adorata*', Kreisler is sent into raptures by the sound of an anonymous soprano voice (Julia Marc's, no doubt); but in 'Kreisler's Musical and Poetic Club' he is led into blacker waters. Surrounded by friends, Kreisler is improvising. The treble keys of the piano have been damaged by dripping candle wax and he can only use the bass register. The lights are put out. Each chord he plays evokes in him an image, which he describes to his listeners. First all is light and beauty, but soon he is caught up in sounds that lead him to a frenzy of terror, visions of the Devil, and despair. Someone relights the candles and puts an end to his trance. In another fragment, Kreisler has gone mad and been locked up. A friend leaves him a guitar. Toying with its strings, Kreisler strikes the basic chord of C major—then smashes the instrument to pieces.

Kreisler is one of the great originals of German fiction, a figure like Falstaff or Mrs Gamp, who seems to run off the page and out of literature altogether: so great is his vivacity, so mercurial his emotions that we want to stay in his company longer. Hoffmann is cleverly both very specific and very vague about him. We know, for instance, that he wears a red cap and Chinese dressing gown, but not where he comes from or who his parents were. The 'editor' who introduces Kreisler's 'papers' to the reader reports that he has now vanished, and was last seen leaving town, sporting two hats and some quill pens stuck like daggers in his belt, when he reappears some years later in Hoffmann's unfinished novel *Kater Murr*, he has become a more conventionally melancholic 'romantic' hero, in love, predictably, with a mysterious girl with a beautiful singing voice named Julia. But apart from his fascination simply as a personality, Kreisler amazingly embodies the crisis of the 'romantic' composer, before such a thing truly existed. The composer outside society, despising it yet expecting it to support him; the composer writing music which tries to tell stories and paint pictures, yet also to communicate incommunicably absolute states of feelings: Kreisler heralds the struggles and aspirations of Schumann, Berlioz, Liszt, and Wagner before any of them had written so much as a note.*

Hoffmann was another fashion over which the great arbiter of German culture Goethe shook his head disdainfully, complaining of the influence and admiration commanded by the 'morbid works of this sick man'. A figure like Kreisler represented just the sort of aberrant unbalanced intensity that he most disliked; *he* preferred to think of music, not as something tortured and indeterminate, but as a means to order and clarity. Music could be sublime without driving one crazy.

Goethe's lifetime overlapped those of Handel and Wagner, and his taste leaned firmly towards the brisk melodiousness of the former: 'moderns' like Beethoven and Weber he found coarse and noisy, ministering to chaos rather than harmony. He liked the clean energies of Bach's keyboard music and the forthright masculinity of the *Marseillaise*; but his ideal was Mozart, whom aged fourteen, he had heard play as a child prodigy aged seven,† and in whose work he sensed a tempered marriage of form and feeling. It was Mozart whose operas were most performed in the court theatre at Weimar, of which Goethe was director; it was Mozart whom Goethe decided should have set *Faust* to music—for he too, in *Don Giovanni*, had confronted the daemonic without, as had Hoffmann, surrendering to it; and it was Mozart's *Die Zauberflöte* for which Goethe devised a sequel libretto.

In all this, Goethe was very much following the contemporary standard of educated musical taste. For the generation after his death in 1791, Mozart was supreme throughout Europe—Hoffmann, in deciding to rate Beethoven's instrumental music a step higher and further was sticking his neck out. 'There is nothing perfect in this world

---

* He also finds his way into English literature in the figure of Julius Klesmer, the Germanic composer, in George Eliot's novel *Daniel Deronda*.

† At the other end of his life, in 1831, Goethe also heard the young Clara Wieck, later Clara Schumann and one of the first of a new breed of piano virtuosi. There cannot have been many others who heard both her and the young Mozart.

except Mozart's music' wrote Thomas Love Peacock: we shall see later how he proselytized his friends on Perfection's behalf.

But among the English intelligentsia a true music lover like Peacock was a rarity. Jane Austen, for instance, found the prospect of a visit to the opera in 1814 'very tiresome' and her heroine Catherine Morland in *Northanger Abbey* remembers the day 'which dismissed the music master as one of the happiest of her life'. In *Emma* Mrs Elton's drooling over music is a measure of her affectation; while in *Sense and Sensibility* the emotion that Sentimental Marianne puts into her piano-playing is regarded as a danger to her mental health.

This is not just Jane Austen's inbuilt puritan reluctance to obey the call to worship at the shrine of music. The English in general took their music differently from the Germans. Apart from all their philosophizing, the Germans had a rich living tradition of composition, a *Kapellmeister* in every town, and a high standard of music teaching— all of which the English lacked. Instead there was a received view, as affirmed by Dr Burney in his famous *History*, that music was only 'the art of pleasing by the succession and combination of agreeable sounds'. Music harmonized life, rather than unsettling it with unnamable yearnings. It was something to enjoy, not worry about or 'experience'. The nation was filled with young ladies of the middle class passing their infinite leisure hours in tinkling away at trivialities on the great toy of the age – the Broadwood cabinet piano, the first mass-produced musical instrument, developed around 1800. Jane Austen herself bought a Broadwood, on which she practised quite assiduously, but her music library contains no Bach inventions, no Haydn or Mozart sonatas, certainly no Beethoven or Schubert; only country-dance arrangements, folk-song arrangements, and some sonatinas by mediocrities such as Dibdin, Bertoni, and Sacchini that today's most un-prodigious twelve-year-old would romp through contemptuously. It is no wonder that Jane Austen found any sort of pretension about music 'tiresome'. Innocent domestic entertainment, the applause of the family circle, was the beginning and end of it: nothing that a tormented soul need worry about.

In 1799 Coleridge wrote his own strictures on musical pretensions, in a poem entitled 'Lines composed in a Concert Room':

> ... I detest
> These scented Rooms, where, to a gaudy throng,
> Heaves the proud Harlot her distended breast,
> In intricacies of laborious song....

O give me, from this heartless scene released,
        To hear our old Musician, blind and grey
(Whom stretching from my nurse's arms I kissed),
        His Scottish tunes and warlike marches play,
By moonshine, on the balmy summer-night
        The while I dance amid the tedded hay
With merry maids, whose ringlets toss in light.

Not Coleridge at his best: the sentiments are first prim, then
maudlin—but the idea of contrasting 'art' music with 'natural' music
was a common one at the time, natural music embracing not only
rustic voices and instruments, but also bird song, the bleating of
lambs, the rustle of trees, and the lapping of water. Wordsworth also
deals with it: lyrically in 'The Solitary Reaper', ploddingly in the
dismal 'On the Power of Sound'. In Germany, Wackenroder invented
a precursor of Kreisler, the Kapellmeister Berglinger, who sickens of
worldly success and longs to run away to the shepherd in the
mountains and hear again the simple folk-songs of his childhood.

Coleridge eventually came round to the harlots and the concert
room. He was dazzled by the singing of Mrs Billington in *The Beggar's
Opera*—'I seem to have acquired a new sense by hearing her,' he wrote
in 1802—and charmed to find himself in the company of the fabulous
Italian prima donna Catalani. More seriously, his life in London
brought him closer acquaintance of the music of the German masters,
on which he reflected in one of his notebooks:

Music seems to have an *immediate* communion with my Life; ... It
converses with the *life* of my mind, as if it were itself the Mind of my
Life. Yet I sometimes think, that a great Composer, a Mozart, a
Beethoven must have been in a state of Spirit much more akin,
more analogous, to mine own when I am at one waiting for,
watching, and organically constructing and inwardly constructed
by, the *Ideas*, the living Truths, that may be re-excited but cannot be
expressed by Words ... yet are themselves untranslatable into any
Image, unrepresentable by any particular Object that I can imagine
myself to be a Titian, or a Sir C. Wren. Yet I wish I did know
something more of the wondrous mystery of this mighty *hot
Magic* ...

What Coleridge means is that the creation of music seems to him far
more like the creation of poetry than it is like the creation of a painting
or a building. It is a subject, or rather a mystery, which he also touched

on in two of his greatest works of the 1790s. At the end of 'Kubla Khan', the poet writes that could he but revive within himself the 'symphony and song' he heard in his vision of the maid singing to her dulcimer, then he too could become a Kubla Khan, building in verse the equivalent of his 'sunny dome' and becoming a great awesome bard, like the Old Testament prophets. In 'The Eolian Harp', written in the tender days shortly after his marriage to the hapless Sara in 1795, Coleridge muses on the title of the poem, 'a box about 3' long, with catgut strings of different thicknesses but tuned in unison attached to its upper surface. It could be placed ... where the wind could catch it and set the strings in vibration' (*Oxford Dictionary of Music*). This popular household toy sits on Coleridge's window ledge and casts 'this soft floating witchery of sound', reminding him of the way that the one life sweeps through the phenomena of 'animated nature', the music constructed by the meeting of the wind and string, as poetry is constructed by the meeting of the mind of man and the images of the world.

That music might serve as a symbol of poetic inspiration struck Shelley as well, although at the time he was quite ignorant of 'art' music and concert rooms. It came to him through the medium of Claire Clairmont's singing, a sound that played over some of the happiest months of his short and volatile life.

In the late winter of 1817, Shelley took a lease on Albion House, an ugly but very solid edifice in the small town of Marlow, about thirty miles west of London. He desperately needed to escape from the latest welter of panic and anger that whirled about him. The previous autumn had seen the terrible suicides of Fanny Imlay and Harriet Shelley, and the consequent beginning of a painful court case to win custody of their children (whom he had not set eyes on for at least two years) from the clutches of Harriet's hated sister Eliza. The likelihood of a nation-wide armed insurrection was also increasing, for all the government's whip-lash efforts to suspend habeas corpus and the rights of public assembly. Shelley was both hopeful and frightened of the possibilities: he begins to sound like every liberal intellectual faced with the prospect of a revolution of the working-class—worried that his own values and place in society might be attacked; worried that, for all the visions of brotherhood, the poor and oppressed might turn out 'illiterate demagogues'.

Shelley wrote a tract for the times, a *Proposal for Putting Reform to the Vote*, in which he argues for annual elections and a limited extension of the male franchise (there is no mention of the possibility of women voting). Moderate as its stance is in comparison to some of his earlier pamphlets, he cautiously signed it as the work of the 'Hermit of Marlow'. Safer to remain anonymous in the climate of repression and censorship, with his moral character under the scrutiny of the courts: not for Shelley the hustings in the market place or parliamentary lobbying. As he grew older he needed his distance more and more. Although he lost nothing of his radical conviction that 'the system of Society as it exists at present must be overthrown from the foundations', his urge to involve himself practically in any overthrowing dwindled.

Spring in Marlow gave his imagination space, solitude, ease. Mary, now the second Mrs Shelley and pregnant again, quietly finished *Frankenstein*, read the horror novels of Charles Brockden Brown, and watched lovingly over her first surviving child William, aged one. Claire came to stay, bringing with her what was described to strangers as a friend's baby, but was in fact her daughter by Byron, Allegra, an innocent destined to tear her life to pieces.

In the blossoming warmth Claire sang. Her music-master compared her voice to 'a string of pearls': even if this was just flattery, she probably was a cut above the average domestic lady singer and she certainly went at her music with her usual gusto, energy, and reluctance to miss any chance of showing off. Shelley was transported. He ordered her a Broadwood piano from London, which was received, enhanced the effect—and was never paid for.

How to snatch a grace from music, this 'mighty hot magic', thought Shelley, how to express the way that the sound, mixed with his secret feelings for Claire, worked upon him?

> My spirit like a charmèd bark doth swim
>   Upon the liquid waves of thy sweet singing,
> Far far away into the regions dim / Of rapture . . .
>
> Her voice is hovering o'er my soul—it lingers
>   O'ershadowing it with soft and lulling wings,
> The blood and life within those snowy fingers
>   Teach witchcraft to the instrumental strings . . .

The idea brought out all Shelley's overwhelming desire to pass beyond, to shed matter and form to reach a state of pure spirit. But he fails to mould it in any sustained way. His poetry about music never suggests actual music. Hoffmann's fantasies about Beethoven and Mozart make the music sharper, focusing the sound into images;

Shelley is only gasping and grasping at something he does not understand.

One of the reasons he had come to Marlow, however, was the proximity of someone who *did* understand—his friend Thomas Love Peacock, who lived nearby with his mother. Shelley had a considerable capacity for hero worship, and he was susceptible to Peacock's influence: through that spring and summer, they walked and talked together in the sun, Shelley drinking in the refreshment of Peacock's philosophy, his scepticism about most current intellectual fashions and his masterly dissection of styles and attitudes. 'There is always a fashionable taste,' booms the formidable Mrs Pinmoney in his novel *Melincourt*, 'a taste for acting Hamlet—a taste for philosophical lectures—a taste for the marvellous—a taste for the simple—a taste for the tender—a taste for the grim—a taste for *banditti*—a taste for ghosts—a taste for the devil—a taste for French dancers and Italian singers, and German whiskers and tragedies.' Peacock's own tastes leaned towards the light of the Ancient Greeks, towards pastoral, comedy, and Mozart, towards the bold erotic energies represented by the myths of Venus and Cupid, Apollo, Pan, and the woodland nymphs. His next novel, *Nightmare Abbey* (1818), gives a satirical drubbing to what he called 'the darkness and misanthropy of modern literature': Byronic brow-clutching, Coleridgean impenetrabilities, Shelleyan castles in the air.

Shelley took no personal offence at this: Peacock helped him to laugh at himself and broke down his prejudice that laughter was always cruel and sneering, the enemy of the Good. More than that, he was deeply fascinated by the spirit of voluptuous paganism that Peacock discussed with him. He put life-size statues of Venus and Apollo in his study; wandered unbuttoned round the woods and fields, his head wreathed in wild flowers, carving Greek letters on the trees; spent hours in a little skiff on the river Thames, lying flat on his back, reading or staring into the infinite blue of the sky.

He was writing an epic poem, *The Revolt of Islam*, 'a story of human passion in its most universal character, diversified with moving and romantic adventures', his first major work since *Queen Mab* and a maturer reconsideration of many of its radical themes. It reinterprets the French Revolution, but preaches a message of hope. What looked like the defeat of Liberty was not final: the hero and heroine may be burnt at the stake, but music is again there to wing them beyond death into the other:

... The pyre has disappeared,
The Pestilence, the Tyrant, and the throng;
The flames grow silent—slowly there is heard
The music of a breath-suspending song,
Which, like the kiss of love when life is young,
Steeps the faint eyes in darkness sweet and deep;
With ever-changing notes it floats along,
Till on my passive soul there seemed to creep
A melody, ...

His message is that we must resist the temptation to despondency.
'Gloom and misanthropy have become the characteristics of the age in
which we live,' he wrote in the poem's Preface. 'Our works of fiction
and poetry have been overshadowed by the same infectious gloom.
But ... I am aware of a slow, gradual, silent change.' This is Peacock's
voice ('the little wisdom and genius we have seem to be entering into a
conspiracy against cheerfulness') made Shelleyan. He would try to
brighten and colour his verse, to make it sing and dance with 'the
luxury of voluptuous delight' that Peacock had put into his pagan
poem 'Rhododaphne'. The culture of the Ancient Greeks grew ever
stronger in his mind as an image of a right-thinking society. 'The firm
yet flowing proportion of their forms; the winning unreserve and
facility of their manners; the eloquence of their speech in a language
which is itself music and persuasion,' he eulogized in his 'Discourse
on the Manners of the Ancient Greeks', written in 1818. 'The
gestures animated at once with the delicacy and the boldness which
the perpetual habit of persuading and governing themselves and
others; and the poetry of their religious rites, inspired into their whole
being.'

Shelley and Peacock were not alone in their paganism. Keats was
writing the pagan *Endymion* in that very spring of 1817 and would go
on to write *Lamia*. His patron, the poet and essayist Leigh Hunt, was
another paganist, a keen musician and a regular visitor to Marlow
where he was noted for his rousing rendition of the *Marseillaise*. He
brought with him his wife Marianne, who set about restoring the
statues of Venus and Apollo in the library, and a gaggle of wild
children, whom Shelley bewitched: he was even wilder than they
were, leading them into crazy and sometimes faintly sinister adventures, pulling faces, inventing hilarious new games, and giving pick-a-
backs on the way home.

In the village Shelley was remembered as a little mad. He took no

meat or strong liquor, only bread, raisins, broth, vegetables, and tea.*
It was said that once he had bought all the crayfish back from the local
fish shop and returned them to the Thames; that he stopped local lads
from their time-honoured pastime of stoning the squirrels. Worst of
all, although evidently a gentleman, he was seen on occasion in public
without either a hat *or* cravat. For all his charitable works, including
the distribution of a job lot of army surplus blankets and weekly
allowances to impoverished lace-makers, Marlow could not take
Shelley altogether seriously.

The idyll of Albion House was over by the autumn. As the days
grew shorter, the sun did not reach the walled garden and the library
which opened on to it became so damp and dank that the books were
coated in mildew. Mary had been successfully delivered of a baby girl
and *Frankenstein* accepted by a good publisher, but Shelley himself
grew restless, and his underlying anxieties manifested themselves in
psychosomatic illness: pains in his chest, his side, his bowels. He
began to worry that he was tubercular, that an English winter would
be the death of him. Escape to Marlow no longer seemed far enough.
What to do about Claire, his unresolved relations with her, and her
hopeless relations with Byron? What to do about Godwin, first cringing, then pestering, then hectoring? How to confront the ominous
political situation in England? He had lost his case for custody of his
and Harriet's children, Chancery having decided, probably wisely, to
foster them out to a disinterested party (Shelley was granted limited
access, but there is no record of his ever having taken advantage of
it). And underneath it all, a festering guilt, projected on to Eliza
Westbrook—it was she, he insisted, who was responsible for Harriet's
suicide.

Early in 1818 Albion House was sold and the Shelley *ménage* made
its way back to the capital to prepare for emigration to the warm pagan
south. One thing alone could have kept the poet in England: the
success of *The Revolt of Islam*. But it was a humiliating failure, and
apart from Leigh Hunt's loyal puff, it met with public indifference and
innuendo from the reviewers about the poet's morality.

---

* Shelley's vegetarianism came and went: Mary on occasion could persuade him to
eat fowl when he was ill and she seems to have remained unimpressed by this side of
her husband's idealism. Keats's friend the painter Haydon memorably describes
Shelley 'carving a bit of broccoli or cabbage on his plate, as if it had been the
substantial wing of a chicken'. Byron was also a sporadic vegetarian; but his motives
were vanity: meat, it was thought, gave you a florid complexion; and he was a
paranoiac weight-watcher.

The last weeks in London were spent in a whirl of glamour. *Frankenstein*, published anonymously, was proving a huge success. The Shelleys spent lavishly and socialized incessantly. Peacock was a constant companion. Together they visited the Elgin Marbles, recently deposited in the British Museum, and regularly took a box at the opera. The current rage was Mozart's *Don Giovanni*, premièred in London some months earlier, and Peacock must have guided Shelley into the subtleties of that masterpiece, which they saw at least five times. Shelley also adored the ballet, and his imagination was, not surprisingly, seized by the ethereal ballerina Mademoiselle Milanie, who, in giving the illusion of flying to music, was fulfilling an effect that Shelley had been trying to convey in the medium of words. Claire the sensation-seeker was enraptured by the Apollonicon, £10,000 and 1,900 pipes' worth of organ, on which six people could play simultaneously.

After they had left for Italy, Peacock would remember to worship at the altar to Pan that he and Shelley had consecrated, only half-jokingly, in the woods near Marlow; Hunt would remember Shelley when he visited the opera house: 'We look up to your box almost hoping to see a thin patrician-cosmopolite leaning out upon us, and a sedate-faced young lady bending in a similar direction, with her great tablet of a forehead, and her white shoulders unconscious of a crimson gown.'

The spell of music was cast over Shelley again, in the last months of his life in 1822, through another and even more unearthly summer idyll, this time in a villa on the edge of the waters of the Bay of Lerici. Shelley was quietly in love with the pretty, kind, not very intelligent Jane Williams, the wife of his new friend and sailing-companion Edward Williams. As he had ordered Claire a Broadwood, so he bought Jane a Spanish guitar and dedicated it to her in one of his most delicate lyrics:

> Take
> This slave of Music, for the sake
> Of him who is the slave of thee,
> And teach it all the harmony
> In which thou canst, and only thou
> Make the delighted spirit glow ...

Jane plucked a few chords and sang only popular ballads and melodies in her pleasant mezzo, but for Shelley there was magic in the air—the dazzling light, the evening wind, the summer moon; the earth

appeared another world. 'Jane brings her guitar, and if the past and
the future could be obliterated, the present would content me so well
that I could say with Faust to the passing moment "Remain thou, thou
art so beautiful." '

But the burden of guilt had become more pressing; the past and the
future could not be obliterated. One night Shelley woke screaming
from a nightmare vision of Jane and her husband covered with blood
and shouting, 'Get up, Shelley, the sea is flooding the house & it is all
coming down.' He ran into Mary's room, only to see his *doppelgänger*
leaning over the bed to strangle her.

A few weeks later Shelley went out with Williams in his beloved
boat, baptized by Byron as the *Don Juan*. It went down in a violent
summer squall, and Shelley's body was washed up some days later,
unrecognizable save for a copy of Keats's 'Hyperion' folded back in
his jacket pocket:

> My life is but the life of winds and tides
> No more than winds and tides can I avail...

On the night before the Shelleys had finally left England in 1818
they witnessed an operatically historic occasion—the first performance in London of Rossini's *Il Barbiere di Siviglia*. What they thought
of it is unfortunately not recorded, but they had exposed themselves to
a disease benevolently infecting Europe, spreading the symptoms of
noise, fun, mischief, and uninhibited gaiety through the virus of music
that was as physically intoxicating as the *Marseillaise* or a tarantella.
'Napoleon is dead, but a new conqueror has already shown himself to
the world; and from Moscow to Naples, from London to Vienna, from
Paris to Calcutta, his name is constantly on every tongue,' proclaimed
Stendhal. 'The fame of this hero knows no bounds save those of
civilisation itself.' Calcutta may be an exaggeration: but as far as
Odessa on the Black Sea, the exiled Pushkin wrote of 'the entrancing
Rossini, Europe's spoilt Orpheus ... always the same, always invent-
ive, he pours out melodies—they effervesce, they flow, they burn like
young kisses.' Mary Shelley heard the peasants singing them, 'not
melodiously but very loud', as they worked in the Tuscan fields.
Before public relations agents, before the gramophone, before radio,
before the railway, Rossini had won what for a mere composer was an
unprecedented celebrity, breaking through the barriers of commercial
success in a way that neither Mozart, nor Beethoven, nor Schubert
ever managed.

Gioachino Rossini was born in Pesaro in 1792, the son of the official town-trumpeter and a seamstress who doubled up as a singer during the local opera season. As a child he had sung in church and narrowly escaped the still common fate of talented boy trebles at the time—castration. He studied at the Bologna Conservatory where, at the age of fifteen, he wrote his first opera. But his first two substantial successes as a composer came in 1813 with the heroic opera *Tancredi*, featuring the sensational hit tune '*Di tanti palpiti*', and the comic *L'Italiana in Algeri*, both commissioned in Venice. From 1814 to 1822 he was based in Naples, for where he wrote a string of tragic operas geared to the impressive talents of his future wife, the Spanish singer, Isabella Colbran; for Rome he produced *Il Barbiere di Siviglia* (1816) and *La Cenerentola* (1817). In 1822 he visited Vienna, where performances of his music precipitated what the newspapers compared to 'an idolatrous orgy ... everyone there acted as though bitten by a tarantula ... this is a true epidemic, against which no physician could discover a prophylactic.' In 1824 he spent six months in England, where by royal request he sang a comic duet with George IV, desperately trying to accommodate the King's atrocious bass; wrote a *Lament of the Muses on the Death of Lord Byron* in which he impersonated Apollo in mourning; and grossed, at today's buying power, over £100,000 from personal appearances. At the end of the year he settled in Paris, where he became director of the Théâtre-Italien. By the time he had written his last opera *Guillaume Tell* in 1829, he was ready to opt out of the competition with changing styles and politics. Although he lived on until 1868, winning new fame as a wit ('*Wagner a des belles minutes, mais des mauvaises quarts d'heure*') and a gourmet (*Tournedos Rossini*), he composed little more.

Stendhal's biography of Rossini, written in 1823–4, covers less than half of his life and stops even before his trip to Vienna. It contains at least a hundred downright inaccuracies, some of them deliberate lies, a lot of unverified third-hand anecdotes, and pages of digression and padding; it leaves out matters of significance and dwells on triviality. But it is also an explosion of energy and joy, sparkling with vitality, blazing with perception and intelligence, a ridiculous masterpiece, wonderfully appropriate to the profligate character of Rossini's own genius.

Stendhal wrote it after his forced return from Milan, and at one level it is a nostalgic revisiting of his years in Italy and the delight in Italian ways and values which he would so memorably fictionalize in *La Chartreuse de Parme*. He had first experienced the Italian idea of pleasure in 1800, as a young officer in Napoleon's 'army of liberation'.

In that year he discovered love, in the enthralling shape of Angela Pietragua, and the glory of Italian opera. 'The first time I ever took pleasure in music was at Novara, a few days before the Battle of Marengo,' he recalled.

> I went to the theatre where they were playing *Il Matrimonio Segreto* [by Cimarosa]. The music delighted me like an expression of love. I think no woman I have had ever gave me so sweet a moment, or at so light a price, as the moment I owe to a newly heard musical phrase. The pleasure came to me without my in any way expecting it: it filled my whole soul. [To live] in Italy and hear such music became the cornerstone of all my thinking.

Consigned as he was to the complacence and dullness of post-Napoleonic France, with its inert institutions and mediocrities in every high place, Stendhal felt banished from life itself. In fact, Stendhal's polemic on Rossini's behalf was out of date by the time the book was published: the Parisians had already come round, and Stendhal was only shadow-boxing with the notion that they were too stuck-up to appreciate music so uninhibited and vivacious. But Stendhal was using Italian culture very much as Madame de Staël had used German—a mud pie to throw at the French confidence in their own superiority. To write about Rossini was to write about everything that France lacked— 'the mad passion for gaiety', 'the art of tranquilly enjoying life'; the glitter of the opera house of La Scala, Milan, with its gossip and intrigue, both political and amorous; and perhaps it also helped to keep in mind the beauty of his unforgotten Milanese love Mathilde Dembowski.

Stendhal had no time for the mystical philosophy of music which floated about in German heads. What he understood was opera, whether comic or tragic, in which the singing voice and the melodic line had prominence. Purely instrumental music appealed to him not at all: he wanted music to have a human, not a superhuman, dimension. He believed that a nation's music reflects the temperamental characteristics of its people; he loved Rossini best when he was most simple, spontaneous, and 'Italianate' and deplored the way this his later work seemed to be selling out to Germanic and Beethovenian complexities of harmony and orchestration. He also admired Rossini for ignoring academic rules of composition; 'the feature which distinguishes the *real* master is the sweeping audacity of his design, the brave impatience revealed in his contempt for niggling detail, the grandiose touches which characterize his creative vision'. Thus the biography gleefully relates all the apocryphal anecdotes about Rossini's slapdash methods of composition, the following being typical.

The opera *Mosè in Egitto* suffered from a weak third act: when it came up to be revived,

> Rossini, who was as usual lounging in bed and holding court to a score or so of acquaintances, was interrupted ... by the librettist Tottola, who came rushing into the room, utterly unmindful of the assembled company, and shrieked at the top of his voice, '*Maestro! Maestro! ho salvato l'atto terzo*' [I have saved the third act]—*E che hai fatto?* demanded Rossini, mimicking the curious mixture of burlesque and pedantry which made up the wretched poet's manner: 'My poor friend, what on earth *could* you do? they'll laugh this time, just as they always do.' 'Maestro, I've written a prayer for the Jews just before the passage of the Red Sea,' cried the wretched snivelling hack, hauling from his pocket an immense wad of papers, all docketed like a lawyer's brief, and handing them to Rossini who promptly lay down again in bed to decipher the tangle of hieroglyphic jottings scribbled in the margin of the principal document. While he was reading, the silly little poetaster was circling the room with a nervous smile, shaking hands and whispering over and over again: '*Maestro, è lavoro d'un ora*' [it is the work of an hour]. Rossini glared at him: '*E lavoro d'un ora, he!*' The scribbler, half terrified out of his wits, and more than ever apprehensive of some catastrophic practical joke, tried to make himself inconspicuous, tittered awkwardly, and glanced at Rossini: *Sì, signor, sì, signor maestro.*' 'Very well then,' exclaimed the composer. 'If it only took *you* an hour to write the words, *I* shall manage to write the music in fifteen minutes!' Whereupon he leapt out of bed and, sitting down at a table (still in his nightshirt), dashed off the music for the *Prayer* in eight or ten minutes, without a piano, and undeterred by the conversation of his friends, which continued as loud as ever regardless of his preoccupations, everyone talking away at the top of his voice, as is normal in Italy. 'Here's your music—take it,' he barked at the librettist, who promptly vanished, leaving Rossini to jump back into bed, convulsed with laughter at Tottola's fright.

Naturally, the Prayer proves a huge triumph, and when it was first heard 'people stood up in their boxes and leaned out over the balconies, shouting to crack the vault of heaven: *bello! bello! o che bello!*' What is more, no doubt lying through his teeth, Stendhal claims that a doctor in Naples once told him that he could quote 'more than forty cases of brain-fever or of violent nervous convulsions among young ladies with an over ardent passion for music, brought on exclusively by the "Jews' Prayer" in the third act.'

Apart from showing himself to be a great teller of stories, the taller the better, Stendhal was also plainly a sensitive listener, sharing with Hoffmann (and George Bernard Shaw) the gift which Shelley signally lacks—that of describing the effect of music *precisely*. He can isolate the reasons for Rossini's success, as well as his limitations, in a few pithy sentences which anyone who has heard a Rossini overture can comprehend:

> The most striking quality in Rossini's music is a peculiar *verve*, a certain stirring rapidity which lightens the spirit, banishing all those grave, half-conscious musings conjured up from the very depths of being by the slow, sad strains of Mozart. And close on the heels of this first quality comes a second, a kind of *freshness*, which evokes a smile of pleasure at every bar. As a result, almost any score seems dull and heavy beside one of Rossini's.... In this quite unleisured century of ours, Rossini has one further advantage: *his music demands no concentration* ...
>
> Light, lively, amusing, never wearisome but seldom exalted— Rossini would appear to have been brought into this world for the express purpose of conjuring up visions of ecstatic delight in the commonplace soul of the Average Man.

He knew, in other words, that first and last Rossini was a brilliant entertainer—and why not?

As with any great popular success, from Shakespeare to the Beatles, there were those who resisted. The half-admiring, half-envious Beethoven looked through the score of *Il Barbiere*, and grumbled, 'Rossini would have become a great composer if his teacher had frequently applied some blows *ad posteriora*.' Hoffmann was sceptical; the painter Ingres thought it 'the music of a dishonest man'; while Coleridge was reminded of 'nonsense verses ... which I know to be meant for a Poem because I distinguish the rhymes.' Mary Shelley wrote to Leigh Hunt's wife in 1819 that 'Nothing is heard in Italy now but Rosini [*sic*] & he is no favourite of mine—he has some pretty airs—but they say that when he writes a good thing he goes on copying it ... for ever and ever.' The French composer Berlioz, standing up for purity and nobility, was exasperated by his 'cynicism, his contempt for dramatic expression and good sense, his endless repetition of a single form of cadence, his eternal puerile crescendo and brutal bass drum'. To no avail: Rossini was hummed from the Black Sea to the fields of Tuscany.

Stendhal's biography of Rossini is significant as an instance of the contemporary fascination with the artist—be he painter, poet, or musician—as 'star' personality, a hero for an age that had grown sick of politics and war. Goethe, Byron, Scott, Pushkin, Madame de Staël, were all literally legends in their own lifetimes: even if their creations were not properly appreciated, they were enshrined in myths perpetuated by press gossip, and surrounded by the aura which we associate with the flash camera and the mysteries of 'no comment'.

Of no figure is this more true than a composer-performer whom Stendhal mentions in one of his all-too-riveting footnotes, and who at the time of writing (1824) was still unknown outside his native land:

> The greatest violinist in Italy, and perhaps in all the world, is Paganini, who is still a youngish man, thirty-five years old, with black, piercing eyes and dishevelled hair. This ardent creature did not stumble upon the secrets of his divine art by dint of eight years' dogged perseverance through the Conservatoire; a hasty impulse inspired by loving *too well* (so the legend goes) resulted in long years of imprisonment; and there, solitary and abandoned in a dungeon which might well have had no issue save to the scaffold, he discovered that the only companion who could console him in his fetters was his violin. Gradually he acquired the art of expressing the very whispers of his soul in sound...

Paganini was a virtuoso, the musician-hero who manifestly did things that no one else could do. His admirers were ready to believe anything. A poor illiterate from the backstreets of Genoa, he had not only murdered his mistress, but had made the G string of his violin out of her gut; his strange walk was caused by pacing round his prison cell with a crossbar between his legs. There were reports of the Devil guiding his bowing arm: he must have sold his soul in the Faustian pact. He held his audiences in such thrall that, as Peacock put it in a review of his London début, 'a single piece of wax, dropping from the side of a candle on the stage, had an effect absolutely startling.'

Paganini consistently contradicted such fictions and later tried suing newspapers that printed them, but he could not kill the legend, and at bottom probably did not really want to. Certainly he made no pretence of being an average sort of fellow. He dressed entirely in black and loped on to the stage like some vulture closing in on its prey.

His body was wasting away from a variety of diseases, of which syphilis was certainly one, and at times he wore spectacles with dark-blue lenses to protect eyes that were sunk deep in their sockets. Later the enormous amounts of mercury he had taken for his pox began to rot his jaw and blacken his teeth: with his violin tucked under his chin he appeared to have no mouth. He made sounds on his fiddle that had never been heard before (including, *hélas*, imitations of farmyard animals) and could play faster, higher, lower, louder, softer, darker, lighter than any of his rivals. If a string broke while he was playing, he would carry on without any audible difference; yet he was never heard to rehearse. He was extremely avaricious and on occasion extremely generous, impulsively giving Berlioz, for instance, 20,000 francs after a moving performance of the latter's *Harold en Italie*. Gaming was probably his worst vice: he bought a Paris casino, above which he lived in a sumptuous sound-proofed apartment and from which he descended at midnight to gamble away the hours of darkness, drinking and smoking cigars to assuage the pain from his crumbling jaw. The place became such a notorious den that the government withdrew its licence and a large portion of his fortune was lost.

Yet for all the theatricality, Paganini was no charlatan. He was considered to be inspired by some metaphysical force, but his real achievement was a solid expansion of the limits of technique, giving the string-player a new set of possibilities to play with: after him, the violin could never sound the same again. He was also, in other ways, the last of his line. The travelling virtuoso was an old phenomenon, older even than the child Mozart; Hoffmann, nearly twenty years before Paganini had left Italy, wrote a *Kreisleriana* sketch about the adulation enjoyed by Milo the Ape, whose hairy hand could span two octaves of the piano and whose years swinging from tree to tree in the jungle made his fingers astonishingly supple. Paganini was like the last magnificent explosion of a firework display: the light of a new musical age was embodied in the Hungarian pianist-composer Franz Liszt who while still a child prodigy in the Vienna of the early 1820s had been blessed with a kiss on the brow from Beethoven. 'Go,' he had said, 'you are one of the fortunate ones; for you will give joy and happiness to many other people! There can be nothing better or finer!'

Thus Liszt lived with something that Paganini lacked—a soul and a mission to sacrifice himself to Art. He would provide what Goethe felt was lacking in Paganini—'a base to this pillar of flame and cloud'.

Liszt's music-making would serve humanity, not Mammon. It would exalt beauty and brotherhood. What, one wonders, would Hoffmann and Shelley have felt at the infinite vistas and dissolving harmonies, the boneless, muscleless reaching-out and -up of Liszt's mighty hot magic?

Chapter 5

'An Alabaster Vase Lighted up Within'

The first letter is long and not very coherent, at times nervous, at times ludicrously melodramatic. 'An utter stranger takes the liberty of addressing you,' it begins,

> I tremble with fear at the fate of this letter. I cannot blame if it shall be received by you as an impudent misfortune. There are cases where virtue may stoop to assume the guise of folly; it is for the piercing eye of genius to discover her disguise, do you then give me credit for something better than this letter may seem to portend. Hope flying on forward wings beckons me to follow her & rather than resign this cherished creature, I jump through at the peril of my Life...
>
> If a woman whose reputation has yet remained unstained, if without guardian or husband to control she should throw herself upon your mercy, if with a beating heart she should confess the love she has borne you many years, if she should secure to you secresy and safety, if she should return your kindness with fond affection & unbounded devotion could you betray her or would you be silent as the grave?
>
> I am not given to many words. Either you will or you will not. Do not decide hastily, & yet I must entreat your answer without delay, not only because I hate to be tortured by suspense, but because my departure a short way out of town is unavoidable & I would know your reply ere I go. Address me, as E. Trefusis, 21 Noley Place Mary Le Bonne.

Byron had received hundreds of such unsolicited letters in the previous four years of his fame. They came from prostitutes proposing assignations in the Park, from provincial love-sick spinsters fantasizing on his poetry, from chorus girls and the married nobility. In his vanity, he ignored almost all of them but troubled to keep the scalps in a trunk, labelled 'Anonymous Effusions', which survives to this day in the office of his publisher John Murray. Miss Baldry of Pimlico: 'I adore you'; Miss MacDonald of Clifton: 'Nothing could give me more joy on earth than a lock of your hair'; poor discarded Susan Boyce of

Drury Lane, a post-marital amusement: 'I remember you once said of women that the more loving they were the more *troublesome*'; the lonely Henrietta d'Ussières who put agony advertisements in *The Courier* and bombarded him with requests to be received as his 'sister'. Others warned him of the damnation hereafter, or asked for literary advice—all these on top of a stream of letters of screaming drunken vindictiveness from that most tedious of Regency figures Lady Caroline Lamb, comparing him in his treatment of her to 'Mefistocles', Richard III, Machiavelli.

The rhetorical strategies of 'E. Trefusis' were transparent and typical, but they had the slight advantage, in March 1816, of catching Byron at a delicate moment. In the middle of separating from his wife Annabella, a torturing process in which pleading had turned sourly into recrimination and now looked like precipitating a scandal that could have cost a good deal more than a reputation in high society, Byron's emotions were rawly sensitive. He was in need of the comfort of being admired, even though he genuinely disliked being openly pursued by women.

However, he did not reply to the 'E. Trefusis' letter and may not even have registered the similarity in the handwriting on a very different style of letter that appeared a few days later, this time signed G. C. B. (his own initials were G. G. B.) and peremptorily demanding an urgent private audience. Did he think, as his biographer Doris Langley Moore has suggested, that the author might have some evidence relating to his wife and their separation? In any case, the G. C. B. he admitted into his presence was none other than the plump, pretty, and brash seventeen-year-old Claire Clairemont, Mary Godwin's stepsister, currently domiciled with, and subsidized by Shelley.

Claire was not just victim of a schoolgirl crush: her motive in aiming so high must have involved an unconscious desire to get one up on Mary—if there was a silent battle going on over Shelley, Claire did not look like winning it; and it may also have contained a genuine desire for a patron who could have launched her into an independent career. Might he, she wondered initially, use his influence at Drury Lane, where he was a member of the Committee of Management, to get her on the stage? 'Are the difficulties of manner and figure to be overcome?' she solicited. 'Is it absolutely necessary to go through the intolerable and disgusting drudgery of provincial theatres before commencing on the boards of the metropolis?' She told him all about her Godwinian background and the Shelley *ménage*—at which one can imagine his Lordship raising an eyebrow in interest. Then she asked him to have a look at 'The Ideot', the novel she had begun on the way back from Switzerland with its Shelleyan heroine, defying all moral convention but 'full of noble affections and sympathies'.

She showed off ruthlessly, writing him long garbled letters analysing her own psychology and coyly cajoling him to take more interest in her—'It is not the sparkling cup which should tempt you,' she wrote, 'but the silent & capacious bowl.' She told him that she loved him: he told her it was 'a fancy'. 'Do what you will, or go where you will, refuse to see me & behave unkindly,' she retorted, 'I shall never forget you.' She paid visits at any hour of the day, and then wrote reproachfully that she had been kept waiting or told that he was out of town; once she even took Mary along to meet him in the Green Room at Drury Lane, presenting him as her smart new friend: Mary was suitably impressed, although quite unaware of what Claire was playing at. Her campaign was swift, daily, and relentless.

To say, as many biographers do, that Claire was Byron's mistress is misleading, even as a euphemism. She simply pushed a man, preoccupied by the bewildering break-up of his marriage and about to leave the country, along the line of least resistance. He never answered her letters, offered her affection, or sponsored her professional aspirations. At most he regarded her emotional performance with contemptuous amusement; but he did take her up on her offer of sex. 'I never loved nor pretended to love her,' he wrote later, 'but a man is a man—& if a girl of eighteen comes prancing to you at all hours—there is but one way ...' This was not dishonesty on Byron's part: all the evidence points to Claire making every advance. 'On Thursday evening we may go out of town together by some stage or mail about the distance of 10 or 12 miles,' she wrote. 'There we shall be free & unknown; we can return early the following morning. I have arranged everything here so that the slightest suspicion may not be excited ... Will you admit me for two moments to settle with you *where*? Indeed I will not stay an instant after you tell me to go.' Byron apparently consented to all this. Her teenage lack of self-respect made her a useful valve through which to discharge some of his present tension, and together they had what he would later describe as 'a good deal' of 'the carnal connection'. Had it not been for a disastrous string of consequences, that phrase would have just about summed up the situation.

Byron left London on 23 April, as soon as his separation papers came through and one short step ahead of the bailiffs. He did not, could not, forbid Claire to follow him: or rather she succeeded in wringing out of him the address of his destination in Geneva. Accompanied by Mary and Shelley (who had that same day received a court judgement over his inheritance that left him still reliant on the problematic charity of his father), she raced ahead of him to Switzerland and put up at a hotel near his villa on the shores of the lake to await his arrival. Her tactics changed. Aware that their relationship would not develop into anything permanent, she proposed a Sentimental friendship—'I would ten times rather be your male companion than your mistress'—but was undeterred even by the realization that 'were I to float by your window drowned all you would say would be "Ah *voilà*".' What she got, of course, was more of the same: sex, and indifference bordering on hostility.

Mary and Shelley, however, went down a good deal better. Byron needed friends, new friends, and Shelley in particular appealed to him as a gentleman, if not a nobleman, with considerable knowledge of poetry and ambitions of his own in that line. He is unlikely to have remembered that in 1813 Shelley had sent him a copy of *Queen Mab* and a note suggesting they might meet.

The relationship which evolved was unequal, and on Shelley's part uneasy. Byron was, after all, an extraordinary celebrity, while Shelley was a comparative nobody. There were times when Shelley did not like what he saw of Byron's high-handedness at all, and Leigh Hunt interestingly points out in his memoir of the two men that although they passed for 'good friends', Shelley—not otherwise noted for impeccable tact—was always studiously careful to address Byron as 'my lord'. One had to be careful: Byron is often loosely compared to rock or movie stars as a figure of international glamour under constant pressure from the attentions of press and public, but he perhaps most resembles them in his personality disorders—paranoiac irritability, an insistence on his status, an addiction to compliment, unthinking self-centredness ('At no time,' wrote one of his first biographers, 'could it be said that Lord Byron was one of those men who interest themselves in the concerns of others'). His virtues—loyalty to old friends and a detestation of cant and pretension among the noblest— became flattened by the poisons of success. 'He is a slave to the vilest and most vulgar prejudices,' confided Shelley to Peacock; and he found Byron's lack of true reverence for the Good and Beautiful appalling. Byron's armour was not a positive idealism, but a scepticism which nobody and nothing escaped, and which bitter experience only nurtured.

But *de haut en bas* Byron warmed to Shelley and Mary, to the point at which he managed to put up with their inevitable appendage, Claire. The two men went off alone together on two lake trips, one of four days and one of eight, talking about Wordsworth's new poem *The Excursion* and visiting the sites and sights associated with Rousseau. Their boat nearly went down in a gale, at the place where the heroine of *La Nouvelle Héloïse* had suffered a similar accident; Shelley calmly announced that he could not swim, and begged Byron not to trouble himself with life-saving.

Back at the villa there was late-night discussion and more of the ghost talk for which Shelley, come the witching hour, had such a fatal attraction: Mary, as a result, had the nightmare which formulated the theme for her first novel *Frankenstein*. The daylight crisis was that Claire was now pregnant by Byron. It was not a matter that he wished to discuss with anyone except Shelley, who managed to negotiate terms—if Claire kept her mouth shut and returned home for the birth, Byron would acknowledge the child and see to its respectable upbringing.

It was not, however, a happy compromise, mainly because Claire was still unwilling to confront the simple but appalling fact that Byron could not tolerate the sight, let alone the sound of her. Back in England, she continued to write him letters so tactless and gauche as to make one's toes curl up with embarrassment. She began with a jaunty tone of mock-horror on the subject of *Glenarvon*, Lady Caroline Lamb's sensational and newly published fictional exposé of her affair with him—'You wretched creature to go about seducing and stabbing and rebelling ... I really am ashamed to hold communion with you'—blithely ignorant that Byron knew nothing about the novel as yet and would only be furious when he did. Then she turned to wheedling intimacies—'If you will write me a little letter to say how you are, how all you love are, and above all if you will say you sometimes think of me without anger and that you will love and take care of the child, I shall be as happy as possible'—before collapsing into imprecations which barely conceal the pain and humiliation she was feeling—'My dearest darling ... I would do anything, suffer any pain or degradation so I might be so very happy as to receive a letter from you ... nothing makes me so angry as when M. & S. [Mary and Shelley] tell me not to expect to hear from you. How proud I should be of a letter to disappoint their impertinent conjectures ...' But she had already thrown her cards away and Byron would have had no compunction about tossing her every communication aside unread: certainly nothing she tried could provoke a response. 'Never was there a collection of love letters so totally without evidence of mutuality,' concludes Doris Langley Moore.

Allegra, the child of this impasse, became Claire's last tragic weapon, used as both shield and spear in the battle to win points off Byron's effortless male superiority. The fresh agony was the passionate love she felt for her baby, on whom she lavished all her most desperate affections. The letters become genuinely poignant:

> She is all my treasure—the little creature occupies all my thoughts, all my time & my feelings. When I hold her in my arms I think to myself—there is nothing else in the world that is of you or belongs to you—you are truly a stranger to every one else: without this little being you would hold no relation with any single human being . . .
>
> We sleep together and if you knew the extreme happiness I feel when she nestles closer to me, when in listening to our regular breathing together I could tear my flesh in twenty thousand different directions to ensure her good and when I fear for her residing with you it is not the dread I have to commence the long series of painful anxiety I know I shall have to endure it is lest I should behold her sickly and wasted with improper management lest I should live to hear that *you* neglected her. . . .

This confusion of feeling would never be resolved. Claire was persuaded that, illegitimate as she was, Allegra stood a better chance of a decent upbringing under Byron in Italy—yet her own experience of him only made her distrust him. Byron wanted a clear-cut situation which gave Claire no room to interfere in his life: he took a conventional view of the responsibilities of a 'seducer', and paid for Allegra to be farmed out, first to approved guardians, then to a boarding school convent. Claire was allowed access, but it cannot be said that he showed much sympathy for the pull of motherhood, and as her ambivalence towards him turned into pure vindictive hatred, a war of attrition ensued.

Claire let off steam in her journals by composing some Byronic caricatures:

> . . . another to be called Lord Byron's receipt for writing pathetic poetry. He sitting drinking spirits, playing with his white mustachios. His mistress, the Fornara opposite him Drinking coffee. Fumes coming from her mouth, over which is written garlich; these curling direct themselves towards his English footman who is just

then entering the room & he is knocked backward—Lord B. is writing he says, Inprimis to be a great pathetic poet. 1st Prepare a small colony, then dispatch the mother by worrying and cruelty to her grave afterwards to neglect & ill treat the children—to have as many & as dirty mistresses as can be found; ... from their embraces to catch horrible diseases ... & to remember particularly to rail against learned women.

His death. He dead extended on his bed, covered all but his breast, which many wigged doctors are cutting open to find out ... What was the extraordinary disease of which this great man died—His heart laid bare, they find an immense capital I grown on its surface—and which had begun to pierce the breast. One says. A new disease. Another I never had a case of this kind before. A third What medicines would have been proper the fourth holding up his finger A desert island.

Soon she decided that she wanted her daughter back—there was even a crazy plan to kidnap her from the convent by means of a forged letter—and Shelley was again forced into the uneasy role of intermediary. His loyalties may have been with Claire, but he was wary of making an enemy of Byron, and he got nowhere. Byron was not prepared to yield: for one thing, if 'Madame Clare' was 'a damned bitch', he also disapproved of some of the radical ideas current in the Shelley household. 'The child shall not quit me again to perish of starvation, and green fruit, or be taught to believe there is no Deity,' he thundered. 'The girl shall be a Christian and a married woman.' The child did perish, but of typhus, in 1822, at the age of five. Byron sent Claire, via Shelley, a lock of Allegra's hair and a message of condolence: but the funeral arrangements were bungled, and Byron refused to pay an extortionate bill for embalming.

Claire never married, became a governess, and kept her loathing of Byron's memory alive until her death in 1879.* She never mentioned Allegra to strangers and erased all mention of her from her journals: a governess could not afford such a sensational indiscretion. Only Shelley comes out of this story with much credit. His handling of two explosive and self-centred people, both of whom he was in a delicate relation to, shows considerable diplomacy and the best of

* The attempt of a Boston sea captain to trick the elderly Claire out of her stash of letters from Shelley and, apparently, Byron inspired Henry James to his short story 'The Aspern Papers'. The confining of the illegitimate Pansy to an Italian convent, in *The Portrait of a Lady*, bears further witness to James's fascination with this episode.

intentions—in stark contrast to the way he had antagonized his father, the Westbrooks, and Elizabeth Hitchener.

Looked at more coldly, it seems an incident very much of its time and the emotions it nurtured. The 1970s were labelled the 'me-decade' by the pundits; it is a phrase one might also apply to the Regency, that era which takes its name from the Regency of the future George IV during his father's final incapacitating madness, 1811–20. Nowadays it is synonymous with a style of affected 'elegance': Beau Brummell, the Brighton Pavilion, striped wallpaper and stucco. There was certainly a spirit of unabashed extravagance about, as embodied in the ball for the Bourbon princes that the Prince Regent gave in 1811 in his new palace of Carlton House, costing £120,000 and featuring a 200-foot banqueting table, at the centre of which stood an elaborately cascading fountain made of solid silver. (The young Shelley was said to have run off copies of a satirical poem on the occasion and tossed them into the carriages of departing guests.)

But elegance and extravagance were just the plaster for a society in which the cracks were becoming inescapably visible. The fun and frivolity of the faces of the upper and middle classes were the mask for fear—not so much of Napoleon, whose star was decisively falling, as of domestic rumblings, akin to those of 1794–5, among peasants and workers noisily banding together as an autonomous political force. Although the largest and most influential of the Protestant sects, Methodism, preached submission to one's lot in life and concentration on the possibility of salvation in the after-life, it also incidentally taught self-help and organization—'the manner in which Methodism has familiarized the lower classes to the work of combining in associations, making rules for their own governance, raising funds, and communicating from one part of the kingdom to another,' wrote the now deeply conservative Southey, 'may be reckoned among the incidental evils which have resulted from it.' Coleridge was present at the public execution of the lunatic assassin of the Prime Minister Spencer Perceval, when he heard an ominously prophetic voice shout from the crowd, 'This is only the beginning.' And throughout the decade the momentum gathered. From the Luddite machine-breaking in 1811 to the discovery of the Cato Street conspiracy in 1820, it seemed that some apocalyptic end was only moments away. In 1814, for instance, the ageing West Country prophetess Joanna Southcott announced that she miraculously bore in her womb the Son of God, who would be called Shiloh (a name that Byron teasingly called Shelley on occasion): the Second Coming was at hand. When she died and the pregnancy turned out to be hysterical, the panic only increased. As Coleridge reflected, it was 'an age of *anxiety* from the crown to the hovel, from the cradle to the coffin; all is an anxious straining to maintain life, or appearances—*to rise*, as the only condition of not falling'.

Such anxiety, such straining to maintain appearances were reasons for the volatility of taste and fashion that Peacock's Mrs Pinmoney catalogues ('a taste for acting Hamlet—a taste for philosophical lectures . . . a taste for the tender—a taste for the grim'). In a time of social mobility, when class barriers became more fluid and buying-power counted for more than rank, individuals judged each other by their style rather than their moral worth. The Regency delighted in snobbishness; it popularized the notion of 'exclusive' clubs. There was a general search for new external ways of defining identity: roles, costumes, niches. 'Everybody must now "move in a circle," ' wrote Jane Austen, 'to the prevalence of which rotatory motion, is perhaps to be attributed the Giddiness & False steps of many.'

One of the most prominent of these new social groupings was the Dandies, men whose only commitment was their own pleasure and physical perfection. They despised the conventions of work, family, the aristocracy (Beau Brummell notoriously managed to 'cut' the Prince Regent and was said once to have asked him offhand to ring the bell for a servant), and grubbing for money. They gambled passionate-ly, but not so much to win as to show that they did not care—in the same way that they duelled and imbibed large amounts of drink. Self-assurance was their cardinal virtue: in their impeccable dress, laconic manner, and choice of friends, they defiantly did things their own way. As Mrs Catherine Gore put it in her novel *Cecil*, a dandy was 'a nobody who had made himself a somebody'.

For the middle classes, the keyword was 'improvement', in the sense of improving one's material resources, specifically that of one's property. There were real social improvements too, as in the new roads built by pioneering civil engineers like Telford and MacAdam which allowed steady travel at an astonishing ten miles an hour! There were also some grand feats of speculative town planning, most notably Nash's Regent's Park in London, money for which was put up by the Prince Regent himself. It is significant however that it was the 'rural' landscaping and *appearance* of the thing that made its effect so impressive. Behind the sweep of the gleaming terraces, the bricks-and-mortar was often shoddily put together, the design poor in detail and practicalities. Nevertheless, in a survey called *Metropolitan*

Improvements, published in 1827, the author James Elmes announces that, 'Augustus made it one of his proudest boasts that he found Rome of brick, and left it of marble. The reign and regency of George the Fourth have scarcely done less ... the absence of a few months from London produces revolutions in sites, and alterations in appearances, that are almost miraculous.'

In interior decoration, 'improvement' took the form of a loosening-up. There was more informality and intimacy, an easier indulgence of leisure and comfort. Conservatories and french windows let in more light and brought garden nearer to house. The steady glow of gaslight was another innovation. Padded sofas and chaises-longues supplanted the old high-backed cane chairs; curtains replaced shutters and carpets covered bare polished floors. Panelled walls were papered, and books formerly kept under lock and key in the master's library were now put on alcoves and shelves in the drawing-room. Side-tables, knick-knacks, and bowls of cut flowers became popular elements of prettification. Smaller houses, of the cottage or villa variety, were even more fashionable than imposing mansions. 'The true impressions of cheerfulness, elegance and refinement,' applauded a contemporary architect, 'are so well understood and so happily united in our modern domestic dwellings that I hesitate not to say we are rapidly advancing to a state of perfection.'

Alongside this relaxation came a much laxer attitude to social intercourse, less insistence on ritual and precedence, with less sexual segregation. The old tradition of the family circle, which required its members to sit for whole evenings in a ring in order to communicate, faded from custom, and it was no longer considered grossly impertinent to engage in private conversation when others were present in the room. Life was thus made superficially a lot more entertaining, for middle-class women in particular, liberated from wigs and stiffened brocades and literally allowed to 'loosen up' in simple but sophisticated clothes made from light cottons and muslins, worn without constricting underwear.

But virtue was not only on the side of the modern, as that most precise analyst of Regency society Jane Austen reveals. From a profoundly intelligent conservative viewpoint, her novels show the dangers of too ready an acceptance of change, ease, and pleasure, reasserting the value of propriety and settled responsibility, through the complex prism of her subversive wit and the true artist's ambivalence about her own moral commitments.

Jane Austen's judgements, in other words, are never simple: for example, the fine old country houses of Kellynch Hall (in *Persuasion*) and Mansfield Park, which should provide a harmonious frame of function and status for the benefit of those who inhabit them, are ruled by inadequate father-figures who fail to command cohesive respect. Sir Walter Elliot is simply vain and trivial; Sir Thomas Bertram is too inert and insensitive to do anything except maintain the shell of the family circle. But Jane Austen looks at the improvements of the younger generation with equal scepticism. The word itself should not be taken at face value: an 'improvement' may be no such thing. One of the improvements instituted by the Rushworth family at Sotherton (in *Mansfield Park*) is to drop the 'fine' custom of assembling the household every morning for prayers. Mary and Charles Musgrove in *Persuasion* have 'modern minds and manners', their house is furnished in Regency chic, and the whole family is frank and friendly; but the heroine Anne Elliot decides that she would rather stay loyal to her more stiff-necked 'elegance' and seriousness. Fresh from the London *beau monde*, Henry and Mary Crawford visit Mansfield Park corroded by the cynicism of Regency values and manners. Mary's relaxation of spirit has allowed her to be happy in the Dandies' playground, where Harriette Wilson was the star among courtesans (her memoirs would net her a cool instant £10,000) and where the genteel minuet and quadrille had given way to the indelicate proximities of the waist-clutching German waltz. Gossiping about her elders, laughing at breaches of decorum, shrugging off her brother's elopement, Mary is the new woman incarnate: uninhibited, restless, generous, again frank and friendly—but in the eyes of Jane Austen and her heroine Fanny, fatally unschooled in moral discipline.

The appetite for novelty bred another phenomenon—boredom. It was in 1812, in the *Edinburgh Review*, that the first recorded instance of the idea of a person being 'a bore' occurs; and in *Don Juan* Byron writes of the 'two mighty tribes' of Regency England, 'the Bores and the Bored'. Boredom had to be countered with sensation, movement, change for its own sake. In *Sanditon*, a fragment of a novel left unfinished at her death, Jane Austen explores the comedy in this hunger for novelty: Sanditon is 'a young and rising bathing place' on the South Coast, attempting to cash in on the vogue for the seaside stimulated by the Prince Regent's patronage of Brighton, but proving unsuccessful at attracting tourists and holidaymakers, despite the public relations efforts of Mr Parker, one of the major investors in the development of the town. Health is the chief local topic of conversation (Jane Austen was herself very ill when she wrote *Sanditon*) and most of the inhabitants and visitors are keenly preoccupied with the latest fads. 'The Sea air & Sea Bathing together were nearly infallible, one or the other of them being a match for every Disorder of the Stomach, the Lungs or the Blood' Mr Parker is reported to think. 'They were anti-spasmodic, anti-pulmonary, anti-sceptic, anti-bilious & anti-rheumatic. Nobody could catch cold by the Sea, Nobody wanted Appetite by the Sea, Nobody wanted Spirits, Nobody wanted Strength ... If the Sea breeze failed, the Sea-Bath was the certain corrective;—& where Bathing disagreed, the Sea Breeze alone was evidently designed by Nature for the cure.' Mr Parker's enthusiasm is set against the 'very quiet, settled course of life' of the Heywood family, whose daughter Charlotte provides the rational eye through which the silliness of Sanditon's innovations is observed.

Improvement for some might also mean expropriation for others, new space for the rich created out of old space for the poor: perhaps ten thousand wretched crofters in the north of Scotland were summarily and forcibly evicted to make way for large 'efficient' sheep farms. William Cobbett, first of a long proud line of free-wheeling campaigning journalists, wrote furiously on behalf of those who had not the resources to defend themselves and their few rights. Profits for the few, unemployment for the many: in 1814 the owner of *The Times* installed two steam-engines to power his presses, quadrupling his print-run and putting most of his printers out of work; in the north, workers in the textile industries smashed up the new machines which threatened their livelihoods by trampling over old and solid working customs. These men, sometimes known as the Luddites, make up another new social grouping of the Regency, their hands as muddied and bloodied as the Dandies' were white and scented. Their own brand of terrorism against property was answered by the full weight of state revenge and the bayonets and sabres of the military. When a Bill proposing execution for 'frame breaking' was put to the House of Lords in February 1812, Byron himself made a magnificent speech pointing out that the deplorable violence had arisen from circumstances of the most unparalleled distress...

You call these men a mob, desperate, dangerous, and ignorant ...
But even a mob may be better reduced to reason by a mixture of conciliation and firmness, than by additional irritation and redoubled penalties. Are we aware of our obligations to a mob? It is the mob that labour in your fields and serve in your houses,—that man

your navy, and recruit your army, ... You may call the people a mob; but do not forget that a mob too often speaks the sentiments of the people ...

This deeply felt plea was made specifically on behalf of the stocking weavers of Byron's own county of Nottinghamshire, where a thousand-odd frames and tons of shoddy mass-produced goods had been destroyed in less than a year. 'Surely, my Lord,' wrote Byron to Lord Holland, a leader of the Whig Party to which he was loosely aligned, 'we must not allow mankind to be sacrificed to improvements in mechanism. The maintenance and well-doing of the industrious poor is an object of greater consequence to the community than the enrichment of a few monopolists by any improvement in the implements of trade, which deprives the workman of his bread ...' With unexpected timidity he adds a PS: 'I am a little apprehensive that your Lordship will think me too lenient towards these men, and half a *frame-breaker myself.*'

The Bill was passed, however, and more troops were barracked in Nottingham. A small wages rise was conceded, but its benefits were cancelled by rocketing food prices, the result of bad harvests and blockades on trade with Napoleon and his allies. May 1812 was a crucial month: the Prime Minister's assassination was followed by riots. A series of anonymous letters was sent to the Prince Regent from Yorkshire, where notices were chalked on doors offering a hundred guineas for his head. 'Provisions cheaper,' the Prince was commanded, '*Bread or Blood*'. For those with time for lighter reading, *Childe Harold's Pilgrimage* had just been published...

Byron never knew his father 'Mad Jack', a soldier, rake, and wastrel who died in 1791. Catherine Gordon was his second wife, a member of one of the most cantankerous Scottish clans and a woman of blunt and fractious temper, which the reduced circumstances in which her husband left her only exacerbated. George Gordon Byron was born in 1788, her only child—something which he later thought significant: '... an odd circumstance.—My *daughter*—my *wife*—my *half sister*—my *mother*—my sister's *mother*—my natural daughter—and myself are or were all *only* children ... [it] looks like fatality almost.—But the fiercest Animals have the rarest number in their litters.'

There were plenty of other reasons for him to have been an unhappy child. His mother's affections were violent and smothering, and their relationship was always an unhealthily intense one. He also had the muddling experience of being sexually initiated aged nine by his nurse May Gray, who was simultaneously giving him hellfire and damnation Bible lessons. His lameness, too, was like the brand of Cain: from his earliest youth, that famous deformed right foot was prodded, pulled about, encased in iron, stared and laughed at, causing him every sort of pain and embarrassment.*

At the age of five, an unexpected death left him heir to the estates and title of his great-uncle, the Fifth Baron Byron; and at ten he and his mother left Scotland to enter upon his inheritance of the shambolic and debt-encumbered Newstead Abbey in Nottinghamshire. By any standards it was a disturbing start to life, in comparison to which Shelley's seems doubly idyllic, full of love, security, fun, companionship and space to run about. In Scotland they would remember 'a wee crockit deevil', an 'ill-deedie laddie' who 'wad take nae telling': there was certainly plenty for him to kick against.

But by the time he arrived at Trinity College, Cambridge in 1805, he had constructed a patina, if not a shell, that allowed him to appear as pretty much the typical young blade of his class and day. He ran up further debts in the course of keeping three horses, two menservants, a tame bear and a carriage; was energetic about his leisure and lazy about learning. He left the university without a degree, flirted with the dandy set and their amusements, wrote bad sentimental and better satirical verse, railing in a tired way against the unsatisfactoriness of the world laid out before him. By this stage of his life, Shelley had developed a much more dangerous and intellectually challenging edge.

It was in 1809, at the appropriate age of twenty-one, that the Byron mythology germinated. In that year he took his seat in the House of Lords and published a poem 'English Bards and Scotch Reviewers' which cocked a snook at the entire literary establishment. But even more striking was that at the point of winning himself a name in the metropolis, he cut and ran. In July 1809 he set out round the Mediterranean, visiting in the course of just over two years Portugal, Spain, Greece, and the Levant. This was not a normal Grand Tour: any sort of continental travel had become unusual during the Napoleonic Wars, despite Britannia's ruling of the waves. It was an adventure, yes, but one with motives of mysterious urgency behind it;

* Its only beneficial side-effect was his prowess as a swimmer, which must have developed as part of a programme of therapy. Swimming was not yet a common sport, least of all among the upper classes: in their relative abilities, Byron was very much the exception, Shelley the rule.

motives which could lead Byron to write from Albania, 'I will never revisit England if I can avoid it'; motives to which we shall return.

But Byron did come back to England and, like so many before and since, wrote a travel book based on his experiences as a long-term tourist in some relatively unknown and colourful terrain. The first two cantos of *Childe Harold's Pilgrimage* were published in the spring of 1812, lightly veiled as fiction and whipped up into verse. The poem was a tremendous success, selling as many as a thousand copies a day; but even more triumphant was the personality of the poet behind it. Witness the emphasis in a letter of the Duchess of Devonshire: 'The subject of conversation, of curiosity, of enthusiasm almost, one might say, of the moment is not Spain or Portugal [scene of Wellington's campaign], Warriors or Patriots, but Lord Byron ... [*Childe Harold*] is on every table, and himself courted, visited, flattered and praised whenever he appears. He has a pale, sickly, but handsome countenance, a bad figure, animated and amusing conversation, and, in short, he is really the only topic ...'

Childe Harold has worn badly. We have lost the habit of reading poetry fast and aloud, which is how this poem was meant to be consumed: analysed closely and read privately it comes across as shallow and tawdry. The medievalisms with which it all begins— 'Whilome in Albion's isle there dwelt a youth ... Childe Harold was he hight'—are on the level of 'in days of old, when knights were bold' and soon peter out; just as the Preface's statement that the poem's theme will be how the 'early perversion of mind and morals leads to satiety of past pleasures and disappointments in new ones' is mere window-dressing. Scratch the surface now and one can detect Byron with a smirk on the other side of his face. He is tossing off verses with the insouciance of an aristocrat; to put in more effort would be bourgeois, beneath his dignity. The whole business is child's play, like a winning streak at the roulette table.

What made *Childe Harold* was not poetic originality, but the first of Byron's many brilliant feats of self-dramatization. In presenting a moody young man (called 'Birun' in the first sketches), sated with pleasures and sick at heart, leaving a mossy old stately home to travel from Portugal to Constantinople, observing politics, geography, and customs, but unable to make real human contact, he could hardly complain when his readers persistently identified the poet with his protagonist. Byron's insistence that he was *not* 'the Childe' only fuelled speculation, as it is so often unclear in the poem which voice the speaker or narrator represents. Just who, everyone wanted to know, was this lonely and antagonized youth whom 'no one loved', this aimless wanderer so badly in need of cheering up?

> Fain would he have joined the dance, the song;
> But who may smile that sinks beneath his fate?
> Nought that he saw his sadness could abate ...

Ironically, Byron had made a thoroughly commercial calculation, in much the same way as those poets he had satirized a few years earlier in 'English Bards and Scotch Reviewers':

> ... when the sons of song descend to trade
> Their bays are sear, their former laurels fade,
> Let such forego the poet's sacred name,
> Who rack their brains for lucre, not for fame:
> Still for stern Mammon may they toil in vain
> And sadly gaze on gold they cannot gain! ...
> For this we spurn Apollo's venal son,
> And bid a long 'good night to Marmion'.

It all comes to look a bit rich: *Marmion*, the sensation of the 1808 publishing season, is one of *Childe Harold*'s most important precursors, on which Byron consciously built his own writing style and structures. Its author was Walter Scott, until *Childe Harold* by far Britain's most popular poet; it was set in sixteenth-century Scotland; and Marmion himself is an out-and-out villain straight out of melodrama, without any of Childe Harold's moping introversion. Nevertheless it was here that Byron found the scale, the swift and broad story-telling, and the trick of breaking it up with interludes of balladry and song, that he put into *Childe Harold*. There was a political dimension too, in the way that Byron—like Scott in his *Vision of Don Roderick* (1811), and many others—exploited the popular sympathy for the freedom-fighters of Spain and Portugal and patriotic concern for the progress of Wellington's campaign there. In all, *Childe Harold's Pilgrimage* was a brilliant capitalization on the literary tastes of the Regency and the large 'leisure reading' market which had opened up for action-packed and exotically set adventure stories in verse. Byron had given the genre a new atmosphere and a new sort of hero; like all overnight successes, he now had to beware of repeating himself. Whatever followed the Childe, it should not be anti-climax.

Where to next? Madame de Staël was in London, waiting anxiously in the limbo between Napoleon's downfall and defeat. She shared the attentions of the town with Byron, who at first found her intellectual broadcasts infuriating: 'A pen behind her ear and a mouth full of ink,' he complained, 'she declaimed to you instead of conversing with you ... never pausing except to take breath ... her society is over-whelming—an avalanche that buries one in glittering nonsense—all show and sophistry ... frightful as a precipice.' Later the exasperation became mixed with a good deal of fondness, and her expertise in the psychology of love was to prove useful when it came to the fall-out of his marriage; but the best advice she gave him came in the form of a hunch about where he ought to concentrate his subject-matter. 'Stick to the East;—the oracle, Staël, told me it was the only poetical policy. The North, South, and West, have all been exhausted; but from the East, we have nothing but Southey's unsaleables ... the public are orientalising.' The author of *De l'Allemagne* could be trusted on such topics.

'Southey's unsaleables' were his vast epic poems, like *Thalaba* (1801) and *The Curse of Kehama* (1810), full of esoteric lore about Eastern religion and customs: they were too long, too complicated, too boring. Byron seized his chance to mine an untapped vein, stripping away the ore and polishing up the gold. In *The Giaour, The Bride of Abydos, The Corsair, Lara,* and *The Siege of Corinth* (1813–16), he gave the public straightforward mystery-romance-and-adventure poems which could easily be read aloud over a couple of evenings, setting them in the more familiar Middle East and featuring a series of swashbuckling love-struck heroes, handy with the scimitar, whose direct descendants are found in the silent films of Rudolph Valentino. Madame de Staël proved right. The sales were astounding (*The Corsair* sold 10,000 copies on publication day, 25,000 within a month) and imitators followed thick and fast. Scott gave up competing in poetry altogether and turned to novel-writing. Byron's friend Thomas Moore went one stage further, producing in *Lalla Rookh* (1817) a compendium of four Eastern poems, linked like the *Thousand and One Nights* by a story in prose. The antique collector and interior designer Thomas Hope wrote a blockbuster novel *Anastasius* (1818) that Byron said made him weep, because he had not written it himself: Hope simply added up all the early Byronic clichés and multiplied them by two.* Shelley used the Eastern colours too, in *Alastor* (1816) and *The Revolt of Islam* (1818), but he could not dent a glutted market.

Byron's 'poetical policy' went on readily meeting, or anticipating,

---

* 'Almost everyone with whom Anastasius comes into contact dies within a matter of weeks, including his three wives, two mistresses, two illegitimate sons, his parents, and his good Christian friend,' writes David Watkin in his study of Hope's work.

public demand. In the first summer of his exile from England, 1816, he returned to Childe Harold and produced a third canto of self-dramatization, this time blatantly using the poem as a vehicle in which to expose the state of his soul after his marital disaster. He addresses the little daughter he may not see again:

> Is thy face like thy mother's, fair child?
> Ada! sole daughter of my house and heart!

and goes on to explain, in highly theatrical rhetoric,

> ... I must think less wildly:—I *have* thought
> Too long and darkly, till my brain became,
> In its own eddy boiling and o'erwrought,
> A whirling gulf of phantasy and flame.

Then he shakes himself—'Something too much of this'—and 'Long absent HAROLD re-appears at last', although it is still continually unclear who the 'I' of the poem is. The public, however, were happy to lap up the confessions and went on to enjoy 'Harold' viewing the carnage of Waterloo and the dust of Napoleon's empire, seeming to stand in a pose of permanently exaggerated dejection, fist on puckered brow. At the close, with as many gasps and sobs as an Italian tenor, he returns unmistakably to himself, standing alone, the world his enemy, thinking about little Ada:

> My daughter! with thy name thus much shall end!
> I see thee not—I hear thee not—but none
> Can be so wrapt in thee ...
> Yet though dull Hate as duty should be taught,
>   I know thou wilt love me—

Lady Byron did not miss the dig, and was naturally furious; but Byron had to pull out all the stops to guarantee the loyalty and sympathy of his readership. These new revelations ensured that the fascination did not abate.

Byron was finishing off this work during the Shelleys' visit to Geneva, and further evidence of his susceptibility is provided by his memory that 'Shelley, when I was in Switzerland, used to dose me with Wordsworth physic, even unto nausea'. Shelley was doubtless trying to explain to him the philosophy of Wordsworth's recent epic *The Excursion*, which he did not understand and which was far removed from any Byronic conception of poetry (Crabb Robinson reported that for his part Wordsworth 'believes Lord Byron to be

somewhat cracked'). Byron may have found the medicine hard to
swallow, but he saw that as a fashionable poet catering to a public, he
should keep up with this important, if apparently reactionary, trend in
modern verse; and so, at the last moment, he slipped in some rhapsodic Wordsworthian stanzas to his new canto:

> I live not in myself, but I become
> Portion of that around me; and to me
> High mountains are a feeling...
> Are not the mountains, waves, and skies, a part
> Of me and my Soul, as I of them?
> Is not the love of these deep in my heart
> With a pure passion?

In Byron's case, the straight answer to these questions is 'No'. Nor did
he make much attempt to iron out the join. Having paid his respects,
he admits he has succumbed to digression:

> But this is not my theme; and I return
> To that which is immediate...

namely, the more familiar tones of

> ... wild Rousseau
> The apostle of Affliction, he who threw
> Enchantment over Passion, and from Woe
> Wrung overwhelming eloquence.

It is as easy to knock down Byron on the grounds of technique as it
is to trace the opportunism of his content. He leans on the short
cuts—dashes, negatives, repetitions, gulps and swoons:

> The wither'd frame, the ruined mind
> The wrack by passion left behind—
> A shrivelled scroll, a scatter'd leaf,
> Sear'd by the autumn blast of grief!

He plods, as Matthew Arnold points out, through the dead rhythm of
lines like

> Dare you await the event of a few minutes'
> Deliberation

and ludicrous rhymes like

> All shall be void—
> Destroy'd!

He is 'little haunted' by what Arnold called 'the true artist's fine passion for the correct use and consummate management of words'.

All this is true: Byron is slapdash, clumsy, and sloppy. He had no grand philosophy of poetry; he was not a spirit dedicated to his art as Shelley and Keats were. He simply discovered that he could do it, do it fast—*The Bride of Abydos*, he claimed, was written in four days, *The Corsair* in ten—and that people bought the results.

It is no use considering Byron now as a serious poet. That is not to say he is a bad or dull one. Even at his worst, he has gusto and rhetorical energy; declaimed aloud and uninhibitedly, he always makes his effect. But he is at his best when he is most spontaneously himself—not the dark angel, wrapped in a voluminous black cloak, but the witty raconteur, shambling, tolerant, worldly, intuitively intelligent rather than analytically intellectual. His masterpiece *Don Juan* has more sheer *fun* in it than anything in English poetry after *The Canterbury Tales*; the sort of comedy that Peacock and Shelley talked about in Marlow seems dry and etched in comparison. The superior smirk behind *Childe Harold* has become exuberant guffawing, and the Byronic hero is not a mystery wrapped inside an enigma, but a naughty Cupid, instinctively sexual and innocent of darker philosophies.

Yet though it now seems the most unaffectedly self-revealing of his works, *Don Juan* was found shockingly cynical when it first appeared. 'It is a *satire* on *abuses* of the present state of society, and not an eulogy of vice,' Byron protested, but few could stomach that as an excuse for the infamous episode in the second canto, when the survivors of a shipwreck, cast adrift without food or water, resort to cannibalism. Sailing through the Bay of Biscay, on his way to Italy with the knowledge of his likely death from tuberculosis looming over him, John Keats read this passage, threw down the book and exclaimed to his companion Severn, 'This gives me the most horrid idea of human nature, that a man like Byron should have exhausted all the pleasures of the world so completely that there was nothing left for him but to laugh & gloat over the most solemn & heart-rending [scenes] of human misery ... '

'Not a single circumstance of it is *not* taken from fact,' Byron stated firmly, but it was the tone that offended, the refusal to ignore the ghoulish and ironic aspects of the situation, and the trivializing brightness of the rhymes. For example, after Juan's dog has been cut up and consumed, Pedrillo, his tutor, falls victim to the lots cast for the next source of food:

The sailors ate him, all save three or four,
  Who were not quite so fond of animal food;
To these were added Juan, who, before
  Refusing his own spaniel, hardly could
Feel now his appetite increased much more;
  'Twas not to be expected that he should,
Even in extremity of their disaster.
Dine with them on his pastor and his master.

Some of the sailors go mad in consequence; another candidate for the chop is spared because he is discovered to be suffering from venereal disease. Byron cannot be quite serious about it, nor can he settle to be funny. Some ensuing stanzas, describing two fathers enduring the slow deaths of their sons, are austerely moving, the rhymes chaste and unobtrusive; but they do not last for long. This black-comedy capacity to mock the sufferings of the innocent, see-sawing between fascination and repulsion, and creating effects of moral ambiguity by boldly focusing on taboos and then recoiling from what is confronted, is original to Byron and constitutes one of his supreme achievements as a writer (unmatched in English literature, except by Dickens, until the mid twentieth century), but it was not much liked.

One of the sources Byron used for the shipwreck was the story of the French frigate the *Medusa*, which went down in 1816 off the coast of Senegal, leaving a hundred and fifty passengers and crew piled on to a makeshift raft and cast adrift without food or shelter. The results were horrifying: mutiny, cannibalism, murder, and insanity took as many lives as disease, starvation, and drowning. Only ten lived to tell the tale, news of which caused scandal and outrage in Paris— especially as the fact that the ship's captain had been a total incompetent, appointed only because he was someone's favourite, gave the affair a marked political dimension. At the very same time that Byron was writing the second canto of *Don Juan*, the young French painter Théodore Géricault* began to work up the huge canvas of *The Raft of the Medusa*, which now hangs in the Louvre. Deeply impressed on a recent trip to Italy by the massy forms of Michelangelo, he depicted the scene as a monumental apocalypse, in which the tone is unmistakably heroic and tragic, the form a single dynamic thrust. The painting

---

* Géricault was himself something of a Byronist, with a mysteriously complicated sex life which biographers have been unable to fathom. He visited England in 1820–1 and made some lithographs to illustrate Byron's oriental poems. There is no evidence that he ever read *Don Juan*.

was displayed at the official *salon* of 1819, surrounded by the insipid and academic canvases of artists concerned only to flatter, please, and sell. It overwhelmed the public with pity and terror; the historian Michelet could later write that 'It was our whole society that he [Géricault] placed on the *Raft of the Medusa*: a portrait so cruelly true that the original refused to recognize herself.' Yet for all the power and energy in Géricault's vision, Byron's version is more unnerving and poignant, more intimately and recognizably human.

For someone so concerned to be shocking, Byron, like so many satirists, was often deeply conservative. His literary tastes, indeed, were anachronistic, if not plain reactionary. The eighteenth century was his ticket. When provoked, he would claim that Voltaire was worth 'a thousand such' of Shakespeare, Dante, and Milton. He rated Dryden and especially Pope far beyond any of his contemporaries. Keats's poetry he thought 'mental masturbation', Wordsworth he did not understand, Coleridge he was personally kind to: soon-dead reputations like those of Campbell, Rogers, and Moore meant much more to him. He detested Southey, but admitted that his *Roderick* (another epic on the theme of Hispanic freedom-fighting) was 'as near perfection as poetry can be'.

Above all, he esteemed Walter Scott: it was, after all, Scott who with *Marmion* and other poems of that sort had set a new pace and stimulated popularity for narrative poetry. Byron handsomely made up for his adolescent gibe in 'English Bards and Scotch Reviewers' by dedicating his drama *Cain* to him and hailing him as 'the Monarch of Parnassus'. Scott's historical novels were the favourite entertainment of his years in Italy—he claimed in 1821 to have read them all 'at least fifty times'. Their personal relations were cordial too, though not intimate. 'Wonderful man! I long to get drunk with him,' wrote Byron in his journal. This would not have been Scott's way at all, however. A sober Tory, yet also a keen improver and speculator, he had trained as a lawyer and was always acutely conscientious about his responsibilities, social and personal. Apart from a lame foot, he shared few of Byron's traits and nothing of his egoism, iconoclasm, or mistrustfulness. The contrast between them was often discussed. Scott was widely regarded as having preserved his virtue despite his celebrity, Byron as having made the devil's bargain. Lady Blessington, reporting on her visit to Byron in 1823, believed that 'had he lived more with men like Scott, whose openness of character and steady principle had convinced him that they were in earnest in *their goodness*, and not making believe, (as he always suspects good people to be) his life might be different and happier.'

But goodness had nothing to do with it. A steadier, happier Byron would not have been so interesting or saleable. His readers wanted him struggling, not happy; and so that muddling idea 'the Byronic Hero' developed, reflected in his verse and distorted by the myths of his personality.

Lord Macaulay defined the Byronic Hero as 'a man proud, moody, cynical, with defiance on his brow, and misery in his heart, a scorner of his kind, implacable in revenge, yet capable of deep and strong affection'. But this does not pin it down. The image passes through many traditions and transformations, projected forward on to Baudelaire or James Dean, and back on to Hamlet and Macbeth. Easier to say what a Byronic hero is not, than what he is: not Mr Knightley in *Emma*, not a man rooted to his responsibilities in the community, rational in his behaviour and incapable of hypocrisy. He is the man he seems to be: the Byronic hero conceals himself.

In his own lifetime, Byron himself was cast into various moulds. 'I have seen myself compared personally or poetically,' he reflected towards the end of his life, 'to Rousseau—Goethe—Young—Aretino—Timon of Athens—"An Alabaster Vase lighted up within"—Satan—Shakespeare—Bonaparte—Tiberius ... to Henry the 8th—to Chenier—to Mirabeau ... to Michael Angelo—to Raphael.'

For the years immediately after *Childe Harold*, he became the scandalous star of Regency London, a super-Dandy whose every movement was chronicled in the tittle-tattle of the town. Those outside that circle regarded him as a Satanic seducer of women, very much in the mould of Lovelace, the amoral rake of Richardson's novel *Clarissa Harlowe* (1747–8). Jane Austen broadly ridiculed the type in *Sanditon*: Sir Edward Denham is a seaside lecher, whom the rational Charlotte Heywood thinks 'downright silly ... very sentimental, very full of some Feelings or other, & very much addicted to all the newest-fashioned hard words'. (There is a significant time-warp here. Jane Austen interprets Sir Edward in the language of Sentimentalism, even though she was certainly familiar with Byron and his poetry. In other words, she sees the character as an old-fashioned phenomenon and misses the novelty of the incarnation. This is perhaps why, compared to the subtlety of the rest of her 'Regency' satire, Sir Edward sticks out as a farcical caricature.)

To a generation younger than Jane Austen, Byron represented

something nobler. He was the critic of British smugness, the jester and jouster against the complacence and conservatism of post-Napoleonic Europe. At his death in 1824 he was also consecrated as the Hero of Missolonghi, the poet who had died armed in the cause of Hellenic liberty and had lived out the swashbuckling of his own fictional creations, the Corsair and Giaour. For the rest of the century, people would remember the shock of hearing the news, as people now remember the moment of Kennedy's assassination. Even the young Thomas Carlyle, who warned against the perils of Byronism and took Goethe as his model, could mourn that 'the noblest spirit in Europe should sink before half his course was run! Late so full of fire, and generous passion and proud purposes and now forever dumb and cold!' His wife Jane Welsh Carlyle, a Byron fan since her teenage years, admitted, 'If they had said that the Sun or the Moon was gone out of the heavens it could not have struck with the idea of a more awful and dreary blank in the creation than the words "Byron is dead".' Fourteen-year-old Alfred Tennyson carved the words 'Byron is dead' on the rocks of a quarry and recalled it as 'a day when the whole world seemed darkened'; in America, the twelve-year-old Harriet Beecher Stowe lay down on the grass and prayed that she might take upon herself a portion of Byron's sufferings, as her Evangelical father preached a hell-fire sermon on the dead poet's wickedness. Within five years of his death, at least thirty Byron biographies, memoirs, and critiques had been published. The poetry was read as confessional, veiled autobiography; Byron was always somewhere to be discovered within it, however unfamilar the costume. From a distance, we can detect more clearly the literary roots of each characterization. The ancestry of Childe Harold includes the name-less melancholy of Hamlet, Werther, and the meditative poetry of the eighteenth century. Even closer to hand, the Childe's elder cousin as it were, is a short novel by the French writer Chateaubriand called *René*, written around 1797–8 while the author was exiled in England, to illustrate a large-scale study of Christianity. Byron is unlikely to have read it, but the similarities to *Childe Harold* are striking, and both works are essentially fantasized versions of personal experience.

René (Chateaubriand used one of his own Christian names, as Byron had contemplated using 'Birun' for Harold) grows up in a picturesque old castle (compare Harold's 'vast and venerable pile', Byron's Newstead Abbey), then wanders the world, lonely and dis-satisfied, eventually coming close to suicide. The only human being he loves is his sister, and she becomes so alarmed at the incestuous overtones to their shared feelings that she enters a convent where she soon dies. René leaves for America and a life of Rousseauan solitude in nature. Chateaubriand frames his story as a lesson in the consolations of religion, but this washes little better than Byron's claim that *Childe Harold* was an attempt to show up the effects of 'an early perversion of mind and morals'. In both cases what sold copies was the voluptuous indulgence of negative emotions. As René admits, 'I realized, with a secret impulse of joy, that grief is not an emotion that one exhausts as one exhausts pleasure.'

René and Childe Harold, Werther and Byron himself were young men produced by and caught up in societies which offered them no definite future, no fixed function or purpose. To that uncertainty their responses are essentially passive. The next manifestation of the Byronic hero, the swashbucklers of the Oriental tales, are by contrast men of power and action, who fight back against circumstances, even though they never seem to have any particular political or ideological axe to grind. Shelley's Laon and Cythna in *The Revolt of Islam* stand for the freedom and enlightenment of humankind; Byron's Conrad the Corsair is neither a Napoleon nor a Robin Hood:

> He knew himself a villain—but he deemed
> The rest no better than the thing he seemed;
> And scorned the best as hypocrites who hid
> Those deeds the bolder spirit plainly did....
> Lone, wild, and strange, he stood alike exempt
> From all affection and from all contempt...

The Byronic hero does not fight against a repressive social order; he cannot be bothered to be a rebel, let alone a revolutionary. Scott's Marmion and Schiller's Karl Moor in *Die Räuber* (The Robbers) both enormously popular heroic figures of the period, have specific angers and targets of revenge; Byron's, in comparison, seem unmotivated.

After his scandal-haunted exile from England in 1816, the clouds of mystery and evil round the Byronic hero swirl even denser. As we have seen, so as to incorporate the *Sturm und Drang* of the last months of his marriage, the Childe Harold of the third canto is a wilder and more tormented creature than he had been in the first and second cantos. Developments in the contemporary theatre presented another set of possibilities: in his days on the committee at Drury Lane, Byron had been enormously impressed by the satanic power in the acting of Edmund Kean as Shakespeare's villains Richard III, Macbeth, and

Iago, and his next major work, *Manfred*, a 'dramatic poem' written in 1817, reads very much like a vehicle for Kean's genius, complete with spectacular scenes of mountain landscapes and spectre-raising. Manfred himself is a mish-mash of Macbeth, Aeschylus' Prometheus, and Goethe's Faust (translated for him verbatim by 'Monk' Lewis during that eventful summer on Lake Geneva). A brooding outcast, his quarrel is not with kings or nations, but something more fundamental. 'My Nature was averse from life,' he snarls at a poor old abbot, who is only trying to help.

Cain, written in 1821, went even further: as far as could be gone. In this version of the biblical story of the son of Adam and Eve who murdered his brother Abel, the malcontent Byronic hero becomes a blasphemer who falls for Lucifer and rails against a cruel and vengeful God, creating life only to destroy it wantonly. No one paid much attention to Cain's final remorse or Byron's claim that he could hardly have presented the Devil talking 'like a clergyman'. The whole business caused a storm of outrage and its author was condemned as an atheist and Jacobin. From a safe distance, Byron could banter: the work was in 'my gay metaphysical style . . . I wrote it when I was drunk. When I reread it later I was astonished.'

There is, however, one further element in the make-up of the Byronic hero which has not yet been emphasized and which is vital to the mystique—a weakness for women and vulnerability to the passions of Love. The Byronic hero is always in search for a mothering he has never had. He wants a woman to stroke his hair, dry his tears, and nurse back the gentle and sensitive side of his nature, thwarted by bitter experience of the world of men. Thus Conrad the Corsair's heart 'was formed for softness—warped to wrong'.

It was this sort of thing that gave Byron's multitudinous women readers a shuddering thrill and released the flood of 'anonymous effusions'. He must be talking about himself, they thought, and I must be the only woman who *understands*. 'How many whose aspects are forbidding, who are incapable of any earthly affections, hide within themselves the warmest feelings,' wrote Claire Clairmont: but Byron had heard that one before. It was the hope of ministering, comforting, and redeeming—that peculiarly poisoned form of sexual love—which obsessed women like his wife Annabella Milbanke. And it is precisely this pattern of feeling which characterizes the behaviour of women *vis-à-vis* latter-day Byronic heroes like Heathcliff and Rochester, as fantasized by two passionate readers of Byron, Emily and Charlotte Brontë.

But what was the Byronic problem? Why had the heroes been 'warped to wrong'? What is their neurosis? About this, they are never clear—some guilt in the past, about which they are now remorseful, created a vacuum ready to be filled in *au choix*. A murder? A maltreated, discarded lover? An illegitimate child? A morganatic marriage? Again, this was something projected on to Byron himself and encouraged by his behaviour—Scott remarked on 'his love of mystifying ... there was no knowing how much or how little to believe'. Even when he purports to be frank, as in the series of *Detached Thoughts* he wrote 'privately' in 1821, he is still tantalizingly self-dramatizing:

74

If I could explain at length the real causes which have contributed to this perhaps *natural* temperament of mine—this melancholy which hath made me a bye-word—nobody would wonder—but this is impossible without doing much mischief—I do not know what other men's lives have been—but I cannot conceive anything more strange than some of the earlier parts of mine—I have written my memoirs—but omitted *all* the really *consequential* & *important* parts—from deference to the dead—to the living—and to those who must be both.

75

I sometimes think I should have written the whole—as a *lesson*—but it might have proved a lesson to be *learnt*—rather than avoided—for passion is a whirlpool which is not to be viewed nearly without attraction from its Vortex.

76

I must not go on with these reflections—or I shall be letting out some secret or other—to paralyze posterity...

Until very recently, scholarly efforts to scrape down to the truth have centred on the break-up of Byron's marriage to the strait-laced bluestocking heiress Annabella Milbanke. She was niece to Byron's best woman friend and confidante, the sophisticated hostess Lady Melbourne, who in 1812 first encouraged him to give up Lady Caroline Lamb (married to her son!) and settle for a safe candidate. Byron agreed in principle, given his view that 'marriage goes no better with esteem and confidence than romance', but was in no great hurry. Only in January 1815, after more than two years of procrastination and several serious affairs, did Byron kneel at the altar with Annabella. He was not enthusiastic. Some weeks earlier he had moaned to his friend Henry Drury, 'I wish [we] would be married at the same time—I should like to make a party—like people electrified in a row by or rather—*through* the same chain—holding one another's hands, & all feeling the shock at once.'

Things were not altogether bleak: there was obviously some affection, and even content, in the early months. Byron called his wife Bell, Pip or Pippin; she called him her Duck. She 'don't bore me', wrote Byron to Lady Melbourne, which for him was a considerable compliment. His bouts of gorging and drinking, followed by periods of self-starvation worried her, however, and she was upset by his irregular nocturnal habits—it seems that he did not like to sleep in the same bed with his lovers, and Annabella's wedding-night defloration took place on the sofa before dinner. There were money problems too—all the fantastic sums delivered for his poetry were swallowed up in the debts on Newstead Abbey. But most sinister of all were his passionate explosions over his past. 'I have done that for which I can never forgive myself,' he told her on the day after the wedding, when she urged him to unburden himself, he replied that she 'could know nothing of the things to which he alluded—good women could know nothing.'

Three weeks after the birth of their baby Ada, Byron and his wife had a marital screaming-match, during which he told her of an affair he had had with the actress Susan Boyce and 'his intention to continue those courses, though tired of her [Susan] personally'. About two weeks later, on 15 January 1816, Annabella left London with the baby, ostensibly to take some deep breaths in the calm of her parents' home. In fact, she never returned and soon announced her desire for a separation. Her charges varied. He was 'insane'; he had shown '*total dereliction of principle*'; he had shot his pistols in the drawing-room while she was upstairs in the throes of labour (Byron claimed he had simply been popping soda-bottle corks!); he had tried to convince her that morality was relative, 'Right & Wrong were merely conventional, & varying with Locality & other circumstances'. A lawyer assured her that she had adequate grounds on the basis of adultery, cruelty, and exposure to the threat of venereal disease.

Byron appeared genuinely upset and baffled by the violence of the volte-face, pressing her for a reconciliation in the belief that she was acting under the influence of her parents and her former governess, a certain Mrs Clermont. He was also increasingly agitated by other gossip about him, some of it viciously spread by Lady Caroline Lamb, and realized that, one way or another, the situation ought to be resolved as soon as possible. The legal wrangling dragged on till April;

Claire Clairmont made her advances. Byron meanwhile had made a crucially bad—and all too typical—public relations error in distributing among his friends two poems he had written, one, a sobbing lyric addressed to Annabella vaunting his own wounded innocence:

> When our child's first accents flow—
> Wilt thou teach her to say 'Father!'
> Though his care she must forego?

the other a satirical sketch of the 'villainous' Mrs Clermont, her origins and ambitions:

> With eye unmoved and forehead unabashed,
> She dines from off the plate she lately washed.
> Quick with the tale, and ready with the lie,
> The genial confidante and general spy—

These were picked up and published by the gutter press, without Byron's consent. But nobody was to know that: all the public could see was a gesture in extremely bad taste, which resulted in the public defamation of two ladies. An enormous hoo-ha ensued. At a ball on 8 April Byron was dramatically 'cut' by a number of his former supporters: Annabella had won a moral victory. Two weeks later Byron left London and England for good. The Whig newspaper the *Morning Chronicle* defended him against victimization; the *Courier* was guarded, the *Morning Post* outraged, and *The Times* virulent—'We shall rejoice to welcome his lordship again to his country,' its leader column crowed, 'whenever his ferocious egotism shall be softened into a capability of an indulgent appreciation of others' opinions and others' feelings, as well as of his own.'

Fifteen-year-old Jane Welsh was one of those who remained loyal. 'Shall I love my Byron less, / Because he knows not happiness' she wrote in her private journal:

> Ah, no! tho' worlds condemn him now,
> Though sharp-tongued fame has sunk him low,
> The hapless wand'rer still must be
> Pitied, revered, adored by me.

The most widespread contemporary rumour about Byron was that he had committed incest with his married half-sister (by his father's first wife) Augusta Leigh. The story first appeared in print in an article written in 1869 by Harriet Beecher Stowe, relating the substance of conversations she had had with Annabella some thirteen years earlier, and it has persisted ever since. Yet the evidence has never added up decisively. It is, for one thing, difficult to account for the strangely conspiratorial relationship between Augusta and Annabella, with the former secretly showing the latter all her letters from him, and the mutual sanctimonious fervour with which they concluded Byron was insane.

Certainly Byron's love for Augusta was very strong—lastingly so—and many are the code-words, hints, blanks and asterisks relating to her in his letters to Lady Melbourne; but it should also be remembered that incest was the fashionable contemporary vice. It carried only a maximum of six months' imprisonment and its social stigma might be compared to that attached to cocaine today. The intense love of brother and sister, often arising between two parties unaware of their relationship until it is 'too late' and doomed by the bigotry of convention, was a common theme of Sentimentalism and its cult of the Love that went beyond Sex. It is a central theme of Chateaubriand's *René*, for example, as it is (more tactfully expressed) of *Paul et Virginie*, and, looking forward, *Wuthering Heights*. It is the theme, one could say, of the relationship between William and Dorothy Wordsworth or Charles and Mary Lamb; and even in the case of Byron and Augusta one may suspect that it was a matter of passionate avowals and stage embraces rather than actual consummations.

Byron himself seemed to be able to live with the thought that the rumour circulated, and *Manfred* is but one of the poems of his exile which play with the *frisson* of incest: the only person in Manfred's life who understood him, he says, was a woman 'like me in lineaments— her eyes / Her hair—her features—all, to the very tone / Even of her voice, they said were like to mine'. Cain, somewhat inevitably given the number of earthly inhabitants at the time, is also incestuously married to his sister Adah.

Incest was, then, at least emotionally conceivable to Byron's educated middle-class readership. There was something else though, which, without exaggeration, would have meant death and ruin: Byron was a lover of boys and had a complicated history in that direction.

This was not fashionable; it was not even acceptable. Sodomy, of either man or woman, was a capital crime in England, brutally enforced. 'Attempted' sodomy was punished with pilloryings of stomach-churning nastiness and feared even more than hanging. Every society, including so-called permissive ones, has its blind spots, areas of human behaviour at which it stops short, and for Regency

England 'Greek love' was one of them. Like all such prejudices, there is an element of the inexplicable about it. Every other European country, from Russia to the USA, had substantially reduced the penalties for sodomy in the Revolutionary period: France decriminalized it entirely in 1791. England alone actually intensified prosecution. The notion of a man having sexual intercourse with another man was considered against nature, and universally condemned. What we call 'homosexuality' and think of as a state of mind—some people are like that, others aren't—was regarded then as simply a repellent physical act like rape, with no authentic emotional content behind it. Even Shelley, who understood the attractions of incest and was in almost every other respect a visionary liberal, could get very little further than this.

The popular press insisted that it was a filthy foreign habit, native to Catholic countries and disgracefully imported. It was also, in that useful journalistic cliché, believed to be 'on the increase'. At all levels of society it was the crime '*inter Christianos non nominandum*', 'that must not be named among Christians'—the crime of 'which good women could know nothing'.

For Byron his involvements with boys remained a source of extreme anxiety. It has also been suggested that 'the love that dares not speak its name' is the key to all the secretive remorse of the Byronic hero, as well as the reverberating evasions in the letters and journals. The retrievable facts are too fragmentary and ambivalent for this to be satisfactorily established, but one can be sure that it was not an aspect of his personality to which he was happily adjusted. For all his defiance, Byron was still a man who would flinch at the word 'Sin': the double-edged instruction delivered by his nurse May Gray must have seen to that from an early age.

It may be assumed that his passage through the unreformed English public school of Harrow, where fifty or more hungry boys would be locked up in dormitories every night completely without supervision, brought Byron his homosexual initiation. Whatever his physical experience—later there would be a rumour that he had 'perverted' three of his schoolfellows—the emotional experience was more overwhelming, nothing less than a discovery of Love and its manifold power. When in the *Detached Thoughts*, he writes 'I never hear the word "Clare" without a beating of the heart,' he was referring not to the 'damned bitch' Madame Claire Clairmont, but an old school friend of his, the Earl of Clare, whose 'excellent qualities and kind affections' he remembered undiminishingly.

This was the idealized love of the Platonic Academy (Byron would not have dared mention it otherwise 'from deference to the dead—to the living—and to those who must be both') in which an older boy patronized a younger one, educating him, contemplating his beauty, and wondering at his innocence and charm. For a hundred and fifty years after Byron's death, until the development of an open psychology of homosexuality, this was the way that the evidence was presented, and to some extent it obviously answers the case. But today it has become impossible to edit out the carnal aspects. Byron did not just 'go through a phase'; he was subject throughout his life to a specific sort of sexual attraction.

At Trinity College, Cambridge, Byron fell into league with the extraordinary Charles Skinner Matthews, who devised a camp argot in which to discuss matters of Greek love, and together they seem to have delved deep into the classical literature of the subject—Greek, Roman, oriental, all of it forbidden. Byron fixed his attentions on the fifteen-year-old Trinity chorister John Edleston. In the words of Louis Crompton, 'Byron in this case achieved something like the palpitating restraint Socrates advocates in the *Phaedrus*, where the male lovers, though burning with erotic desire, restrict the expression of their emotions to "the sight, the touch, the embrace".' In one touching incident, Edleston gave his mentor a cornelian stone. Embarrassed by the humbleness of the gift and afraid that Byron would scorn it, he burst into tears. Such sincerity made Byron himself melt, and he commemorated their feelings in a little poem entitled 'The Cornelian':

> Some, who can sneer at friendship's ties,
>   Have for my weakness, oft reprov'd me;
> Yet still the simple gift I prize
>   For I am sure the giver lov'd me.

This could be presented as the stuff of adolescence, pure and sacred friendship, and the poem does not hesitate to specify the masculine pronoun. When he separated from Edleston, who took up a post with a London merchant, Byron could respectably pour his heart out to a woman friend, comparing himself and Edleston to all the other respectable same-sex attachments, from the biblical David and Jonathan to the Ladies of Llangollen.* But Sentiment was one thing, sodomy quite another.

---

* In 1778 Lady Eleanor Butler, thirty-nine, and Sarah Ponsonby, twenty-three, 'eloped' to set up home together in rural Wales, where they lived for the rest of their

In 1809, after a period of heterosexual promiscuity and dandaical pursuits in London and Brighton, Byron reached the age of majority. In a sudden access of unexplained panic, he decided to embark on his Grand Tour of the Mediterranean. The war made any European travel dangerous; his lawyer advised him that his finances were in a parlous state and needed his attentions, but Byron was hysterically adamant. 'If the consequences of my leaving England, were ten times as ruinous as you describe, I have no alternative. There are circumstances which render it absolutely indispensable, and quit the country I must immediately.' What may have worried him was an agreement he had made with Edleston in 1807 that they should live together when Byron reached his majority and which he now wished to evade. If so, he ironically left England for shores where he could practise his predilections freely. At the first port of call, Lisbon, he and his travelling companion John Cam Hobhouse, a friend from Cambridge, stopped symbolically to gaze at the palace whence in 1784 the writer William Beckford, author of the oriental fantasy novel *Vathek*, had fled after he had been accused of sexual relations with a sixteen-year-old boy. They moved on to Albania, a wild and unvisited land known for its complete acceptance of the 'revolting passion': it was from here that Byron wrote his previously quoted letter to the effect that 'I will never revisit England if I can avoid it'. In Constantinople, he received the alarming but unconfirmed news that John Edleston had been 'accused of indecency'. During the autumn of 1810 he wrote from Greece to Hobhouse, who had returned to England, asking him to 'tell M that I have obtained above two hundred pl & opt Cs and am almost tired of them'. 'M' was Charles Skinner Matthews; 'pl & opt Cs' stands for *plenum et optabilem coitum*, meaning, let us say, 'complete and long-desired coition'; and Byron was reporting back the number of his conquests. It was in Athens too that he took under his protection a Greek boy, Nicolo Giraud, who taught him Italian and became the beneficiary of his will to the tune of £7,000.*

In London in 1814, Byron wrote in his journal that Hobhouse had

told me an odd report,—that I am the actual Conrad, the veritable Corsair, and that part of my travels are supposed to have passed in

lives. They wore men's clothes and shared a bed, were visited by the great and the good, and celebrated as an instance of the highest Sentimental friendship. There was no suggestion that their relationship was genitally sexual and it may not have been. See Elizabeth Mavor, *The Ladies of Llangollen* (1971).
* The most complete account of Byron's Grand Tour from this angle is contained in Louis Crompton's exhaustive but fascinating *Byron and Greek Love* (1985).

piracy. Um!—people sometimes hit near the truth; but never the whole truth. H. don't know what I was about the year after he left the Levant; nor does any one—nor—nor—nor—however, it is a lie . . .

Byron had plenty of girls on his travels too, and when he finally returned to England in the summer of 1811, he was plagued with gonorrhoea, as well as being exhausted and penniless. Within three months of his arrival, he had three deaths to assimilate: first, his mother's; then, in a swimming accident, that of Charles Skinner Matthews; then the news that John Edleston had died of tuberculosis. To a man of Byron's temperament, it must have seemed like divine admonition: 'Some curse hangs over me and mine,' he wrote. The series of laments he wrote in memory of Edleston, now carefully masked under the name of Thyrza, may signify the conscious decision to bury a part of himself:

> One struggle more, and I am free
>> From pangs that rend my heart in twain;
> One last long sigh to Love and thee,
>> Then back to busy life again.
> It suits me well to mingle now
>> With things that never pleased before:
> Though every joy is fled below,
>> What future grief can touch me more?

But he made one last idiotic mistake—that of revealing certain details to the first and most difficult mistress of his years of fame, Lady Caroline Lamb (this may incidentally explain her propensity for dressing herself as a pageboy while in pursuit of Byron). When the time came for revenge, she was quite ready to circulate this potentially fatal information round the town. Annabella too was exposed to similar revelations—or at least drunken talk which not even a good woman could fail to understand—during their last tempestuous weeks together; it has even been suggested (by Hobhouse for one) that it was a violent attempt to sodomize her that caused her precipitate flight to her parents. In any case, it is difficult for us now to realize with what horror this little history would have been received, and how, at the wrong moment, in the wrong ears, it could have brought out the mob. Byron was lucky to get out of England without being lynched.

Whether Byron's years in Italy held any lovers of his own sex is completely unknown, although speculation has been fuelled by

Shelley's impenetrable statement in a letter to Peacock that in Venice Byron 'associates with wretches who seem almost to have lost the gait & physiognomy of man, & who do not scruple to avow practices which are not only not named but I believe seldom ever conceived in England'.

Then in the last months in Greece, we gather that Byron had taken 'under his protection' the fifteen-year-old son of a genteel but impoverished Greek widow. Lukas Chalandrustanos became Byron's last love, and not his happiest. Pretty, vain, and grasping, Lukas took full advantage of the infatuation, strutting about in the gorgeous gold-trimmed uniform he was bought and screwing Byron for everything he could get. The Hero of Missolonghi may have been the most famous man in Europe, but he was also approaching middle age, overweight and balding. His teeth were falling out; he was constantly in pain and giddy from what the doctors could only hopelessly diagnose as 'rheumatic fever'. Worst of all, he was lonely and uncomforted by a callow boy whom he had pathetically tried to please and impress. The last lines of poetry Byron ever wrote are more melancholy and touching than anything in *Childe Harold*:

> Thus much and more—and yet thou lov'st me not,
>   And never wilt—Love dwells not in our will,
> Nor can I blame thee—though it be my lot
>   To strongly—wrongly—vainly—love thee still.

But that little knot of real suffering was swallowed up in a greater myth, as witnessed by the obituaries and statues to the warrior-poet, by the tear-stained teenagers prostrate on the grass. Lukas Chalandrustanos was quietly and firmly suppressed: a hero did not die trying to fondle a silly foreign boy. The biographies and memoirs which soon jostled in the bookshops had other tales to tell, some of them very tall indeed.*

Oneupmanship played an important part in this. The final fascination of all idols is the revelation of their clay feet, and to claim some uniquely telling and intimate glimpse of the real Lord Byron was an

---

* The manuscript of Byron's own memoirs were ceremonially burnt in his publisher's office a few days after the news from Missolonghi came through. They were unlikely to have revealed anything except the heterosexually erotic, but the story of Byron's love for boys did survive in an obscure pornographic poem *Don Leon*, the provenance of which is still hotly contested. See Doris Langley Moore, *Lord Byron: Accounts Rendered* (1974) and *The Late Lord Byron* (1961), and Louis Crompton, op. cit.

obvious way to make oneself interesting. That unstoppable spinner of good yarns Stendhal was an early culprit. In his chatty volume *Rome, Naples et Florence* (1817) he turned a brief and perfunctory encounter with the great man at a Milanese dinner party in 1816 into an evening with him at the Venetian opera in 1817: Byron wrote politely to correct the error. Undeterred Stendhal informed the author of one of the pulp biographies rushed out within months of Byron's death that he had spent 'several months in the society of this great poet' and in a memoir essay of his own claimed to have noted in him 'much petty vanity, a continual and puerile fear of appearing ridiculous and ... some of that hypocrisy which the English call *cant*'. Even nastier was Leigh Hunt, who had been the glad recipient of considerable bene-factions from Byron, including an un-repaid loan of £200 and free accommodation for him, his ailing wife, and six rampageous children: Byron described trying to help him 'like pulling a man out of a river who directly throws himself in again'. Hunt's *Lord Byron and Some of his Contemporaries* (1828) was widely considered to have gone below the belt when it knocked mean, conceited and selfish Byron against angelically selfless Shelley, and Hunt subsequently had to make some rather shabby retractions. One story in it rings macabrely true: having ceremoniously burnt Shelley's drowned remains on the beach near Viareggio, Hunt and Byron got hopelessly drunk and drove back through the pinewoods singing and howling with laughter.

It also became common to claim some point of superiority or priority over Byron. In his memoirs Chateaubriand would announce that during his sojourn in England he had dreamed up *René* sitting under an elm in a churchyard in Harrow, 'in the same shade in which later, in his turn, the poet came to dream of Childe Harold.' He then goes on to detail, with a show of magnanimity, 'the coincidence of the two leaders of the new French and English schools having a common fund of nearly parallel ideas and destinies'—the important point being that he, Chateaubriand, was always the one to have been there first.

Another kind of envy had a more creative issue. Byron's fellow-poets could not just gossip about him: they were confronted by an eclipsing fame and achievement which had to be grappled with, and perhaps—for influence can deaden—defeated. History has not judged Byron to be anything like as great a poet as Wordsworth in terms of depth and power of emotion, but *Childe Harold* changed the terms for contemporary poetry much more dramatically than anything in the *Lyrical Ballads*, and all over Europe it was Byron who was pondered as the embodiment of the modern poetic spirit. 'I despair of rivalling Lord Byron, as well I may,' complained Shelley after reading some of *Don Juan*, 'and there is no other with whom it is worth contending.'

From an older generation, Goethe concluded that Byron was 'undoubtedly the greatest genius of our century', thus reciprocating an earlier compliment from Byron, who had dedicated his poetic tragedy *Sardanapalus* to the Sage of Weimar, the author of *Faust* and 'the greatest genius that the age has produced'. These elaborate courtesies conceal a trail of misunderstandings, misinterpretations, and pure ignorance. The two perhaps most formative figures of nineteenth-century European culture never met or even corresponded directly (although there was much fluttering in the Weimar dovecots at a second-hand report that Byron planned to visit Goethe on his return from Greece). Byron's German was effectively non-existent, beyond a small repertory of swear words—this is what might have been expected, since German, it may be recalled, was not thought of as a gentleman's language—and his picture of German literature was limited by what Madame de Staël's *De l'Allemagne* had sketched for him. Goethe had a certain reading knowledge of English, but not much more than is farcically revealed by his attempt at the age of seventeen to impress his sister with some 'english veses' he had composed:

I pray thee be not haugty thereof

A SONG OVER THE UNCONFIDENCE TOWARDS
MY SELF

> An other tought is misfortune
> Is death and night to me:
> I hum no supportable tune,
> I can no poet be....

Are they not beautifull sister? Ho yes! Senza dubbio ... Often Sister I am in good humor. In a very good humor! Then I go to visit pretty wifes and pretty maiden.... I am diligent, I am mirthy, and I am luky. Adieu.

This incompetence did not diminish Goethe's enormous admiration for English literature and he keenly kept in touch with its latest developments, as he did with all the modern literatures of Europe. Byron reached him in 1816, the same year that *Faust* reached Byron on Lake Geneva, when 'Monk' Lewis improvised some translations from it: Byron liked the idea of Faust and his devil pact, and something of that play's atmosphere and theme found their way into *Manfred*, while Werther's sorrows also figure in the hinterland of Childe Harold's melancholy. Hence the courtesy of the dedication. But for Goethe, the impact of Byron was much more resonant, like an echo to a long unanswered call. Byron seemed like the son he had never had (the neurotic and dimwitted August von Goethe was a bitter disappointment to his father) or even an *alter ego*, the man he never was. If Goethe was dedicated to moral, spiritual, and physical health and wholeness, then Byron was the opposite, divided in soul, flaunting his inner sickness, yet still impelled by some magnificent daemonism, some heroic power or force of nature which put him beyond ordinary considerations. A Byron or a Napoleon could not be judged alongside other men: like Goethe himself, they were world-makers with a Destiny.

In many respects, this was as fanciful a picture of Byron as anything dreamed up in the fan-letters of his lady admirers. One of Goethe's chief sources of biographical information was Lady Caroline Lamb's rubbishy novel *Glenarvon* which turned Byron into the anti-hero of a Gothic fantasy, complete with black cloak and manic laugh. Goethe read it under the impression that it was largely true. He was particularly taken by one episode in which Glenarvon/Byron emerges as the murderer of the jealous husband of a woman he was making love to—this, Goethe decided, must be the guilty secret that generically haunted the Byronic hero: in fact it was only Lady Caroline's elaborate embroidery of an incident in which Byron had helped to rescue a Muslim girl from being executed for adultery.

Goethe's critical opinions of Byron's poetry are quite unhelpful and even eccentric. He shuddered at the 'immorality' of *Don Juan*, and in suggesting that it 'manifested the most savage hatred of humanity [and] the deepest and tenderest love of mankind', quite missed its fundamental and constant good temper. He was much more impressed by a Gothic novel, *The Vampyre*, published anonymously in 1819, which, like many others, he believed to be Byron's. Unfortunately, having dubbed it his 'best work', he was mortified to ascertain that the author was not Byron at all, but the wretched doctor, John Polidori, much put upon during the Shelleys' visit to Lake Geneva. *Cain* he admired for its fearless destruction of Old Testament dogma and repression, its brash intellectual vulgarity quite invisible even to him; later he was bowled over by dramas like *Marino Faliero* and *Werner* which now seem the merest fodder for opera libretti.

But the Byron that Goethe created was the image of more than a poet, 'only Shakespeare and the Ancients his superior'. It was also the focus for all sorts of unanswered questions about the nature of genius, the mystery of human aspiration, and the balance between action and contemplation, poetry and worldly deeds.

In the second part of *Faust*, that fantastic stew of everything Goethe thought about everything during the last years of his life, Byron is embodied in the Ariel-like form of Euphorion, the child born of the union between Faust and Helen. Euphorion lives by the motto '*immer höher muss ich steigen*', 'ever higher must I climb'. He will be free, he will dance and sing: others counsel caution, but Euphorion follows only the dictates of his own desires. He rushes to Greece, with the headstrong mission of liberating others as he is liberated himself, only to fall dead in battle. The chorus celebrate his elevating example.

Euphorion is the distillation of conversations Goethe had with his disciple Eckermann, in which he continually circles round the phenomenon of Byron, trying to catch at his motivations and explain his significance. Byron's 'disposition ... always leads him into the illimitable';

'If he had but known how to endure moral restraint ... That he could not was his ruin; it may be said he was destroyed by his own unbridled temperament.

'But he was too much in the dark about himself. He lived impetuously for the day, and neither knew nor thought what he was doing ... Everywhere it was too narrow for him, with the most perfect personal freedom he felt confined; the world seemed a prison. His Grecian expedition was the result of no voluntary resolution; his misunderstanding with the world drove him to it. ...

'His revolutionary turn, and the constant negation and fault-finding is injurious even to his excellent works. For not only does the discontent of the poet infect the reader, but the end of all opposition is negation; and negation is nothing. If I call *bad* bad, what do I gain? But if I call *good* bad, I do a great deal of mischief. He who will work aright must never rail, must not trouble himself at all about what is ill done, but only to do well himself. The great point is, not to pull down, but to build up; in this humanity finds pure joy.'

The troubling irony for Goethe was that Byron did not 'build up'. The medium of his power was doubt and gloom rather than light and joy. In acknowledging this, Goethe had to retreat on one of his first principles. 'To all your excellency says of Byron,' says Eckermann,

'I agree from the bottom of my heart; but however great and remarkable he may be as a talent, I much doubt whether a decided gain for *pure human culture* is to be derived from his writings.'

'There I must contradict you,' said Goethe; 'the audacity and grandeur of Byron must certainly tend towards culture. We should take care not to be always looking for it in the decidedly pure and moral. Everything that is great promotes cultivation as soon as we are aware of it.'

This is an important point. It was Byron's audacity and grandeur, his capacity for broad strokes and tremendous public gestures which brought him victory over the nitpickers, and over the next half-century heroic Byron or the Byronic hero would be emulated in many ways. In the cause of national liberty, for instance. Following the example of Missolonghi, the Hungarian poet Sandor Petöfi would die at Szegesvar on the battlefield of Hungarian freedom from the Austrian yoke; his leader Lajos Kossuth bore a much-remarked physical resemblance to Byron. In Italy Mazzini and Cavour would invoke the memory of Byron's support for the Carbonari. Throughout the Europe of the 1820s, youths of a sensitive poetic turn longed to go and fight for the independence of Greece—since Byron's sponsorship, the cause, like the Spanish Civil War over a century later, of everything young and brave and golden.

An easier option was to become a drawing-room Childe Harold. Hordes of pale, sulky young men dressed in black and tried to make themselves look neurotic and interesting; authorship of a little poetry was a standard excuse for being bad-tempered, unreliable, and unremittingly seductive. Others went to further lengths to imitate the Great Original. In 1826–9 the impoverished but flamboyant German aristocrat Count Hermann von Pückler-Muskau made a Grand Byronic Tour, embracing Newstead Abbey, Goethe in Weimar, and Greece and the Orient, where his adventures included swimming up to the cataracts of the Nile and 'rescuing' some beautiful slave girls. Fervently insistent on his own freedom, he had the grace to understand that others might want a modicum of that commodity too: Byronism might be affected, but it was also generous.

But there had to be a way forward past the Colossus, towards another horizon. One poet who made the voyage out into new waters was the Russian Alexander Pushkin (1799–1837). If Goethe watched over Byron with a paternal eye, then Pushkin was the sparring younger brother, defiantly cutting his own tracks. He too only knew Byron from a distance, since he never travelled abroad or mastered more than the feeblest English. Translations into French prose were the principal source of his knowledge of Byron's poetry; Russians were not even sure how to pronounce the name, vacillating between *Beer*-on, Bi-*ron*, *Bay*-ron.

Pushkin discovered Byron in 1820. A bright young man of St Petersburg with radical leanings and even more obvious inclinations to enjoy life to the full, he was banished to the South for some early poems coloured with hints of anti-tsarist views. After an ill-advised swim in the virus-ridden Dnieper, he ended up racked with fever 'in a Jew's hovel, delirious, without a doctor, only a pitcher of lemonade', and was rescued by his charming friends the Raevskys—Tolstoy would have appreciated them—who took him home to the lush beauties of the Caucasus region, nursed him back to health and gave him a taste of the family life that his own chilly and disagreeable parents had failed to provide. The Raevsky children were also fervent Byronists and taught Pushkin some English, using *Childe Harold* as a textbook. Pushkin was soon won over from his previous taste for soft French elegance: in comparison Byron seemed full of that red-blooded energy and boldness of spirit that Pushkin wanted to inject into Russian literature, then still a feeble thing. Even more than in Germany, writers suffered from the fear that French was the only true language of art and cultured speech: Russian was an embarrassment, something which one shouted at the servants. Pushkin would have none of it. He stood up and spoke in his native tongue, making it sound beautiful, moving, witty, direct, and bequeathing his country as valuable an inheritance as Dante or Shakespeare.

But first there was Byron to deal with: in the early 1820s Pushkin used the models of *The Corsair* and *The Giaour* to fashion long exotically located romance-and-adventure poems like *The Fountains of Bakhchisarai*, *The Prisoner of the Caucasus*, and *The Gypsies* (on which Mérimée would base his story *Carmen*). In another department, he was delighted in 1821 to discover that Calypso Polichroni, the daughter of a gypsy fortune-teller with whom he had a brief affair, also claimed to have been involved with Byron. Then, after Byron's death in 1824, a certain impatience against the general adulation set in. 'Byron's genius paled with his youth,' Pushkin claimed. 'He was created completely topsy-turvy; there was no gradualness in him, he suddenly matured and attained manhood, sang his song, and fell silent': a strange view, but one that suited Pushkin's sense of his own mounting powers. In 1825 he wrote an elegy, not, as might have been expected, to Byron, but to a more distant tragic hero of poetry and politics, André Chénier. He was sceptical about the fuss over the burning of Byron's memoirs:

> We know Byron well enough. We have seen him on the throne of glory; we have seen him in the torments of his great soul; we have seen him in his coffin in the midst of a Greece's rising from the dead. Why should you want to see him on a chamber pot? The mob greedily reads confessions, memoirs etc., because in its baseness ... it is in rapture at the disclosure of anything loathsome. 'He is small like us; he is loathsome like us!' You are lying, you scoundrels: he's small and he's loathsome, but not the way you are—differently.

And he was beginning to think about Shakespeare:

> How paltry is Byron as tragedian in comparison with him! This Byron who never conceived but one sole character, [who] has parceled out among his characters such-and-such a trait of his own character; his pride to one, his hate to another, his melancholy to a third etc., and thus out of one complete, gloomy, energetic character he has made several insignificant characters.

In 1823 Pushkin started on his most celebrated work *Eugene Onegin* and airily announced it to be 'in the genre' of Byron's *Don Juan*—'a novel in verse'. By 1825 he was adamantly denying the connection: 'Nobody esteems *Don Juan* more than I do (the first five cantos; I have not read the others)* but there is nothing in common with *Onegin* in it.' Pushkin had gracefully taken what he wanted from Byron and left behind the rest: in his undogmatic, unprogrammatic way, he knew that he had to write out of himself, not in imitation or servility. A sonnet he wrote in 1830 movingly defends his freedom:

> Poet! Don't value the people's love,
> Ecstatic praise's momentary uproar will pass,

---

* Later he read on until Canto IX, and would have encountered a reference to an ancestor of his in Canto VII, stanza xvii: 'Koclobski, Korakin, and Mouskin Pouskin / All proper men of weapons.'

　　Curiously enough, Pushkin's remarkable successor Mikhail Lermontov (1814–41) also has an ancestor mentioned in *Don Juan*: 'Arseniew, that great son of slaughter' (Canto IX, stanza ix) was his great-grandfather. Lermontov's novel *A Hero of our Time* (1840), which falls outside the chronological scope of this book, stands as one of literature's most searing and subtle portraits of a Byronic temperament. See Laurence Kelly, *Lermontov* (1977), especially Appendix 1.

You will hear the fool's censure and crowd's cold laughter,
But stay firm, unmoved and calm.
You are King; live alone. Travel along
The path of freedom, inspired by a free mind,
Realizing the fruits of your heartfelt thoughts,
And demanding no reward for your noble work.
Reward lies in you yourself. You are your own best judge,
Best able to assess what you yourself have done.
Does it satisfy your rigorous appraisal?
If it does satisfy, then let the masses scorn it,
Let them spit on the altar on which your light burns,
Let them rock your tripod in childish play.

Eugene Onegin is, first and foremost, the work of such a free poet, effortlessly being himself; but it is also both a delicate analysis of Byronism and a delicate tribute to one loved feature of Byron's *Don Juan*—the narrator's comfortably chatty relationship with the reader, which seems to get friendlier and more intimate as the poem progresses. Thus Byron:

But for the present, gentle reader! and
    Still gentler purchaser! the bard—that's I—
Must, with permission, shake you by the hand,
    And so your humble servant, and good bye!

And thus Pushkin:

Reader, I wish that, as we parted—
whoever you may be, a friend,
a foe—our mood should be warm-hearted....
God grant that from this little book
for heart's delight, or fun, you took,
for dreams, or journalistic battle,
God grant you took at least a grain.
On this we'll part: goodbye again!

These narrators are like story-tellers sitting in the same room, and relating their tale especially for *you*. They assume to know what sort of person you are and the sort of thing you enjoy. Sometimes they let you into secrets, sometimes they firmly close the door. They wag their fingers at the characters in the book, then turn and ask the reader to indulge their foibles. They may decide to tell the story straight or they may amble off into an amusing digression. They admit to love for the poem they have made. They might even have enjoyed each other's company!

But Pushkin's relaxation is actually much more disciplined than Byron's. *Don Juan* has no plan, no plot; *Eugene Onegin*, although also published serially over a period of years, does. In *Don Juan*, it is Byron's voice that we listen for, and all the other characters come and go at that voice's command: none of them develop as human beings, nor do their inner lives move our emotions. Pushkin criticized Byron for 'parcelling out among his characters such-and-such a trait of his own character', but in his much less egocentric way, without a trace of the puppet-master, he does something comparable. Certainly there is in both Tatyana and Onegin much of his own personality and predicament—which is why he can communicate them with such a fine blend of sympathy and detachment, and why the reader ends up feeling he knows them so well.

Onegin is a St Petersburg dandy who has carefully nurtured his persona, taking three hours a day over his toilet and running the gamut of cynicism, boredom, and alienation. I knew him myself, the narrator tells us: there was something about him—

> I liked his quality, the dream
> which held him silently subjected,
> his strangeness, wholly unaffected
> his mind, so close and so precise.

He comes to the country to claim an estate and encounters Tatyana, a bookish and lonely girl wrapped up in the world of Sentimental novels. It is a meeting of two unhappy introverts. Like Marianne Dashwood in *Sense and Sensibility*, Tatyana's mistake is to proceed on the assumption that life—and love—must be the same as it is in books. She decides to fall in love with Onegin and sends him a bold confessional letter. Onegin rejects her, but with surprising sensitivity and kindness—only to go on to stir up trouble by flirting with Tatyana's sister Olga, who is being courted by his friend Lensky, another figure of Sentimental high-mindedness. After a duel in which Lensky is killed, Onegin vanishes. Tatyana pays a visit to his house and takes some of his books off the library shelf: Byron, of course, and

> two or three novels where our later
> epoch's portrayed, survived the ban,
> works where contemporary man
> is represented rather truly,
> that soul without a moral tie,

> all egoistical and dry,
> to dreaming given up unduly,
> and that embittered mind which boils
> in empty deeds and futile toils.

She begins to realize what has made Onegin into the person he is:

> ... this freakish stranger,
> who walks with sorrow, and with danger,
> whether from heaven or from hell,
> this angel, this proud devil, tell,
> what is he? Just an apparition,
> a shadow, null and meaningless,
> a Muscovite in Harold's dress,
> a modish second-hand edition,
> a glossary of smart argot...

Olga marries a dashing Lancer with unseemly haste; Tatyana goes to Moscow.

Some years later, Onegin returns, apparently a changed man. But how, the narrator asks:

> Is he a Melmoth, a Childe Harold,
> a patriot, a cosmopolite,
> bigot or prude? or has he quite
> a different mask? is he becoming
> someone like you and me, just nice?

At a ball, he sees Tatyana, now a well-married and impressively sophisticated woman. The tables have turned: Onegin is now the one in love and writing passionate letters. Tatyana receives him and, not without a little crowing, adopts his role of the preacher of good sense. No, she is not happy in her new life; yes, she is still in love with him, but life is not like books. She has cast her lot and must live with the consequence. Onegin is left standing—at which point the narrator tantalizingly rings down the curtain.

The tone of *Eugene Onegin* is not heroic or epic. Byron's Juan wanders the world and meets with adventure, but *Eugene Onegin*, like Jane Austen's novels, turns on lives which are framed by a limited set of domestic possibilities. It is significant that Pushkin soon gave up on an attempt to write an account, in the Childe Harold manner, of Onegin's ennui-filled wanderings after the duel with Lensky. We are not Byronically free, Pushkin knows; desires are not satisfied, understandings not reached, escapes not made. Most of the time is spent putting up with disappointments; but then people change their minds or decide to cheer up and get on with things. *Eugene Onegin* accepts and explores such ordinary feelings, alongside the self-deceptions, fantasies and ironies which colour them.

Living under a regime of petty and sometimes tyrannous repression, Pushkin learnt to take what pleasure he could and be grateful for it. Byron may have complained bitterly about the fetters of fame and the hell of other people, but in comparison to the Russian he was as free as the wind. When he visited the cell in Ferrara in which the poet Tasso had been unjustly incarcerated, Byron insisted on having himself locked in, as though trying to make his imaginary prison concrete. Pushkin needed to make no such experiment: the reality was too near at hand to play about.

After the failure of the Decembrist uprising, which resulted in a poet friend of his being hanged for treason, Pushkin tried to opt out of politics. Byron's Greek expedition redeemed his reputation for posterity, as he knew it would; but Pushkin had no wish to be a hero, and became steadily less favoured among the young and frustrated. Back in St Petersburg, uncomfortably close to a new tsar who allowed him an insidious amount of rope, he decided to buckle under the shadow of censorship. Life must come first. He quoted some words from Chateaubriand's *René*, '*Il n'y a de bonheur que dans les voies communes*' ('Happiness is only to be found on the common highways'), married, and had children. 'It is quite possible to live without political liberty,' he wrote, 'but without the inviolability of the family it's impossible.' In the event, he was less than ordinarily successful. His beautiful wife Natalya was vain and self-centred, passionate only for the glamour of court society. In 1837 her flirtation with a handsome French baron led to a duel in which Pushkin, as if pursuing the fate of his own creation, the infatuated poet Lensky, was killed. The Tsar allowed Natalya a pension and she remarried. It was a somewhat heartless business.

Pushkin's compromises—and they were not easy ones—would never have attracted Byron, who imperiously assumed that absolute freedom was his by right. But his claims have come to ring hollow and the bulk of his hero-centred poems now read like dead matter; whereas Pushkin is still for the Russians what Jane Austen is for the English—a writer with whom one feels intimate, a comfort in times of trouble, sane, sincere, and trusted. 'Pushkin, not a memory, but a state of being,' wrote the twentieth-century poet Marina Tsvetaeva, 'Pushkin—forever and fromever.' Pushkin, a writer as friend but not, like the magnificently misunderstood Byron, an idol hungry for worship, 'An Alabaster Vase lighted up within'.

Chapter 6

Shakespearomania

We are so used to thinking of Shakespeare at the summit of literature, the standard by whom everyone else is ultimately measured, that
it is hard to appreciate that for a hundred and fifty years after his death
in 1616, his achievement was patronized in cultured circles with a
certain amount of scepticism. Throughout the seventeenth and most
of the eighteenth centuries the literati strongly believed that every
work of art should have a definite form, shape, and purpose, reflecting
and endorsing the values of a well-ordered civilization like that of
Imperial Rome: by such criteria, Shakespeare looked excessive and
inconsistent, lacking in sophistication and polish. His plays were
imperfectly constructed, mixing comedy and tragedy and confusing
distinctions of social class; his verse, however full of beauties, was
marred by indecency, puns, repetitions, and other copybook faults; his
plots were often improbable and sprawled through time and space; he
taught no clear moral lessons, neglecting the great principle of fiction,
that the good end happily, the bad unhappily. He was, in sum, a naïve
genius without a classical education, and posterity felt no compunction about tidying up the mess. Shakespeare was rewritten, cut,
adapted, and cannibalized to fit the new taste. In 1681, for instance,
Nahum Tate produced a version of *King Lear* which omitted the Fool,
invented a love interest between Edgar and Cordelia which results in
marriage, and rounded off the proceedings with Lear and Gloucester
walking off into the sunset of peaceful retirement.

But through the latter half of the eighteenth century in that great
move of European taste towards the primitive and sincere, the reasons
for admiring Shakespeare almost reversed. What had seemed naïveté,
even crudity, could now be regarded as truth to Nature, while his
irregularities evinced his powers of feeling and imagination, not his
inability to be lucid and courtly. Scholars such as Edmund Malone
assembled more authentic editions of the texts (although these did not
become current in the theatre until much later); forgers simultaneously turned their craft to the production of a stream of faked
Shakespearean manuscripts. The facts of Shakespeare's life became a
subject of popular speculation, his personality surrounded by a pen-

umbra of awe. Not only a great playwright and poet, Shakespeare was also set up as a great human being—'superior to all mankind', Horace Walpole called him in 1778. Nine years earlier the finest actor of the century, David Garrick, had begun the glamorization of a dirty little Midlands market town, Stratford-upon-Avon, with a grand Jubilee celebration. No play was performed, but tribute was paid to the Bard's birthplace with fireworks, a ball, an oratorio, and a horse race. The climax of the festivities proved comically disastrous. A Shakespearean fancy-dress procession was aborted; Garrick's declamation of a specially composed ode to the Swan of Avon was ruined by a cack-handed barber who slashed Garrick's face during his morning shave, and by 'hateful drizzling rain' which caused the river to break its banks. The whole event was said to have lost Garrick £2,000 and gained him only a galling amount of ridicule in the press. But nothing could stop what soon became labelled 'Shakespearomania', the cult of a phenomenon as English as the weather. Henry Crawford in Jane Austen's *Mansfield Park* (1814) puts it thus: 'Shakespeare one gets acquainted with without knowing how. It is part of an Englishman's constitution. His thoughts and beauties are so spread abroad that one touches them everywhere, one is intimate with him by instinct.'

This has a trace of the old-fashioned view of Shakespeare as a writer best anthologized into 'thoughts and beauties': more advanced tastes were beginning to appreciate the plays as delicately structured wholes, which should not be tampered with lightly. Between 1808 and 1819, Coleridge lectured extensively on this theme, using Shakespeare's example as a means of developing a theory of 'the principles of poetry', demonstrating Shakespeare's ability to embrace complexity and contradiction into unity—the form miraculously attuned to content, language to character and meaning, in a realism that was poetic not pedantic—without resorting to any of the externally imposed 'rules' of classical procedure. His appreciation of the subtleties of Shakespeare's psychology was also acute, and he marvelled at the openness of Shakespearean morality, which never wags an admonitory finger and loves a Falstaff as well as a Cordelia.

Yet Coleridge's thoughts on Shakespeare are as tantalizing and confusing as so much else in his *oeuvre*, surviving only as they can be assembled from fragments and the notes taken by members of his audiences. For all the town's appetite for talk about Shakespeare, Coleridge was too unreliable a performer to make the lecture courses the success they should have been. 'They were but indifferently attended, and scoffers were not unfrequently among the number, among my personal acquaintances not a few,' reminisced Crabb Robinson of the 1811–12 lectures. It was the old Coleridge story, with no way of telling whether you would end up with an evening of brilliant and incisive insights or one of doped-up ramblings. On one occasion, Crabb Robinson's diary relates, 'He surpassed himself in the art of talking in a very interesting way, without speaking at all on the subject announced. According to advertisement, he was to lecture on *Romeo and Juliet* and Shakespeare's female characters. Instead of this he began with a defence of school flogging' and continued through 'the character of the age of Elizabeth and James I, as compared with that of Charles I; distinguished not very clearly between wit and fancy; referred to the different languages of Europe; attacked the fashionable notion concerning poetic diction; ridiculed the tautology of Johnson's line, "If observation with extensive view", &c; and warmly defended Shakespeare against the charge of impurity.' Sudden illness and peremptory cancellations were other box-office deterrents: on one characteristic occasion, Coleridge turned up late at the hall, looking puffy and worried, claiming that his lecture notes had been pickpocketed as he was walking up the Strand.

This is a psychologically interesting excuse, inasmuch as the schoolboy Coleridge had himself once been wrongly apprehended as a pickpocket in the Strand; and he would be guilty of another sort of pickpocketing, namely that of plagiarizing his lectures from the work of the German critic A. W. Schlegel, Madame de Staël's camp-follower. When some virtually word-for-word parallels were presented to him, he brazenly disclaimed the implication: impossible, he said, I did not even possess a copy of Schlegel's writings on Shakespeare at the time—but then he would surreptitiously jiggle the dates. Schlegel and I had both read deep into Kant and our minds moved in the same direction; such things happen by coincidence.

Coleridge had at least taken advantage of the most developed Shakespeare scholarship of the day, for Schlegel stands at the pinnacle of the half-century in which the Germans had discovered Shakespeare. He translated seventeen of the plays into sensitive and imaginative verse which is still current today in German theatres, accepted as a work of German literature much as Scott-Moncrieff's translation of Proust is among English speakers. He investigated Shakespeare's sources and the works of his contemporaries, insisting on the importance of establishing accurate texts and understanding the social context in which they were all rooted. Where he crucially anticipated Coleridge was in emphasizing that Shakespeare was a self-conscious artist whose plays uncovered their layers like a flower: he pointed out, for instance, how in *Romeo and Juliet*, hero and heroine, Capulet and Montague, Mercutio and the Nurse, and so on, functioned in parallel and contrast both poetically and dramatically. To us this may seem obvious: then, it represented a major advance on what had gone before, a serious attempt at a scholarly and objective reconstruction of Shakespeare.

Others in Germany had only mined for precious metal to adorn their own theories, sieving away what they saw as inferior ore. The *Sturm und Drang* movement, for instance, took garishly caricatured versions of Macbeth, Iago, and Richard III as the basis for the violent bombast of their own hero-villains and looked no further. The great actor-manager Friedrich Schröder may be remembered for introducing Shakespeare to German theatre audiences in the 1770s, but it was a Shakespeare translated into prose, in which Hamlet wins the day and Juliet gets to talk to the dying Romeo. Ludwig Tieck turned *The Tempest* into an opera along the lines of Mozart's *Die Zauberflöte*—he loved in Shakespeare what he saw as an unanchored dream world; Hoffmann, like so many since, sank himself into Hamlet, whose irony and alienation re-emerge in the figure of Kreisler. Even Goethe, whose admiration for Shakespeare was lifelong and fervent, squinted. At his theatre at Weimar he produced Schiller's translation of *Macbeth*, turning the witches into something like the chorus of a Greek tragedy, not cackling hags but temple priestesses, declaiming their prophecies in mellifluously measured tones. Shakespeare may have been the writer closest to Nature, but Nature for Goethe had to be pleasingly harmonious, and rough edges needed honing down: in 1812 he proposed that *Hamlet* would work much better in the theatre if the play ended after the bedroom scene, with the climactic revelation that the rat behind the arras whom Hamlet stabs to death was Claudius after all, not Polonius! Later he came to the conclusion that Shakespeare was simply not an effective dramatist—too many scene changes and minor characters, not enough clarity of action: far better to read and reflect on him in the privacy of one's own mind.

This was not sour grapes: one of Goethe's strongest instincts was intellectual self-preservation, and he must have realized the necessity of keeping his distance from such a potentially overwhelming influence. Anyone who studied Shakespeare too closely, he commented, would discover that he 'had already exhausted the whole of human nature in all its tendencies, in all its heights and depths, and that in fact there remains for him, the aftercomer, nothing more to do'. He was to some degree right. Shakespearomania did not altogether work for the good of modern literature, least of all in England.

There was young John Keats, for instance, who first started thinking about Shakespeare seriously on holiday in the Isle of Wight in 1817, at the moment of dedicating the great adventure of his life to Poetry. 'He has left nothing to say about nothing or any thing,' was his daunted conclusion. But a writer is a human being as well as a monument of words, and Keats also found Shakespeare comforting and companionable: 'I felt rather lonely this morning at breakfast so I went and unbox'd a Shakespeare,' he wrote, just after the Isle of Wight; later, 'I never quite despair and I read Shakespeare.' He became an intensely personal presence, an invisible friend to the young poet: in what position did Shakespeare sit when he began 'To be or not to be'? he wondered; and was he not more like Hamlet, 'in his common every day life than any other of his Characters'? Perhaps the most moving evidence of this intimacy is contained in the first letter he wrote to his beloved brother and sister-in-law in America, after the terrible death of Tom Keats, at which Keats himself had patiently ministered. Needing to feel as close as possible to them, and comparing the disembodied way in which they must communicate to that of immortal spirits, he writes, 'I shall read a passage of Shakespeare every Sunday at ten o Clock—you read one at the same time and we shall be as near each other as blind bodies can be in the same room.'

Nor was it just an emotional relationship. Keats learnt important lessons in poetic technique from the sonnets in particular; and of all the familiar 'Romantic' poets, it was he who most artfully wove his own threads into the tapestry of Shakespearean language, emulating its rich and fine excess, its shot density of imagery and complexity of mood, as well as what every English Literature student knows as the quality 'which Shakespeare possessed so enormously ... *Negative Capability* ... when man is capable of being in uncertainties, mysteries, doubts, without any irritable reaching out after fact & reason' (although this, in fact, is only the extension of a commonplace of criticism: Shakespeare's unself-conscious gift for thinking himself 'in to the Thoughts and Feelings of Beings in circumstances wholly & strangely different from our own', as Coleridge's version of 1802 put it, had been celebrated since the middle of the eighteenth century).

But in terms of writing for the theatre Keats got nowhere. Even if he did not feel, as Goethe suggests, that the possibilities had been exhausted, so powerful was the notion of Shakespeare as the ideal that he made no attempt to find a modern form and subject-matter or to look anywhere but backwards for inspiration. Keats's failure here was typical of his generation: anybody trying to write a serious drama inevitably modelled it, to some extent, on five-act blank-verse tragedy in the Shakespearean style. The dream was partly fuelled by the prospect of money and success beyond anything most books of poetry could hope to excite: Keats wrote his wretched *Otho the Great* thinking that 'were it to succeed ... it would lift me out of the mire ... My name with the literary fashionable is vulgar—I am a weaver boy to them—a Tragedy would lift me out of this mess.' The hope proved vain, as it did for Wordsworth, Southey, Lamb, and Shelley—their tragedies were all either abortions or pastiches, dutiful copies of the Old Master never transformed into art by any fresh feeling, vision, or experience, and thus stillborn on the page. None of them, for one thing, had Shakespeare's practical experience of the medium. At best it was only the minor dramatists of the Elizabethan and Jacobean period that were genuinely echoed: Shelley's *The Cenci*, for instance, almost works as a blood-bath melodrama along the lines of *The Revenger's Tragedy* or *The White Devil*. Coleridge, whose play *Remorse* caused a brief ripple at Drury Lane in 1813, recognized this in a remark recorded in *Table Talk*:

> There's such a divinity doth hedge our Shakespeare round, that we cannot even imitate his style. I tried to imitate his manner in the *Remorse*, and, when I had done, I found I had been tracking Beaumont and Fletcher, and Massinger instead. It is really very curious. At first sight, Shakespeare and his contemporary dramatists seem to write in styles much alike: nothing so easy as to fall into that of Massinger and the others; whilst no one has ever yet produced one scene conceived and expressed in the Shakespearean idiom.

It is Byron, once again, who stands a little apart. His historical tragedies, such as *Marino Faliero* and *The Two Foscari*, are as flat and stiff as any of his peers', but they do at least have the negative virtue of not trying to pursue the Shakespearean atmosphere and effect. With his preference for the eighteenth century, Byron was still capable of confessing to the old view of Shakespeare as 'a man of great genius but no art ... the *worst* of models, though the most extraordinary of writers', and he avowed that he had been more influenced by the neo-classical dramas of the Italian Alfieri and the Ancient Greeks than by Shakespeare: his plays were written to be read not acted, he said, and he had concentrated on keeping them austere in colour and strong and simple in action.

Another influence on Byron's drama was, surprisingly, a contemporary woman playwright of Scots birth. Joanna Baillie is now almost totally forgotten, even among feminist academics dredging the catalogues for third-rate women novelists, but in her day she was rated astonishingly high. For Walter Scott she was 'the best dramatic writer since the days of Shakespeare and Massinger', for Southey, 'an honour to English literature'; Byron himself called her 'our only dramatist since Otway and Southerne' (in other words for the best part of a century) and reflected less reverently: 'Voltaire asked why no woman had "written even a tolerable tragedy" [and] replied, "The composition of a tragedy requires testicles."—If this be true Lord knows what Joanna Baillie does—I suppose she borrows them.' Yet even in the joke is the acknowledgement that Joanna Baillie *had* written 'tolerable' tragedies, not mere fustian.

Her life story is a quaint one, interesting for being so dull. Today we tend to assume—and indeed everything else in this book may seem to bear out—that to write about turbulent emotions implies a writer with a turbulent biography, but in the case of Joanna Baillie the equation does not hold. She was born in 1762, into an old and venerable family—her father was Professor of Divinity at the University of Glasgow and her brother a distinguished physician who at one time treated Byron's club foot. The Scottish respect for learning meant that she was more comprehensively educated than her English contemporary Jane Austen, becoming an accomplished musical performer as well as a keen amateur mathematician. In 1784 she moved to London with her widowed mother and sister, and it was there, according to the *Dictionary of National Biography*, 'whilst imprisoned by the heat of a summer afternoon, and seated by her mother's side engaged in needlework, that the thought of essaying dramatic composition burst upon her'.

Joanna Baillie had one particular and in some respects original theatrical principle. Each of her plays was an exploration of one specific and extreme emotional state—Hate, Fear, Hope, Love—and the way that an individual can become dominated by it to the point of monomania. It was this powerful central focus that Byron was to emulate and which won her considerable critical acclaim. However, no one could claim that she treated her themes with any degree of subtlety or insight. Instead the bones were clothed in the trappings of the Gothic horror-fantasies which were as popular on stage as they were in the Novel. Her plays are full of gloomy medieval castles, caverns, convents, and mountain retreats. Bells toll, doors creak, phantoms howl, and innocent women scream. The elaborate stage directions include a good deal of staggering and raising-of-arms-and-eyes-to-heaven. At the climax of her most successful play *De Monfort*, for example, the protagonist 'shrinks back with horror, runs furiously, and, dashing his head against the wall, falls upon the floor.'

But beneath all this overt frenzy, the play—a study of obsessive hatred—did not have enough substance to establish itself. The verse is blank in both senses, and from an opening scene in which servants prattle about their masters to the 'song' interlude,

> Pleasant is the mantling bowl
> And the song of merry soul,
> And the red lamp's cheery light;
> And the goblet glancing bright,
> Whilst many a cheerful face around
> Listens to the jovial sound,
> Social spirits, join with me:
> Bless the God of jollity.

the play is full of the usual feeble pseudo-Shakespeareanisms. But no one else had anything much better to offer.

De Monfort's, and Joanna Baillie's, finest hour came in 1800, when the incomparable brother-and-sister team of John Philip Kemble and Mrs Siddons acted the play in a splendid production at Drury Lane, further graced by an epilogue composed by the Duchess of Devonshire. After that burst of éclat, Joanna Baillie found little luck in the theatre—only seven of her twenty-eight published plays were ever performed—but her standing as a literary figure was maintained for some years. In 1806 she moved to Hampstead, and although we now associate that London village with the cabal of young radicals like Keats and Shelley who clustered round Leigh Hunt, at the time it was she who was its most celebrated inhabitant, visited by 'many friends eminent in science, in art, and in society'. She was liked for her meekness and modesty, for the way in which she never shirked her feminine dutifulness. Keenly charitable to the poor, she made her own puddings and paid devoted attention to her blind and aged mother. There was no unbecoming bluestocking arrogance in her. 'If I had to present anyone to a foreigner as the model of an English gentlewoman, it would be Joanna Baillie,' said Wordsworth. 'She carries her literary reputation as freely and easily as the milkmaid in my country does the *leglen*, which she carries on her head and walks as gracefully with it as a duchess. Some of the fair sex, and some of the foul sex, too, carry their renown in London fashion on a yoke and pair of pitchers,' cooed Walter Scott.

What would this paragon of womankind have thought of the unhealthy effect one of her plays had in a sordid little apartment down the hill from Hampstead in St Pancras?—where one night in October 1814, Shelley and Claire sat up late talking (Mary, as usual, having gone to bed early). The conversation gravitated to the horrors of the supernatural, and by two o'clock in the morning, the two of them were 'awe-struck' and 'hardly daring to breathe'. Shelley's journal records how it was to a Gothic-Shakespearean play by Joanna Baillie, published in 1812, that their imaginings turned:

> Shelley says to Jane [Claire's preferred name at the time] 'Good night'; his hand is leaning on the table; he is conscious of an expression in his countenance which he cannot repress. Jane hesitates. 'Good night' again. She still hesitates. 'Did you ever read the tragedy of Orra?' said Shelley. 'Yes—how horrible you look—take your eyes off.' 'Good night' again, and Jane ran to her room.

Claire's journal continues: 'I placed the candle on the drawers & stood looking at a pillow that lay in the very middle of the Bed—I turned my head round to the window & then back again to the Bed— the pillow was no longer there—it had been removed to the chair.' She ran out in a fit of terror at the apparent *poltergeist* to find Shelley, who takes up the story: 'Her hair came prominent and erect; her eyes were wide and staring, drawn almost from the sockets by the convulsions of the muscles; the eyelids were forced in, and the eyeballs, without any relief, seemed as if they had been newly inserted, in ghastly sport, in the sockets of a lifeless head.' His idea of calming her down consisted of taking her back to the fireside and 'engaging in awful conversation relative to the nature of these mysteries'—with the result that by dawn 'her horror and agony increased even to the most dreadful convulsions. She shrieked and writhed on the floor.' Mary, one notes, did not bother to intervene.

Orra had something to answer for that night. It was Joanna Baillie's treatment of the state of 'superstitious fear': the eponymous heroine is a cheerful and charming maiden who makes her first entry 'tripping gayly, and playing with the folds of her scarf'. Her weakness is a penchant for ghost stories and when she refuses to marry the repulsive dwarf Glottenbal, he imprisons her in an isolated castle, where with sadistic malice he inflicts a diet of the horrors on her, finally driving her insane. For Shelley and Claire, the parallels needed no pointing.

Joanna Baillie sank inexorably into obscurity: critical attacks on her by Hazlitt and the *Edinburgh Review* delivered fatal blows. An oddity is that in the 1830s two of her plays were translated into Sinhalese, after the Chief Justice of Ceylon decided that they constituted an efficacious means of raising 'the minds of the inhabitants of that island, and of eradicating their vices'. She lived on to 1851 and the age of eighty-eight: the writer and reformer Harriet Martineau remembered how she 'had enjoyed a fame almost without parallel, and had outlived it. She had been told every day for years, through every possible channel, that she was second only to Shakespeare,—if second; and then she had seen her works drop out of notice so that of the generation who grew up before her eyes, not one in a thousand had read a line of her plays:—yet was her serenity never disturbed, nor her merry humour in the least dimmed.' We might also commemorate her as an original of the demure spinster with the paradoxical ability to write lurid murder stories or torrid romances.

Every generation interprets the art of the past through its own perspectives, and Shakespeare in particular has changed his profile according to the tastes and exigencies of different eras and cultures. Joanna Baillie, for instance, took up some of the more violent and sensational elements of his plays—their melodramatic extremes, if you like—and cast them into the moulds of the Gothic fantasy and psychological horror story popular in her day. But it wasn't just a matter of literary vogue meeting another literary vogue: there was something in the breadth and power of Shakespeare's genius that struck deep into the heart and mind of Revolutionary Europe. He was the dramatist who matched up to the historical drama of the time, with all its emotional over-heatedness and sense of chaos and reversal. Those who had watched the rise and fall of Robespierre, Napoleon, and Byron could appreciate the force of Hamlet, Lear, Macbeth, Othello, Richard III, heroes lurching between good and evil.

The great bodying-forth of this *modern* Shakespeare came in the acting of Edmund Kean (1789–1833). This small, wiry man with a rasping voice and penetrating jet-black eyes, often thought to have been of gypsy origin (he himself preferred to claim that he was the bastard son of the Duke of Norfolk), brought a style of tempestuous naturalism to the interpretation of the major Shakespearean roles: imagine a first glimpse of Marlon Brando after years of watching John

Gielgud, and you have something of the shock he inflicted on his audiences. The illusion he gave was of spontaneity—'something genuine and unconscious', wrote Leigh Hunt, 'something that moved, looked and spoke solely under the impulse of the immediate idea'—and a unique nervous volatility which many critics tried to translate into words—'his fixed gaze, his starting up, his turning about, his letting fall a speech, then suddenly snatching it up again with the greatest energy, his way of going quickly off, then returning slowly but unexpectedly' was the version of the German novelist Tieck; Hazlitt, who more closely than anyone else recorded Kean's art, spoke of 'the rapidity of his transitions from one tone and feeling to another, [his] propriety and novelty of action, preserving a succession of striking pictures and giving perpetually fresh shocks of delight and surprise'.

A longer view shows, however, that Kean was not quite the original he appeared to be. His background was conventionally theatrical: he was born near the proverbial trunk, if not actually in it, and had the usual start as a stage 'infant prodigy' of no great note, followed by years of drudgery as a teenager performing Harlequin acrobatics in variety shows around the provinces. And it was the usual mixture of ruthless ambition and luck that brought him out of mediocrity. In 1810 he started filling notebooks with classical tags and gems from the poets, which he was clearly memorizing as part of an effort to get ahead and pass himself off as a gentleman. He also began to play leading roles and worked at his interpretations with ferocious energy: the famous spontaneity was in fact the result of meticulous rehearsal. He was also determinedly different. The reigning king of the London stage was John Philip Kemble, an actor whose portrayals were cerebral and decorous, full of noble bearing and beautifully modulated verse-speaking (he was an asthmatic and thus lacked the breath control to rant); Kean seems to have looked more to the dubious example of George Cooke, an actor who teetered on insanity, tottered into alcoholism, spent long spells in the debtors' prison, and who on a half-sober night could flame up and electrify the dampest audience. But Kemble was near retirement, and Cooke had left England for America in 1810: by 1814 London was ready for a new star, and Kean moreover was ready for London.

There were only two principal theatres at the time, Covent Garden and the newly rebuilt Drury Lane; the former held the solid box-office draw of Kemble; Drury Lane badly needed someone to counter it, and decided to scout for talent round the touring companies, each of whose leading tragedians would be given a one-night chance to show their worth. Kean's turn duly came. On a filthy January night, after a single brief rehearsal and to an auditorium three-quarters empty, he played Shylock in *The Merchant of Venice*, wearing not the red wig traditionally symbolic of a comic approach to the part, but a black one: this Shylock was a real and dangerous villain. The audience was impressed, the management encouraged, but it was Hazlitt's unequivocal review for the *Morning Chronicle* which clinched it: 'for voice, eye, action, and expression no actor has come out for many years at all equal to him', he reported. In the way of such things, the pitch of the public's curiosity rose from mild to feverish, and when two weeks later Kean appeared as Richard III, the house was packed and alive with anticipation. It was again a performance which played up the villainy of the character, featuring some spectacular explosions of violence, set against moments of eerie introspection, such as Richard's brooding before the Battle of Bosworth, when Kean stood in front of the royal tent, moodily tracing patterns in the sand with his sword. The result was a triumph, and Kean was confirmed as the greatest actor of his generation, the formal anointing taking place when Garrick's elderly widow summoned him to sit on her husband's chair (something no one had done since his death thirty-five years earlier) and then bequeathed him Garrick's box of stage jewels.

But Kean did not have the temperament to ride life, let alone success smoothly. Paranoiacally sensitive and often insanely demanding, he was not calmed by recognition. First he fell ill and the press announced alarming reports of his 'spitting blood'; then he recovered and gave his Hamlet, in which he was generally considered miscast, although there was another wonderful touch after the angry cry of 'Get thee to a nunnery ...' when Kean's Hamlet was suddenly overcome with tenderness and remorse, pressing Ophelia's hand silently to his lips. The reviewer's ready superlatives were already turning against him: Crabb Robinson, for instance, came late to Kean having read all the newspapers, and confessed disappointment— 'my expectations were pitched too high.'

His career was as volatile as his acting style, and he was by no means universally applauded. He had only two further indisputable triumphs—Othello, and Sir Giles Overreach in Massinger's *New Way to Pay Old Debts*, in which he scaled such a climax of evil intensity that audiences became frozen with terror (Byron, it was said, fell into an epileptic convulsion). He passed briskly through the gamut of modern pseudo-Shakespearean roles, including Joanna Baillie's Monfort, but none of them ever caught on, partly because the plays were inherently so weak, and partly because Kean's genius was such a limited one—he was not a chameleon actor with a broad emotional range; romantic and comic roles were beyond him; he did not have the light touch. In Hazlitt's words, he was 'all passion, all energy, all relentless will', and there were periods when audiences and critics tired of it.

It was not just that on a bad night he could seem ranting and mannered, ready to fall back on a series of well-tried effects, such as high-pitched gabbling. It was also that he was becoming increasingly cantankerous both on and off stage, and regularly the worse for drink. The nadir of his reputation was reached in 1825, when Alderman Cox, a member of the Drury Lane management committee, sued him for £2,000 damages in a case which involved the revelation of Kean's long-term and faintly ludicrous affair with none other than Mrs Cox. In the wake of the scandal, he was left by his long-suffering wife, whom he had married back in 1808, years before his elevation; worse, the charismatic tragedian was shown up as a trivial adulterer, who wrote silly love notes, bundled whores into his dressing room, and got a thrill from staring at his mistress clad in nothing but the breeches he wore for Richard III.

After this and other sordid revelations, the gallery found it hard to take his Othello seriously, and Kean's last years were spent mostly on tour, his extraordinary art sinking into routine and then into decrepitude. But it was kind of Fate to allow him to collapse finally on the stage of Drury Lane, scene of his first triumphs, while playing Othello to the Iago of his own son Charles. He died a couple of weeks later, in March 1833, having survived for some years on a suicidal diet consisting of virtually nothing except brandy.

The fascination of Kean grew on the fashionable aesthetic criteria of the times. Keats, following a dictum of Hazlitt, wrote that 'the excellence of every art is its intensity', and Kean's acting was the very distillation of that intensity. Like many aspiring young playwrights Keats dreamt of Kean's patronage carrying his play *Otho the Great* to success and wrote the leading part with him in mind; more than that, he hoped that he could 'make as great a revolution in modern dramatic writing as Kean had done in acting'. He also published an ecstatic Hazlitt-esque appreciation of Kean, marvelling at his 'intense power of anatomizing the passion of every syllable ... Kean delivers himself up to the instant feeling, without a shadow of a thought about anything else.' For the intellectuals, then, the great actor was no longer regarded as a mere entertainer or mimic, holding the mirror up to

Nature, but as an *artist* 'spontaneously' inspired, very much as they liked to think a poet or a Paganini might be, with some daemonic power. Yet a Kean was still ultimately an interpreter; a genius perhaps, but only by virtue of his mediumship of the greater genius of Shakespeare. In Italy there flourished an ancient craft which further refined the idea of the actor as creative artist. Tommaso Sgricci, a Pisan law student, had won international celebrity for his soirées, at which the audience would be invited to present him with any theme, on which he would immediately improvise a long poem in either blank or *terza rima* verse, complete with the appropriate gestures and dramatically modulated declamation: subjects might range from Samson and Delilah to Charles I, and the speed and fluency of his performances appeared miraculous. Homer was thought to have been the first of these *improvvisatori*, spectacular evidence that spontaneous poetic inspiration was more than a myth.

During the Christmas of 1821 Shelley, Mary, and Claire went to hear Sgricci at a theatre in Pisa, and in their characteristic ways were mightily impressed. Mary, cautious, intellectualizing: 'I am inclined to think that in the perfection in which he possesses this art it is by no means an inferior power to that of a *printed poet*'; Claire, rapturous: 'A great poet resembles Nature—he is a Creator and a Destroyer, he presides over the birth & death of images, the prototypes of things— the torrent of his sentiments should flow like waves one after the other, each distinctly formed and visible yet linked between its pre- decessor and its follower as to form between them both by beauty and necessity an indissoluble connection'; while Shelley, as Richard Holmes has suggested, was inspired to the writing of his most rhapso- dic and 'free-form' poem, *Epipsychidion*, the hymn to Emilia Viviani. Byron knew Sgricci too, but was more interested in the gossip: 'He is also a celebrated Sodomite,' he wrote to Hobhouse, 'a character by no means so much respected in Italy as it should be; but they laugh instead of burning and the women talk of it as a pity in a man of talent ...'

The *improvvisatore* intrigued Pushkin as well.* In a haunting, unfinished story, 'Egyptian Nights', he contrasts the Russian Charsky, who tries to lead an outwardly normal life, keeping his writing of

---

* In 1835 the thirty-year-old Hans Christian Andersen published his first major work, a novel entitled *The Improvisatore*. One might also mention a book published in 1821 by a then freshman at Oxford University, Thomas Lovell Beddoes. This collection of macabre tales in verse, *The Improvisatore*, purports to be authored by a wandering minstrel, medieval descendant of Homer.

poetry a thing apart and joyously private, with the mysterious black-bearded figure from Italy who bursts in on him one evening. He is a poor wandering *improvvisatore*, for whom Charsky arranges a soirée. The theme of Cleopatra is undertaken and he warms to it: 'His face became terribly pale; he trembled as if in a fever; his eyes sparkled with a strange fire; he pushed his dark hair off his forehead with his hand, wiped his lofty brow, covered with beads of perspiration, with his handkerchief ... then suddenly stepped forward and folded his arms across his breast ... The music stopped ... The improvisation began ...'

What is poetic inspiration, where does it come from, and can it be commanded? Pushkin asks. 'Every talent is inexplicable,' he answers—and leaves the story unfinished, the enigmatic record of a period in his life when he felt barren and empty. These things are mysteries.

Coleridge was yet another poet deeply engaged by such questions—'Kubla Khan', for instance, poses as the utterance of an *improvvisatore*, or at least as a spontaneous poetic chant formed beyond the realms of reason. But Coleridge compared himself to the divinely inspired psalmists of the Bible rather than to a Sgricci and his stagey footlit glamour. The cult of the star performer he found distasteful; poetry was not the stuff of a theatrical turn, but a manifestation of human creativity. And he was sceptical of the way that a Kean 'took over' Shakespeare. His famous remark that watching Kean resembled 'reading Shakespeare by flashes of lightning' was not altogether a compliment. That flash dazzled in the darkness, blinding those who witnessed it to the steady glow that should emanate from the organic whole of Shakespeare's poetic drama. People were going to the theatre 'not to see a play' but Kean 'in some one part' of it.

Coleridge might have been considerably more indignant at, or baffled by, the audiences witnessing the season of Shakespearean tragedy presented by a company of English actors in Paris during 1827–8. Here it was truly a matter of '*seeing* a play'—for virtually no one in attendance understood more than the odd word of Elizabethan English, and even the most zealous received the drama only through the medium of an antiquated and inaccurate prose translation which they attempted to follow through the performance. But the impression of colour, passion, violent contrasts of mood and pace, as well as an unfamiliar style of acting—vigorous, uninhibited, and 'realistic'—was overwhelming. The stars were John Philip Kemble's younger brother

Charles, Kean's rival William Macready (Kean himself came later, much heralded but too tired and demoralized to be anything other than a relative disappointment*), and the pretty but second-rate Harriet Smithson, whose inadequacies, obvious enough to sophisticated London audiences, proved inaudible and invisible to the gullible French; the most appreciated plays were *Hamlet* and *Romeo and Juliet*. Shakespeare was virtually unknown to the French stage, in any identifiable form, and the effect of the English actors on Paris was electrifying. For the young lions—Alfred de Vigny, Charles Sainte-Beuve, Gérard de Nerval, Hector Berlioz, Alexandre Dumas, Eugène Delacroix, Victor Hugo, all there for the first night of *Hamlet*—it was like discovering a new religion. Berlioz fell in love with Harriet Smithson and later married her, disastrously: what is more, 'Shakespeare, coming upon me unawares, struck me like a thunderbolt. The lightning flash of that discovery revealed to me at a stroke the whole heaven of art, illuminating it to its remotest corners. I recognized the meaning of grandeur, beauty, dramatic truth ... I saw, I understood, I felt ... that I was alive and that I must arise and walk,' he records in his memoirs, pathetically confessing, 'I may add that at that time I did not know a word of English.' Alexandre Dumas was even more fulsome: 'I realized in fact, that, after God, Shakespeare had created more than any other human being ... It was the first time that I had seen on the stage real passions, animating men and women of flesh and bone ... *O Shakespeare, merci! O Kemble et Smithson, merci! Merci à mon Dieu! Merci à mes anges de poésie!*'

Five years earlier, in 1822, another troupe of English actors performing *Othello* in Paris had been laughed off the stage. Some of the animosity had been purely xenophobic, the bitter after-taste of Waterloo— '*A bas avec les Anglais!*' was shouted from the gallery, '*Shakespeare, c'est l'aide-de-camp de Wellington!*—but there was also genuine derision directed against Shakespeare's aesthetics. The prejudices of Voltaire and other eighteenth-century critics had never been broken. A tragedy should not feature a hero in black face, revolve around so ludicrous an object as a handkerchief, nor end with the heroine meeting the grotesque fate of being smothered by a pillow. Why was all the ranting and falling about necessary? Why was formal elegance of gesture and voice so neglected? And even worse, why did Shakespeare not observe the basic rules of classical drama which

---

* The legend, however, was soon fixed by Alexandre Dumas' play *Kean* (1836), which portrays the actor as a wild and lusty genius, cramped and finally destroyed by the establishment and the narrowness of its moral values.

insisted on the action taking place within one day, inside one clearly defined area, preferably a monarch's palace? Such low and chaotic nonsense as *Othello*, penned by an enemy barbarian, was an insult to *la gloire* of France, to the perfect good manners of Racine and Corneille, and their immaculate verse in strict alexandrine metre, treating of high-born personages locked in high-toned moral dilemmas.

Such was the argument of the supporters of the state-sponsored and controlled Comédie-Française, an institution which stood like a rock at the centre of French arts and letters, upholding the standards and traditions of a hundred and fifty years; and it was an argument loaded with ideological implication. After Napoleon's downfall, a chastened France, straitjacketed by war reparations, had restored the monarchy and become subject to a cautious and conservative government anxious to keep order, avoid unsettling new ideas, and win back lost respect from the rest of Europe. An official periwigged theatre was symbolic of periwigged politics, reflecting a state which could keep the rabble from breaking down the doors.

From 1824 the reaction hardened. A new king, Charlex X, had come to the throne and proved a good deal tougher than his predecessor, insisting on his appointment by Divine Right and the domination of the Catholic Church. There were many French men and women who could accept this reversal of thirty-five years of change as the price of stability, and some even relished the mystique and ritual entailed—it is significant that the most popular reading of the day was Scott's 'Waverley' novels and Chateaubriand's *Le Génie du Christianisme*, both of which ignored recent history to fall back into a dimmer past of faith, chivalry, and ceremony. Meanwhile that strange word 'Romantic' floated around the *salons* like a miasma, although there were scarcely two literary hostesses, two journalists, who could agree on what it exactly meant. Scott and Chateaubriand qualified under most definitions: they were Romantics because they could see the poetry of a Gothic cathedral, a pine forest in the mist, a knight in armour. Madame de Staël's *De l'Allemagne* had given the lead here, and A. W. Schlegel's Lectures (which had influenced her directly) were also translated and discussed. Romanticism was the art of the north, full of religion and the medieval; Classicism was the art of the South, full of reason, light and clear lines. Even Byron found it all a trifle baffling: 'I perceive that in Germany, as well as in Italy, there is a great struggle about what they call "Classical" and "Romantic,"' he wrote in 1820, 'terms which were not subjects of classification in England, at least when I left it four or five years ago.' But if London didn't yet care, Paris did: by the mid 1820s Romanticism was definitely *in*, and Classicism was *out*.

In 1823 Stendhal had taken the distinction a stage further and somewhat blurred it. He published a pamphlet entitled *Racine et Shakespeare* aimed, like his *Vie de Rossini*, at puncturing French pretensions and complacence—in this case, the stuffiness of the Comédie-Française in particular. '*Romanticism*,' he claimed, 'is the art which presents to people the literary works which, in the current condition of their customs and beliefs, are susceptible of giving them the most pleasure. *Classicism*, on the other hand, presents them with the literature which gave most pleasure to their great-grandfathers.' Sophocles and Racine had been Romantics in their own day; but Shakespeare is *still* a Romantic because he wrote at a period of history with similar problems and preoccupations to those of the early nineteenth century. Modern French dramatists should not copy or imitate Shakespeare, but learn from him 'the art of giving to our contemporaries precisely the sort of tragedy of which they have need'. So Shakespeare could be a modern, and Romanticism the banner for modernism: it is this twist that explains the difference in the receptions given to the English actors in 1822 and 1827.

The matter soon reached the Académie-Française, the institution charged (as it is to this day) with preserving the purity of French language and literature. In 1824 it issued an edict condemning 'Romanticism' as a foreign infection; but the young lions who met for cakes and *eau sucrée* at the Sunday evening *salon* of Charles Nodier only laughed. They had their magazine *La Muse Française*, as short-lived as the Schlegels' *Athenäum*, but as provocative and influential; and they could turn to listen to the poetry of the young Victor Hugo, destined for greatness.

Victor Hugo (1802–85) was a golden boy—'*l'enfant sublime*' Chateaubriand called him. Son of a Napoleonic general, his early poetry and a novel had won him a royal pension and the Légion d'Honneur before he was even twenty-five. No one, least of all himself, doubted his fertility of imagination or his energy and tenacity. Politically, he moved away from his youthful royalism towards out-and-out republicanism, but it was in literature that he was the effective revolutionary. A collection of his poems, *Odes et ballades*, published in 1826, confirmed his promise and showed him the heir to André Chénier, that 'Romantic among the Classics', in his efforts to unshackle French verse from the tyranny of Racinian alexandrine regularity. He then turned to the challenge of the theatre and began work on a vast reconstruction of a day in the life of Oliver Cromwell: more like a pageant than a play, its chief inspiration was Scott's 'Waverley' novels, but the concept intrigued no less than the great actor Talma who for almost forty years had been supreme at the Comédie-Française. He had pushed through several reforms—notably one which allowed historic-ally accurate costuming—and was now nearing retirement, bored with a lifetime of impersonating kings and emperors. At dinner one night he sat next to Hugo and asked for a Romantic drama to crown his career. No finely chiselled verses, he begged, but a hero 'with the variety and movement of real life, who wasn't all of a piece, who could be tragic and ordinary, a king who was also a man'. Hugo was moved by the request, but Talma had died shortly after and *Cromwell* grew to unstageable pro-portions—a fantasy or at least a deliberate experiment.

The possibilities fell into place with the arrival of the English actors and their 'authentic' Shakespeare. Hugo reeled out of the first night of *Hamlet* as punch-drunk as his *confrères* Dumas and Berlioz, and, it is said, went straight home to start work on the famous '*Préface*' to *Cromwell*, a manifesto for all the Romanticism that had been ferment-ing in Paris over the past decade. '*Shakespeare, c'est le drame*,' Hugo announces, and he comes to France a liberator, showing how contra-ries can be made harmonious, how different styles, moods, idioms, and sorts of people can coexist in one work of art: Hamlet can talk prose to a gravedigger, shout obscenities at Ophelia, parry ironically with Rosencrantz and Guildenstern, and commune in verse with the depths of his soul. It is this path, says the '*Préface*', that the 'modern muse' must follow. Drama must not cut itself off from the fullness of life, but realize that 'not everything in creation is humanely fine, that ugliness exists alongside beauty, deformity is close to grace, the grotesque but the reverse of the sublime, evil of good, shadow of light'. Where Hugo further advances on Stendhal's version of the Romantic is in the emphasis he puts on changing the *language* used in tragedy as radically as the subject-matter. Instead of the relentless metrical security and limited vocabulary of the alexandrine *style noble*:

Titus m'accable ici du poids de sa grandeur:
Tout disparait dans Rome auprès de sa splendeur;
Mais, quoique l'Orient soit plein de sa mémoire,
Bérénice y verra des traces de ma gloire.   (Racine, *Bérénice*)

there would be 'verse free, open, straightforward, daring to say every-thing without prudery, to express everything without affectation'. It is this flinging-wide of some long-closed, long-guarded gates that Hugo achieved for French poetry:

J'ai dit aux mots; soyez république! Soyez
La fourmilière immense, et travaillez! Croyez,
Aimez, vivez!—J'ai mis tout en branle, et morose,
J'ai jêtê le vers noble aux chiens noirs de la prose ...

(I said to Words: be republican! be a great ants' nest, and get to work! Believe, love, live! I set everything in motion, and moodily threw *vers noble* to the black dogs of prose)

So however oppressive the example of Shakespeare was to aspiring English dramatists, elsewhere he brought the torch of freedom. It was the same in Russia as in France: Pushkin thought of his great tragedy *Boris Godunov*, written in 1825, as Romantic and Shakespearean not because Tsar Boris's unclean conscience recalls that of Macbeth and Claudius, but because it was wide-ranging in time and space, high and low, grotesque and sublime.

The young Romantics of Paris were lucky above everything in the support of one influential state official. A certain Baron Isidore-Justin-Séverin Taylor, a naturalized Frenchman of English parentage, was appointed director of the Comédie-Française in 1825. A young man with both imagination and diplomatic charm, he appreciated that the new drama had to be admitted to his theatre if it was not to ossify completely—but that it should be admitted carefully and by degrees. Early in 1829, he presented a rough and hairy prose melodrama by Alexandre Dumas, *Henri III*. On one side, the event caused joy: after the first night a coven of Romantics danced a derisory fandango around a bust of Racine in the foyer. On another side, disgust: seven classicists from the Académie unsuccessfully petitioned Charles X to stop such nonsense and sack the subversive Baron Taylor. Later that same year Taylor commissioned from his friend Alfred de Vigny a translation of *Othello*. As *Le More de Venise*, the plot tidied up and the verse put into standard alexandrines, it passed off moderately and paved the way for the ultimate battle—to be fought over a new verse tragedy by a Frenchman, Victor Hugo, written according to the principles of the '*Préface*' to *Cromwell*.

The date for the launching of this bomb, code-name *Hernani* and taking a violent episode from Spanish history as its basis, was set: 25 February 1830 would be, in the words of Théophile Gautier, 'the greatest event of the century, since it marked the inauguration of free, young, and new thought over the debris of old routines'. The campaign was brilliantly handled. Dismissing the resident paid claque, the Baron gave Hugo four hundred free tickets for each of the first four performances. These were distributed all over the student and artist *quartiers* of Paris, marked in red with the word *Hierro*, the Spanish for iron, and bearing with them the responsibility for the honour of Romanticism, of youth, hope, and the future of poetry. The press further obliged with a rush of features, previews, reports, outrage and gossip.

Red was to be the colour of the day—red against what Gautier called *le grisâtre*, the greyness of Classics and Academies and alexandrines; red the colour of *l'étendard sanglant*, the bloody standard celebrated in the *Marseillaise*. Five hours before the première the long-haired upholders of *Hierro* assembled outside the Comédie-Française, truculent, excited, and prepared for trouble. Gautier wore a stunning red doublet; others were in Spanish costume or some form of fancy dress. A crowd pelted this bizarre parade with fruit and vegetables, and the young Balzac was hit by a cabbage. Five hours before curtain up, to avoid further public disturbance, the Romantics were let into the auditorium. Sitting in the darkness and cold, they passed the time by reciting Hugo's poetry, singing songs, and making farmyard noises. Some had brought picnics—*petit pain*, chocolate, rough garlic sausage—and since the administration had forgotten to open the lavatories, the stink of food and urine soon grew obnoxious. In due course, the eleven hundred paying members of the audience were let in, and the pitch was set for hostilities to commence.

From the very first line, it was clear that Hugo was not going to disappoint either side by compromising. Even if its 'Shakespeareanness' now looks dubious or superficial, *Hernani* was certainly defiantly Romantic in effect. All the rules were broken, and broken gleefully. Instead of the smooth and rounded flow of couplets, Hugo favoured impassioned rhetorical outbursts and short, sharp exchanges—

Est-il minuit?

Minuit bientôt!

—like the volley of question-and-answer which opens *Hamlet*. Such flagrant novelties caused a rumpus. Indeed, between the cheering, booing, catcalls, the bursts of applause answered by whistling and hisses, it is surprising that anyone managed to hear a word of the play at all. By the end of the evening, no one could be sure who had won: not the poor actors, for sure, although there was universal enthusiasm for the elderly doyenne Mademoiselle Mars, who had bravely sustained the part of the beautiful girl beloved of the hero. But the 'greatest event of the century'?

At subsequent performances the barracking continued, but soon the whole business of *Hernani* became no more than a circus: good copy for the newspapers, thrilling fun for anyone lucky enough to find a ticket, and a rich source of satire for the little boulevard theatres who presented parodies with titles like *Oh! qu' Nenni* and *Ni-i-ni*. And in the end *Hernani* stuck, the critical judgements and purists' complaints irrelevant in the face of such excitement. Shakespeare was vindicated, Romanticism had triumphed, but something real—some sense of the isolation of intellectual struggle, of writing out of need and desire, anger and vision—was lost.

Through the summer of 1830, there was a brief and bitter revolution on the streets of Paris, in which two thousand lost their lives: red was again the colour of Paris as blood saturated the cobbles and trickled into the gutters. Charles X slunk out of the country, having attempted to seize unconstitutional power after he had failed to win an election. In his place came the mild-mannered and gentlemanly Louis Philippe of the House of Orléans, ushering in an era of moderate liberalism and hard-headed bourgeois morality. Money, as the great chronicler of the time Balzac recognized, could do anything now: the prevalent ethic was to take as much as you could get, by any means, and live to enjoy the material pleasures that money magicks up. And under this new dispensation, with its luxury and leisure and wealth and glitter, Romanticism became comfortably fashionable, on view at the opera, available in the shops, visible on every menu and billboard—the small coin of art, pretty, sentimental, and entertaining; familiar, unchallenging and unchallenged. The avant-garde was now represented by a band of anarchist bohemian eccentrics, the *Bousingots* (possibly intentionally connoting the English 'boozing') who sported leather sailors' hats and roamed the streets of Paris at night, blowing noisy public raspberries—their aim little more than outraging dullness, scrawling clever rude *graffiti* on the walls of decency.

For those outside the charmed circle and exploited by it, there were new forces—socialism, machinery, unemployment, factories, ideas and actualities undreamt of by a Rousseau, a Goethe, a Shelley. For many others, anxious to forget that since 1780 hundreds of thousands had died that they should have liberty, there were fortunes to be made and trains to be caught.

History reveals no full stops, no neat demarcations; but this is the beginning of another of its chapters.

*

The world's great age begins anew
   The golden years return,
The earth doth like a snake renew
   Her winter weeds outworn:
Heaven smiles, and faiths and empires gleam,
Like wrecks of a dissolving dream . . .

Oh cease! must hate and death return?
   Cease! must men kill and die?
Cease! drain not to its dregs the urn
   Of bitter prophecy.
The world is weary of the past.
Oh, might it die or rest at last!

                       Shelley, *Hellas*, 1821

Were we required to characterize this age of ours by any single epithet, we should be tempted to call it, not an Heroical, Devotional, Philosophical, or Moral Age, but, above all others, the Mechanical Age. It is the Age of Machinery, in every outward and inward sense of that word; the age which, with its whole undivided might, forwards, teaches and practises the great art of adapting means to ends. Nothing is now done directly, or by hand; all is by rule and calculated contrivance. For the simplest operation, some helps and accompaniments, some cunning abbreviating process is in readiness. Our old modes of exertion are all discredited, and thrown aside. On every hand, the living artisan is driven from his workshop, to make room for a speedier, inanimate one. The shuttle drops from the fingers of the weaver, and falls into iron fingers that ply it faster. The sailor furls his sail, and lays down his oar; and bids a strong, unwearied servant, on vaporous wings, bear him through the waters. Men have crossed oceans by steam; the Birmingham Fire-king has visited the fabulous East; and the genius of the Cape, were there any Camoens now to sing it, has again been alarmed, and with far stranger thunders than Gama's. There is no end to machinery. Even the horse is stripped of his harness, and finds a fleet fire-horse yoked in his stead. Nay, we have an artist that hatches chickens by steam; the very brood-hen is to be superseded! For all earthly, and for some unearthly purposes, we have machines and mechanic furtherances; for mincing our cabbages; for casting us into magnetic sleep. We remove mountains, and make seas our smooth highway; nothing can resist us. We war with rude Nature; and, by our resistless engines, come off always victorious, and loaded with spoils.

These things, which we state lightly enough here, are yet of deep import, and indicate a mighty change in our whole manner of existence. For the same habit regulates not our modes of action alone, but our modes of thought and feeling. Men are grown mechanical in head and in heart, as well as in hand. They have lost faith in individual endeavour, and in natural force, of any kind. Not for internal perfection, but for external combinations and arrangements, for institutions, constitutions,—for Mechanism of one sort or other, do they hope and struggle. Their whole efforts, attachments, opinions, turn on mechanism, and are of a mechanical character.

Carlyle, Signs of the Times, 1829

... but most she loathed the hour
When the thick-moted sunbeam lay
 Athwart the chambers, and the day
 Was sloping toward his western bower.
  Then, said she, 'I am very dreary,
   He will not come,' she said;
  She wept, 'I am aweary, aweary,
   Oh God, that I were dead!'

*

... The air is damp, and hush'd, and close,
As a sick man's room when he taketh repose
  An hour before death;
My very heart faints and my whole soul grieves
At the moist rich smell of the rotting leaves,
  And the breath
  Of the fading edges of box beneath,
And the year's last rose.
  Heavily hangs the broad sunflower
   Over its grave i' the earth so chilly;
  Heavily hangs the hollyhock,
  Heavily hangs the tiger-lily.

Tennyson, Mariana and Song, both written in 1830

'It seems to me that the young men who were my contemporaries, fixed certain principles in their minds and followed them out to their legitimate consequences, in a way which I rarely witness now. No one seems to have any distinct convictions, right or wrong; the mind is completely at sea, rolling and pitching on the waves of facts and personal experiences ...'

Coleridge, Table Talk, 21 September 1830

Goethe is dead. He died on March 22, 1832, that memorable year in which the world lost its greatest celebrities. It is as if death had suddenly become aristocratic, and sought to designate particularly the great ones of this earth by sending them contemporaneously to the grave. Perhaps death wished to found a House of Lords in the shadowy realms of Hades, in which case its selection was well made. Or, perhaps, on the contrary, death sought during the past years to favour democracy by destroying those great celebrities, and their authority over the minds of men, and thus to bring about an intellectual equality. Was it out of respect or from irreverence, that death spared the crowned heads during the past year? In a fit of abstraction, death did raise his scythe over the King of Spain, but he recollected himself in time, and spared his life. During the past twelve months not a single king has died. *Les dieux s'en vont*—but the kings are still with us.

Heine, The Romantic School, 1833

There is no more love. There is no more glory. A thick night covers the earth. And we shall be dead before the dawn.

Alfred de Musset, 1836

> With deep distress I contemplate our generation
> Its future stretches on to darkness, emptiness.
> Knowing too much, lost in equivocation,
>   It grows towards old age in idleness.
>   For we are rich, from infancy or almost,
> In all our fathers' faults, their hindsight and their wit,
> And life, like a smooth road without a goal, has dulled us
>   Like guests who at an alien banquet sit.
>   To good and evil shamefully indiff'rent
> We wilt yet in the slips, before the lances' shock ...
> In danger's face—we offer no resistance,
> Cowed by authority, a servile flock
>   So some poor fruit, too early come to ripeness,
> Void of delight—for palate as for eye,
> Might dangle waif-like midst Spring blossoms' brightness,
> Aware—even as they bloom—that it must die!
>
> Our brain is all dried up by arid learning,
> And, jealously, from our best friends we hide
> Our dearest hopes and even the noble burning
>   Of passions which our sceptic minds deride.

Our lips have scarcely touched the cup of pleasure
   Yet by this caution we've not saved our strength;
Fearing excess, we have drawn off a measure
   From every joy—and left all flat at length.

Great works of art and high, poetic dreaming
Wake in our minds no sweet responsive thrill
And, avidly we hoard the dregs of feeling,
A miser's wasted talent—buried still.
And casual all alike our loves and hatreds,
We make no sacrifice to love or ire.
The coldness in our souls holds nothing sacred,
   Yet in our blood seethes fire.
Bored by our ancestors' delights uproarious,
Their conscientious, childish revelry,
We, hastening joyless on to grave inglorious,
Look back in irony ...

A sullen multitude not long remembered
We'll flit earth's face and leave no mark,
No seed of fruitful thought have we engendered,
   No work of genius, no living spark
To light the ages for our heirs and citizens to come ...
Who will dismiss us with a scornful epitaph
As, seeing his heritage despoiled, a son
   Writes off his bankrupt father—with a laugh.
                Lermontov, *Meditation*, 1838

Acknowledgements

I am grateful to John Calder (Publishers) Ltd for permission to quote extracts from *The Life of Rossini* by Stendhal, translated by Richard Coe, and to the estate of the late Sir Charles Johnston for permission to quote extracts from his translation of *Eugene Onegin* by Pushkin.

Thanks are also due to the following for permissions to reproduce photographic material: Roger-Viollet, Paris, nos. 1, 2, 3, 9 and 16; Deutsche Schillergesellschaft, no. 4; the Trustees of the British Museum, nos. 5 and 6; the Trustees of the National Museums and Galleries on Merseyside (Walker Art Gallery), no. 7; The Ashmolean Museum, Oxford, no. 8; the Trustees of the Victoria and Albert Museum, no. 10; the Bodleian Library, Oxford, no. 11; Scottish National Portrait Gallery, Edinburgh, no. 15.

Select Bibliography

Chapter 1

The major work on André Chénier in English is Francis Scarfe, *André Chénier: His Life and Work* (1965); Scarfe has also compiled a selection of Chénier's *Poems* (1961).

On Enlightenment Europe, see Peter Gay, *The Enlightenment* (2 vols., 1967, 1970), Ernst Cassirer, *The Philosophy of the Enlightenment* (1951), and John Lough, *L'Encyclopédie* (1971). *The Indispensable Rousseau*, ed. Hope Mason (1979) provides a range of texts in translation. The literature on the French Revolution and its antecedence is vast: I would recommend Alfred Cobban's lucid and concise *History of Modern France*, vol. 1 (1965); George Lefebvre's *The French Revolution* (2 vols. 1962, 1964) is the most influential modern interpretation; George Rudé's *Revolutionary Europe 1783–1815* (1964) and *The Crowd in the French Revolution* (1959) are excellent; E.J. Hobsbawm's *The Age of Revolution 1789–1848* (1962) is less elegant but wider ranging. On English history specifically, see Élie Halévy's *England in 1815* (1949 edn.), magisterial and unsurpassed; likewise E. P. Thompson's *The Making of the English Working Class* (1963). Texts connected with the intellectual ferment surrounding the Revolution can be found in *The Debate on the French Revolution*, ed. Cobban (1960) and *Burke, Paine, Godwin and the Revolution Controversy*, ed. Butler (1984).

On Wordsworth, see Mary Moorman's biography William Wordsworth (2 vols., 1957, 1965). The Oxford Authors series has the best modern text of the poetry, attractively presented—*William Wordsworth*, ed. Gill (1984); see also *The Pedlar, Tintern Abbey, The Two-Part Prelude*, ed. J.Wordsworth (1985), for an introduction to the complex and fascinating subject of Wordsworth's developing drafts. Outstanding recent critical works include John Danby, *The Simple Wordsworth* (1960), Geoffrey Hartman, *Wordsworth's Poetry 1787–1814* (1964), and Mary Jacobus, *Tradition and Experiment in the 'Lyrical Ballads'* (1976). H. W. Piper, *The Active Universe* (1962) explains the philosophical hinterland, and H. Crabb Robinson, *On Books and their Writers*, ed. Morley (1938) gives vivid contemporary sketches of the poet and his circle.

On Coleridge, see The Oxford Authors series *Samuel Taylor Coleridge*, ed. Jackson (1983) and *Selected Letters*, ed. Jackson (1987). There is no standard modern biography at the time of writing (spring 1987), although E. K. Chambers' *Coleridge* (1938) and John Cornwell's *Coleridge: Poet and Revolutionary 1772–1804* (1973) both have their virtues; and Richard Holmes—

253

author of a useful little introduction to Coleridge's thought in the Past
Master series, *Coleridge* (1982)—is currently working on one of which there
are high expectations. For Coleridge's prose, see the enjoyable selection in
Inquiring Spirit, ed. Coburn (1951); Professor Coburn is also the editor of the
still incomplete transcription of Coleridge's astonishing *Notebooks* (6 vols. to
date, 1957–   ). Three outstanding and original perspectives on Coleridge
are contained in E. S. Shaffer, '*Kubla Khan*' *and The Fall of Jerusalem* (1975);
William Empson and David Pirie, *Coleridge's Verse: A Selection* (1972), featuring Empson's unforgettable reinterpretation of *The Rime of the Ancient
Mariner*, and Norman Fruman's profound and controversial study of Coleridge's plagiarism, *Coleridge, The Damaged Archangel* (1972). John Colmer's
Coleridge: Critic of Society (1959) is useful. See also J. Simmons's critical
biography of *Robert Southey* (1945) and Molly Lefebure's life of Sara Coleridge, *The Bondage of Love* (1986).

On Shelley, see *Complete Poetical Works*, ed. Hutchinson and Matthews
(1970) and his *Letters*, ed. Jones (2 vols., 1964). Richard Holmes's lyrically
written and sensitive biography *Shelley: The Pursuit* (1976) can be read
alongside the more academically rigorous Kenneth Neill Cameron, *The
Young Shelley: Genesis of a Radical* (1950) and *Shelley: The Golden Years*
(1974). The huge edition, still incomplete, of documents and letters relating
to *Shelley and his Circle* (7 vols., to date, 1961–   ) held in the Pforzheimer
Library makes, at the very least, riveting browsing.

For Godwin, see *Enquiry concerning Political Justice*, ed. Carter (1971),
Caleb Williams, ed. McCracken (1982), and Peter H. Marshall, *William
Godwin* (1984).

Chapter 2

On madness, see Michel Foucault, *Madness and Civilisation*, tr. Howard
(1971); Ida McAlpine and Richard Hunter, *George III and the Mad Business*
(1969); and Roy Porter, *A Social History of Madness* (1987). A. Alvarez's *The
Savage God* (1971) is a provocative study of suicide; also M. Miller 'Géricault's Paintings of the Insane', *Journal of the Warburg and Courtauld Institutes*
(1940–1).

For the tradition of literary Melancholy, see *The New Oxford Book of
Eighteenth-Century Verse*, ed. Lonsdale (1984); Goethe's *The Sorrows of Young
Werther*, tr. Bogan and Mayer (1971) and Jane Austen's *Sense and Sensibility*,
ed. Tanner (1969). On Chatterton, see Linda Kelly, *The Marvellous Boy*
(1971) and Richard Holmes, 'Thomas Chatterton', *Cornhill Magazine*
(1970). A. D. Harvey's *English Poetry in a Changing Society 1780–1825* (1980)
is interesting on the matter of popular taste at the time. Roy Porter's *English
Society in the 18th Century* (1982) is fresh and involving.

For Coleridge's pathology, see especially Fruman op. cit., Alethea Hayter,
Opium and the Romantic Imagination (1968), Molly Lefebure *Coleridge: A
Bondage of Opium* (1974), and Carlyle's comments, reprinted in *Carlyle:
Selected Works*, ed. Symons (1956).

On German culture, see Henri Brunschwig, *Enlightenment and Romanticism in 18th Century Prussia* (1974); Roger Cardinal, *German Romantics in Context* (1975), Alan Menhennet, *The Romantic Movement* (1981), and Rene Wellek, 'German and English Romanticism', *Studies in Romanticism* (1974). *The Penguin Book of German Verse*, ed. Foster (1957) has a sound basic selection of the poetry of the era, with English prose translations.

For Kleist, see Joachim Maass' biography *Kleist* (1983)—stolid as it is, there is no real alternative; a selection of Kleist's prose, letters, and essays in *An Abyss Deep Enough*, ed. Miller (1982); and the best edition of Kleist's stories in English, *The Marquise von O— and other Stories*, tr. Luke and Reeves (1978). For Hölderlin, see *Selected Poems*, ed. Leishman (1954); *Selected Verse*, tr. and ed. Hamburger (1985); *Hymns and Fragments*, tr. and ed. Sieburth (1984)—all with good introductions. *Hyperion* is disgracefully unavailable in English. See also Shaffer, op. cit.

For Goethe, the most engaging introduction is Eckermann's *Conversations with Goethe*, reprinted in Everyman's Library (1970) and Thomas Mann's historical novel *Lotte in Weimar* (1968 edn.). Also T. J. Reed's brief *Goethe* (1984) in the 'Past Masters' series: more substantial are Reed's *The Classical Centre: Goethe and Weimar* (1980) and W. H. Bruford's *Culture and Society in Classical Weimar* (1962).

Chapter 3

On the situation and expectations of women in the period, see D. M. Stenton, *The English Woman in History* (1957); Patricia Branca, *Women in Europe since 1750* (1978); Jane Rendall's excellent *The Origins of Modern Feminism* (1985), with a useful bibliography; Linda Kelly, *Women of the French Revolution* (1987). For Jane Austen, Marilyn Butler, *Jane Austen and the War of Ideas* (1974); for Mary Hays, *Letters of Mary Hays*, ed. A. F. Wedd (1925) and the reissue of *Memoirs of Emma Courtney* (1987).

For Mary Wollstonecraft, her *Vindication of the Rights of Woman*, ed. Kramnick (1975); further texts in *The Mary Wollstonecraft Reader*, ed. Soloman and Berggren (1983); and *Collected Letters of Mary Wollstonecraft*, ed. Wardle (1979). Best of the many biographies is Claire Tomalin's, *The Life and Death of Mary Wollstonecraft* (1974); see also Richard Holmes, *Footsteps* (1985) and Virginia Woolf's essay in *Collected Essays*, vol. iii (1957).

No modern edition of Madame Roland's memoirs and letters is available: see instead Gita May, *Madame Roland and the Age of Revolution* (1970), also M. J. Sydenham, *The Girondins* (1961).

For Mary Shelley, see Holmes, *Shelley* and *Footsteps* op. cit.; *Mary Shelley's Journal*, ed. Jones (1947) and *The Letters of Mary Shelley*, ed. Bennett (2 vols. 1980, 1983). Jane Dunn's *Moon in Eclipse* (1978) is a readable biography of Mary; Ellen Moers' *Literary Women* (1977) has some challenging thoughts about Mary's fiction. See also *The Journals of Claire Clairmont*, ed. Stocking (1968). Nora Crook and Derek Guiton's *Shelley's Envenomed Melody* (1986) is a remarkable study of the poet's sexual pathology, specifically his paranoiac terror of venereal disease; *Shelley on Love*, ed. Holmes (1980) assembles his more refined thoughts on the matter.

By far the best biography of Madame de Staël is J. Christopher Herold's supremely elegant and witty *Mistress to an Age* (1959). Little of her work is available in modern English editions except *Corinne*, tr. Rutgers (1987): for French readers, there is *Madame de Staël: Choix de textes*, ed. Solovieff (1974). See also Harold Nicolson, *Benjamin Constant* (1949) and *Adolphe*, tr. Tancock (1964 edn.) For Rahel Varnhagen, see Hilde Spiel's essay in *Genius in the Drawing Room*, ed. Quennell (1979); Hannah Arendt's biography *Rahel Varnhagen* (1958) is hard going and concentrates on her Jewishness.

For the male view, Stendhal, *Love*, tr. Sale (1975); Alexander Pushkin, *Letters*, tr. and ed. Shaw (1963).

For Dorothy Wordsworth, her *Journals*, ed. Moorman (1971) and Robert Gittings and Jo Manton's biography *Dorothy Wordsworth* (1985): Norman Fruman's review of this book in the *Times Literary Supplement*, 28 June 1985, is well worth hunting out.

Chapter 4

Rousseau's letter to Malesherbes is translated by the author from R.A. Leigh's edition of his *Correspondance Complète* (1965–   ). On nature, and man's relation to it, see Keith Thomas, *Man and the Natural World* (1983); Piper op. cit.; Basil Willey, *Nineteenth-Century Studies* (1949) and M.H. Abrams *The Correspondent Breeze* (1984) for Coleridge in particular: also M.H. Abrams, *Natural Supernaturalism* (1971), Stephen Prickett, *Coleridge and Wordsworth: The Poetry of Growth* (1970), and Raymond Williams's *The Country and the City* (1973), for a markedly social and socialist perspective.

On music in the period, see Alfred Einstein, *Music in the Romantic Era* (1947); Henry Raynor, *A Social History of Music: from the Middle Ages to Beethoven* (1972); Peter Le Huray and James Day's substantial collection of contemporary musicological texts, *Music and Aesthetics in the 18th and Early 19th Centuries* (1981); Hector Berlioz, *Memoirs*, tr. Cairns (1969 edn.). For opera, see two fascinating monographs, John Rosselli, *The Opera Industry in Italy* (1984) and Alice M. Hanson, *Musical Life in Biedermeier Vienna* (1985). Also Winton Dean, 'Opera under the French Revolution', *Proceedings of the Royal Music Academy* (1967–8).

Hoffmann's work is not satisfactorily available in English: *Selected Writings*, tr. Kent and Knight (2 vols., 1969) includes the complete text of *Kater Murr*. For a biography, see H. Hewett-Thayer, *Hoffmann: Author of the Tales* (1948); on music, see R. Murray Schafer, *E.T.A. Hoffmann and Music* (1973), which includes some of *Kreisleriana*.

On Goethe and music, see Romain Rolland, 'Goethe and Music', *Musical Quarterly* (1931).

On Peacock and Shelley, see Howard Mills, *Peacock: his circle and his age* (1969) and *Memoirs of Shelley and other essays*, ed. Mills (1970); Marilyn

Butler, *Peacock Displayed* (1979); and John Buxton, *The Grecian Taste* (1978). For Jane Austen and music, Patrick Piggott, *The Innocent Diversion* (1979).

Rossini: Stendhal, *The Life of Rossini*, tr. Coe (1970) and Herbert Weinstock, *Rossini* (1968); Paganini: Alan Kendall, *Paganini* (1980); Liszt: Alan Walker, *Franz Liszt 1811–47* (1983).

Chapter 5

The most important name in modern Byron scholarship is undoubtedly that of Leslie Marchand, author of the standard biography *Byron* (3 vols., 1957), satisfyingly abridged as *Byron: A Portrait* (1971). Marchand is also the editor of *Byron's Letters and Journals* (12 vols., 1973–82)—from which a one-volume selection was made (1982). For the text of the poetry, use The Oxford Authors *Byron*, ed. McGann (1986). See *Byron: The Critical Heritage*, ed. Rutherford (1970) for early criticism.

Doris Langley Moore's books *The Late Lord Byron* (1961) and *Lord Byron: Accounts Rendered* (1974) delve illuminatingly into nooks and crannies of Byron's biography, particularly matters relating to his death and posterity. Louis Crompton's *Byron and Greek Love* (1985) explores his homosexuality; Philip W. Martin, *Byron: A Poet before his Public* (1982) contains astringent judgements of Byron's poetry; P. L. Thorslev's *The Byronic Hero* (1962) explores the various versions and developments of the phenomenon; G. Paston and Peter Quennell's *To Lord Byron* (1939) transcribes and analyses the fan letters; *Byron: Interviews and Recollections*, ed. Page (1985) usefully gathers many eye-witness accounts of the man and his manners.

See also R. G. Grylls, *Claire Clairmont* (1939); for Scott, A. N. Wilson, *The Laird of Abbotsford* (1980); Lorenz Eitner, *Géricault* (1983); and on Gothic literature, David Punter, *The Literature of Terror* (1980).

On Regency England, its façades and realities, see Halévy and Thompson, op. cit. and D. M. Low, *That Sunny Dome* (1977); also Ellen Moers, *The Dandy* (1960), Alison Adburgham, *The Silver Fork Society* (1983), T. A. J. Barnett, *The Rise and Fall of a Regency Dandy* (1981), and Harriette Wilson's amusing and scurrilous *Memoirs* (1983 edn.). For Jane Austen's analysis of her times, see Q. D. Leavis, 'Jane Austen and a changing society', in *Collected Essays*, vol. 1 (1983) and Butler, *Jane Austen*, op. cit.

On Byron and Goethe: E. M. Butler, *Byron and Goethe* (1950); on Pushkin, David Magarshack's biography *Pushkin* (1967) and John Bayley, *Pushkin: A Comparative Commentary* (1971). Texts in English include *Eugene Onegin*, tr. Johnson (1977) and *The Bronze Horseman and other poems*, tr. Thomas (1982). *Pushkin on Literature*, ed. Wolff (1986) collects both his formal and off-the-cuff criticism.

Chapter 6

On changes in Shakespeare's reputation, see *Shakespeare: The Critical Heritage*, ed. Vickers, vols. 2–6 (1974–83). On the English theatre, see J. W. Donohue, *Theatre in the Age of Kean* (1975) and two outstanding biographies,

H. N. Hillebrand, *Edmund Kean* (1933) and Raymund Fitzsimons, *Edmund Kean* (1976). For Joanna Baillie: Bertrand Evans, *Gothic Drama* (1947). Also *Coleridge's Shakespeare Criticism*, ed. Raysor (2 vols., 1930), Jonathan Bate, *Shakespeare and the English Romantic Imagination* (1986), and *Letters of John Keats*, ed. Gittings (1970).

For Shakespeare in Germany: Roy Pascal, *Shakespeare in Germany 1740–1815* (1937) and L. M. Price, *English Literature in Germany* (1953). Fruman, op. cit. explores Coleridge's relation to German Shakespearean scholarship.

For France and the French Romantics: W. D. Howarth, *Sublime and Grotesque: French Romantic Drama* (1975); Linda Kelly, *The Young Romantics* (1976); D. G. Charlton, *The French Romantics* (2 vols. 1984); and Joanna Richardson's biographies of *Théophile Gautier* (1958) and *Victor Hugo* (1976).

Index